LAND ACKNOWLEDGEMENT

The City of Chicago required us to obtain its permission to use the site upon which we realized our project. However, Indigenous scholars and activists inspire us to ask exactly to whom the Chicago Architecture Biennial's participants are indebted. We recognize that Euro-American settlers stole the land, on which our project was anchored, from its original inhabitants. We recognize that federal, state and municipal governments enabled, authorized and then silenced this theft. We acknowledge this site is located on the traditional homelands of the Council of the Three Fires—the Ojibwe, Odawa and Potawatomi Nations—as well as the Miami, Ho-Chunk, Sauk and Fox, the Kiikaapoi (Kickapoo), Peoria and the Očeti Šakówiŋ (Sioux) Nations. We pay our respect to the land, the elders and the Indigenous people who called this area home: the rightful owners and original stewards of this land.

EDITORS' NOTE

The editors would like to acknowledge the importance of the careful and evolving use of language. There is ongoing discussion about the capitalization of the words "Black", "Brown" and "Indigenous" when used in racial, ethnic and cultural contexts, and the editors take the position that the form of these terms, either capitalized or lower case, must be deliberate and considered. Where these terms have appeared in this book, contributors have engaged in a conversation about their preference—where there has been no preference, these terms have been capitalized to signify a shared cultural and racial identity, consistent with other racial and ethnic identifiers (such as Asian or English).

TABLE OF CONTENTS

INDEX OF THEMES

SOIL LAB **INTRODUCTION**

With this anthology, we set down in print an examination of the making of the project Soil Lab, the Danish contribution to the 2021 Chicago Architecture Biennial.

We realized early on in this process that to try to tell the story with our own words would be futile, as the project was made by more than our own hands (and heads): neighbors, high school students, carpenters, bricklayers, ecologists, ceramicists, archeologists, a mathematician, retirees, artists, architects and bicycle mechanics. People working night shifts joined us after breakfast. People who were skilled or unskilled, but all enthusiastic and eager to make. While it has not been possible to identify and give credit to everyone who has contributed to the development of the project, it is important to us to acknowledge that they exist. We present this book as the product of the sustained and diligent work of a network of intersecting and overlapping communities, which we are fortunate enough to be learning from and with. In these pages are some of the people we met in the process, the people with whom we built the structure, and those who helped us navigate and make sense of it. This is as much their story as it is ours, and this book is dedicated to them, to the Soil Lab community we made during the summer of 2021. In a sense, the project is described here through the many contributors:

the characters, the context, the materials, the method and the madness of it all.

We realize that this by no means puts these matters to bed, but instead of keeping us awake at night, we now let them out into the world, in the hope that they might provide guidance or a starting point or provoke discussion. We hope that this publication can help those setting out on similar trajectories.

While we may be more experienced now than when we started out, we have only scratched the surface. This book is intended as an open-ended study of the five main themes: availability, community, soil health, material culture and the architecture of public space. You will find illustrations and drawings, photo essays, "how-to" manuals, short stories, essays, anecdotes, architectural reviews, personal interviews and factual and empirical research.

The photographs in this book have been made by Benita Marcussen, Will Quam, Jay Simon, Sandra Steinbrecher and Amara Abdal Figueroa. The graphic design is by Studio Atlant and editing by Eleanor Beaumont.

We will forever be indebted to Maxwell Rodencal for his enthusiastic teamwork, his help and support, and to Traci Wile who acted as our project manager, our cultural translator and our friend. They both gave their knowledge, their time, their humour and themselves in abundance, and without them both, Soil Lab would not have been possible.

This project took us on a fantastic yet very fast and challenging journey, and while there are many things that didn't come to pass, things that didn't work out as intended or hoped, a project was made. It was a project made as the result of our collective energy, our conversations and collaborations, our late evenings and our early Zoom calls. The project was more than the physical thing that was built on South Pulaski Road. By its very nature it was an architecture of storytelling, an architecture of bricks, of relationships and of soil: it was an architecture of, by and for community. This is a story of a project, a discovery of a place and a celebration of that community.

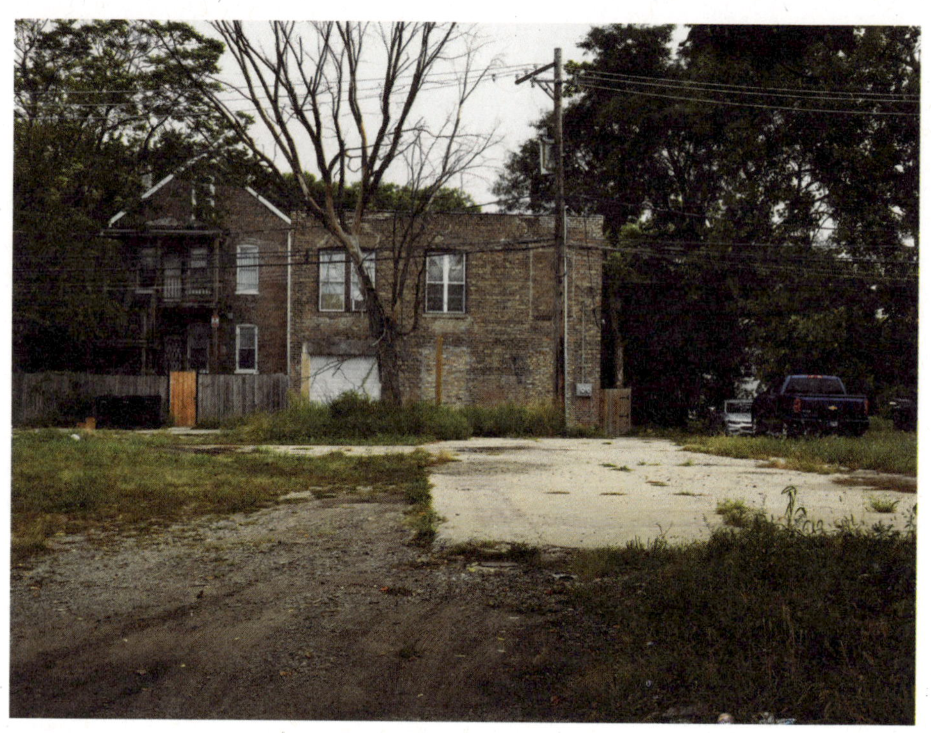

Catherine Fennell

BENEATH THE PAVEMENT

Catherine Fennell signed up as a participant in one of our rammed earth workshops. It wasn't until we were back-to-back, tamping inside a 7-by-1.5-foot box, in the hot late August sun, that Cassie explained her connection to the area. As it transpired, she had been following the Soil Lab project for several months from a distance, in connection with her own research concerning urban landscapes formed through residential demolition. From those early conversations on-site grew a deep respect for a friend and mentor who helped us navigate sensitively the challenging context we found ourselves in.

In early 2019 I overheard an unexpected conversation between two middle-aged men—unexpected because it involved a landscape far from the one unrolling right before us. Their badges told me their names, employers and destination that morning: they were soil scientists, both on their way to an annual professional meeting being held that year in San Diego. As the Pacific Ocean took shape beyond the bus windows, they began to trade remarks about land use. One noted that California's southern coast had never really been an ideal place for large-scale agriculture. Not enough fresh water, he observed, too sandy. Given that, he continued, the tangle of tourist hotels and entertainment venues flashing by made sense. "It's not like this is Chicago," his companion chuckled, "all that prairie" "paved over" in "concrete and asphalt." Beneath the pavement, the prairie.

Just where did this prairie go, the glacial till upon which so much dark, well-drained nutrient-dense silt and sod had settled? The men on the bus offered one answer: rapid industrialization had swallowed up the continent's most fertile soils as Chicago rose to industrial prominence in the late 19th century and kept right on sprawling across its hinterlands. They are not alone in imagining a vanished prairie; Daniel Burnham, one of Chicago's most renowned architects and planners, peppers his 1909 masterplan for the city with references to a primordial prairie filled with "only" "waving grasses" and "brilliant wildflowers." He laments the loss of the prairie, even while he proposes it as the testing ground for an orderly and endless urban growth.

A different kind of answer emerges with the recognition that this landscape was in fact never—save its flowers and grasses—empty. Indigenous groups had long reckoned with this watery landscape. They developed a network of portages and trails, and in the process they transformed a soggy place into a hub of intra-continental trading and transit. Euro-Americans plonked their "city in a garden" on top of that infrastructure. Beneath the pavement, then, was maybe never really the prairie. Beneath the pavement, a swamp.

In the summer of 2021, Soil Lab landed on a vacant lot in a western part of Chicago now known as North Lawndale. The name "Lawndale" was always a misnomer, historian Beryl Satter suggests, dreamed up in the 1870s by developers who had hoped that its lush connotations would attract middle-class residents. "[T]he only grass to be found [even then]," Satter writes, "was in its two city parks." Development took off in the aftermath of Chicago's Great Fire in 1871, as industrialists came in search of sound places to rebuild their factories and warehouses. Czech, German and Irish immigrant laborers followed close on their heels. They settled into the brick cottages, row houses and townhomes that came to line the manufacturing facilities, also made of brick. Such "fireproof" constructions could only emerge following efforts to drain the soggy ground. In a city gripped with feverish expansion, those efforts proved uneven. To this day, local property owners reckon regularly with flooded basements, the effect of so much hasty construction upon unstable ground. Beneath the pavement, no longer just a swamp. Beneath the pavement, the fill.

By the 1930s, Lawndale—as it was originally known—had become one of Chicago's densest and most populous areas. Russian and Polish immigrants began arriving during the early decades of the 20th century, chasing manufacturing work. Yet, more established residents would not rent to them. Scholars like Matthew Jacobson and Karen Brodkin underscore how American race politics at the time positioned Jewish immigrants as adjacent to—yet not quite—"white." While Jewish newcomers faced discrimination, Satter shows that some did manage to acquire vacant lots upon which they constructed large apartment buildings to meet growing housing demands within their community.

And so Lawndale became increasingly dense as it became increasingly Jewish. It would not remain that way: as housing opportunities increased in the 1950s for Jewish people elsewhere, wealthier residents left to pursue them. Speculators, brokers and investors sensed an opportunity. They bundled together properties and offered them to yet another group that had begun arriving in the 1930s and 1940s: Black migrants from the American South. Newcomers relied on contract sales to acquire property because intense and violent forms of racial discrimination shut them out of favorable mortgage arrangements available to other Americans. They faced exorbitant down payments and interest rates for substandard housing. High demand meant that unscrupulous brokers could forgo regular maintenance. When a buyer got behind on their payments, brokers simply evicted them, retained past payments and cycled the deteriorating property into another unfair yet utterly legal contract sale. Above the pavement, another swamp: this one mired in American racism, its trenchant inequities and scandalous profits.

Chicagoans often narrate the vacancy that besets West Side neighborhoods like North Lawndale through a singular event: the civil disturbance that followed the assassination of Martin Luther King Jr in 1968. King had lived in Lawndale while community organizing in the urban Northern states. To hear many tell it, his assassination unleashed a destructive rage characterized by arson, looting and property destruction. When bulldozers finally cleared away the rubble, this story goes, they left behind gluts of vacant lots that still plague these neighborhoods today. As powerful as this narrative may be, it papers over what historical maps and the recollections of long-term residents make clear. Buildings in these areas had begun to disappear already in the 1940s. Over the next six to seven decades these buildings fell in fits and starts. Some fell to urban clearance and renewal projects aimed at combatting "blight," others to smaller-scale demolitions aimed at containing devaluation, residential flight and deindustrialization, and others to ensuing neglect and inadequate maintenance. Such protracted demolition has opened ample space for new and long-term residents. More than a few will wax agrarian when speaking of the lots they have come somehow to occupy, acquire, build, cultivate or speculate upon. "The little fields," some will say when referring to these places; "the prairie" say others. Amid another swamp, and the violent clearings it pressed upon buildings and their inhabitants, yet another prairie.

Those closest to the ground know that if they stand now in a "prairie," it is an especially peculiar one. Car parts, garbage sacks and matted clothes clot its grasses and wildflowers. When it rains, a young gardener explained to me in 2019, and when it thaws, "the earth just births glass." She is far from the only gardener to have noticed the glass, brick, slag, tiles, pipes, wood and wiring but also the clinkers, paint chips, carpets, bottles and dishes that well up with the weather. A long-practiced—albeit no longer permitted—disposal strategy in the region had wreckers repurposing demolished buildings to fill the "holes" that demolition opened within the landscape. They folded building debris *into* remaining foundations, tamped the pile down and drove away. The concaves and mounds that now dot vacant lots on Chicago's West Side have emerged as building debris has subsided. Those who work this strange ground know that for every discernable object it yields, there is much more that they cannot see. The young gardener I spoke to worries about the toxins that her cats and dogs might be ingesting but also spreading as they tramp around vacant lots, lick their paws and snuggle with her inside. Beneath this strange prairie, more fill, and so much of it unknown.

The open call to participate in the Chicago Architecture Biennial, to which Soil Lab's designers responded, defined a vacant lot as "an area of land within an urban setting that is not built upon." It stressed that like many of the 10,000 vacant lots owned by the City of Chicago, the lot Soil Lab eventually occupied was "rough" and "raw" with "limitless potential." It welcomed proposals that would route such potential through the theme of *The Available City*. Soil Lab's proposal did just that by focusing on local vernacular architecture and vernacular materials. The proposal drew inspiration from North Lawndale's ubiquitous brick architecture. It also imagined mobilizing ancient construction techniques that directed would-be builders, as one of the designers put it, "to the earth in front of you and the shovel in your hand." Above the earth, but also through it, the bricks.

Limits to potential nevertheless ensued. Some limits were logistical: materials held up in customs, team members held up by travel restrictions. Others emerged from the site itself, from the fact that most vacant lots that do not appear built upon have in fact been built upon in the past. The ground is not exactly "earth" but rather the residue of demolitions driven by devaluation, discrimination and displacement. Those residues are anything but transparent; they are perhaps even something unhealthy. Lab tests, for instance, showed on-site soils to have substantial levels of lead, a potent neurotoxin common in American paints and gasolines until the late 1970s. Having no budget or time for remediation, the biennial's coordinators advised Soil Lab that no ground should be broken. The rammed earth blocks would be built on-site from material brought in. Those blocks would rest atop a wall of standard bricks, and that wall would have to rest on the concrete pad that remained on-site, a remnant of past building.

The designers felt the disappointment of thwarted plans. And yet this strategy to contain rather than free up available materials conforms to common regulations in the United States. For generations, Americans have been told that lead and other toxins pose relatively few health risks when held behind a clean and even layer of paint, wallpaper or tile, or covered up by a firm barrier. Soil Lab's lot had the benefit of an existing concrete slab. Other lots in the biennial used wood chips to create a barrier. Behind the walls of obsolete residential buildings, beneath the pavement and mulch that cover the vacant lots they become, the byproducts of late industrial capitalism.

Soil Lab raised its pavilion on the extant concrete pad. Over the fall of 2021, it hosted several workshops about bricks, brick making and ceramics. Despite efforts to retain the space for community use, rumors had it that the lot would eventually go to affordable housing construction. Little remains of the structure today. Indeed, the City of Chicago announced the sale of some 4,000 vacant lots on the South and West Sides in October 2022. On the West Side, these sales will bolster conventional housing developments designed to maximize property tax revenue. As much as the biennial's vacant lots might have embodied "limitless potential," and as much as the biennial might have sketched out numerous visions for realizing such potential, vacant lots are becoming "available" only to the most mundane development imaginations. Across the vacant lot, and its latter-day prairies and clearings, the predictable horizons of urban growth would seem to be unrolling yet again.

In the face of impending vacant land sales in places like North Lawndale, it would be possible to fold a project like the biennial into broader revaluations fueled by so many booms and busts and so many demolitions and displacements. Yet such a conclusion would ignore the challenge posed by Soil Lab's thwarted designs, and more pointedly by residents who have been breaking local ground in their efforts to raise plants and animals and recreation and gathering spaces, amid utter uncertainty about what these grounds hold. Rather than repave the material footprints of racism and industrial life by looking past them, these efforts insist on engaging with their risks, uncertainties, even their pleasures. They challenge urbanites to consider what it would mean to build self-consciously in—but also with—a world in which the dump is not so much elsewhere as it is everywhere, albeit it in radically uneven distributions. Beneath the pavement, then, lies the outlines of the most sobering and clear-eyed beach.

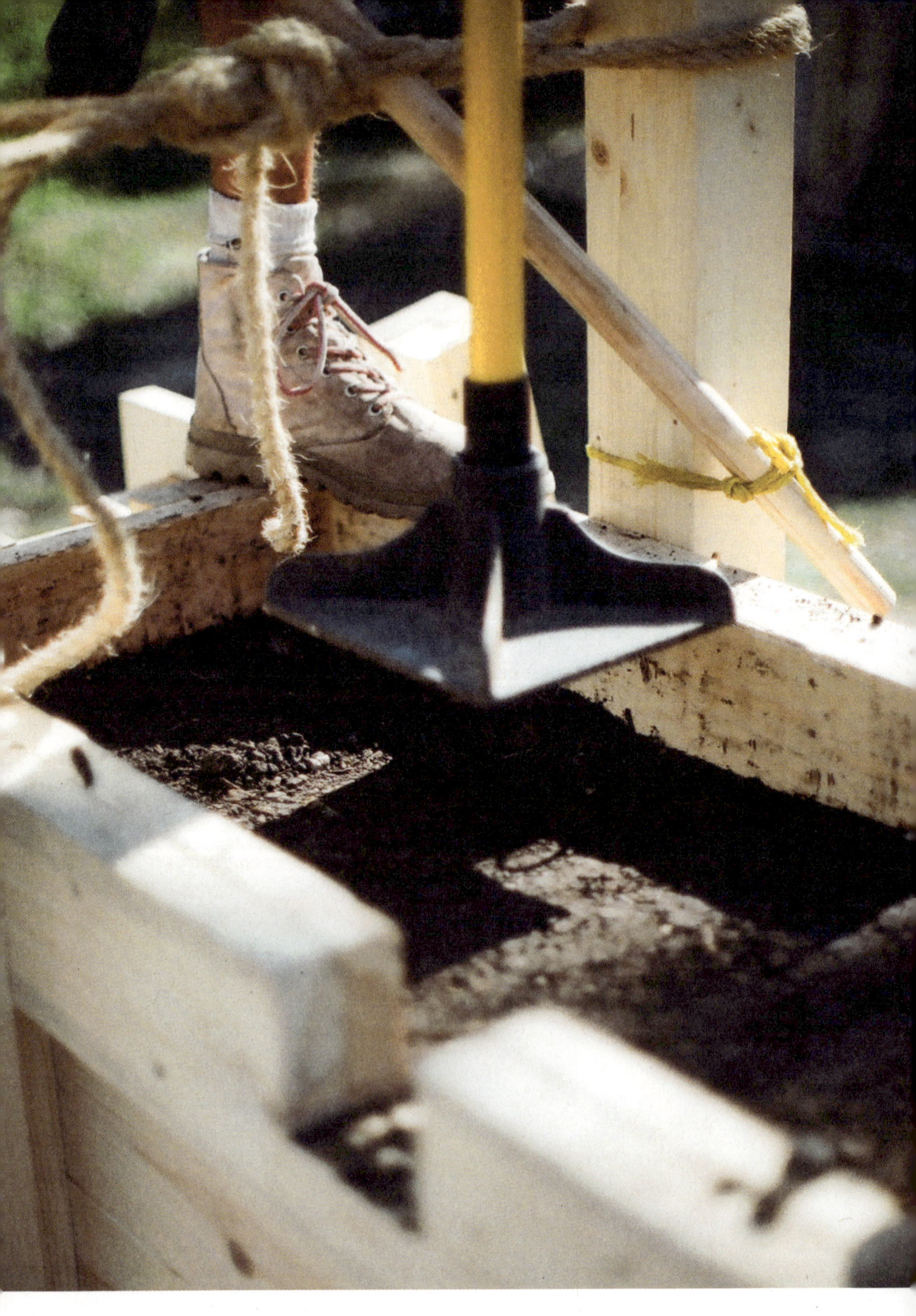

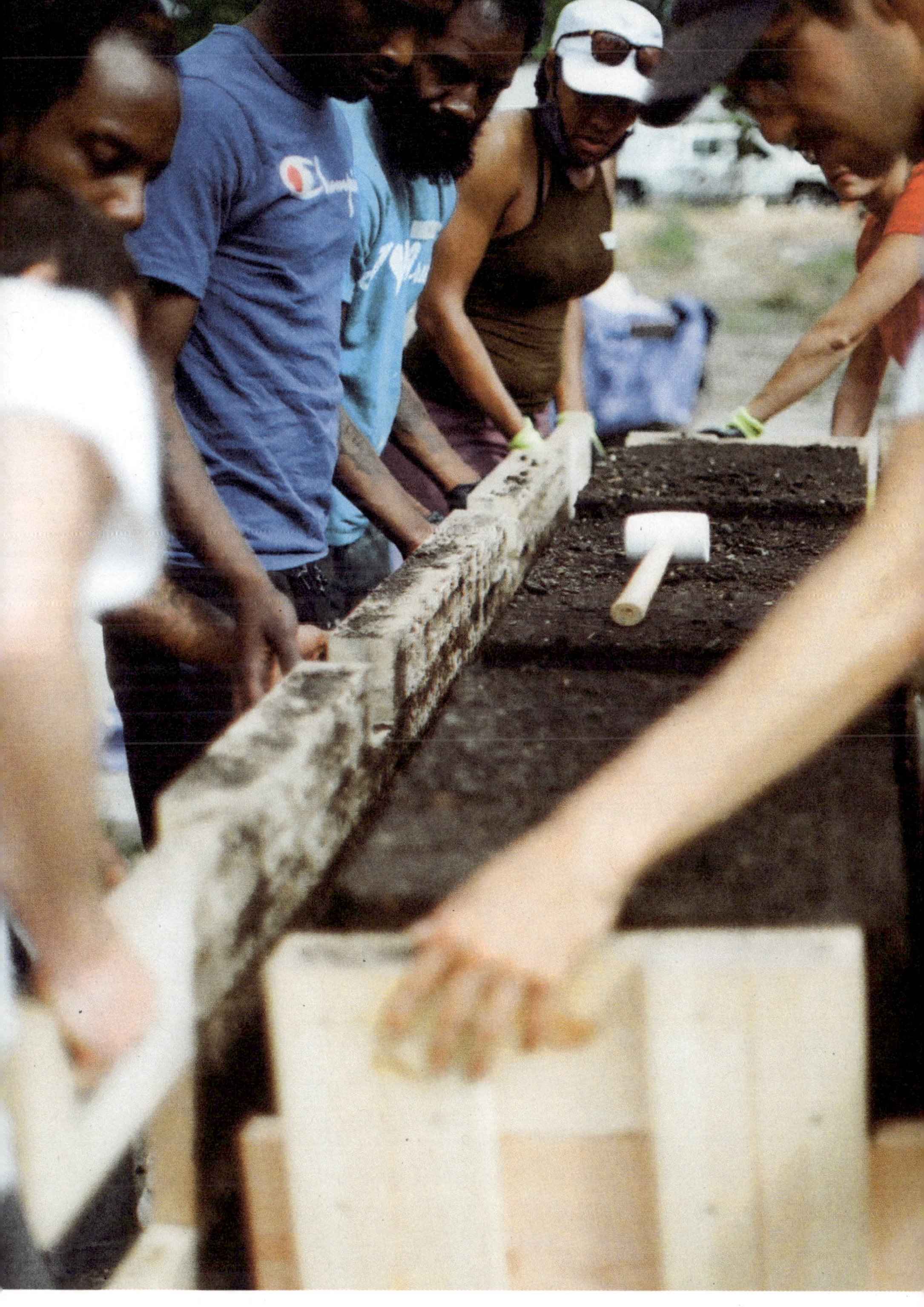

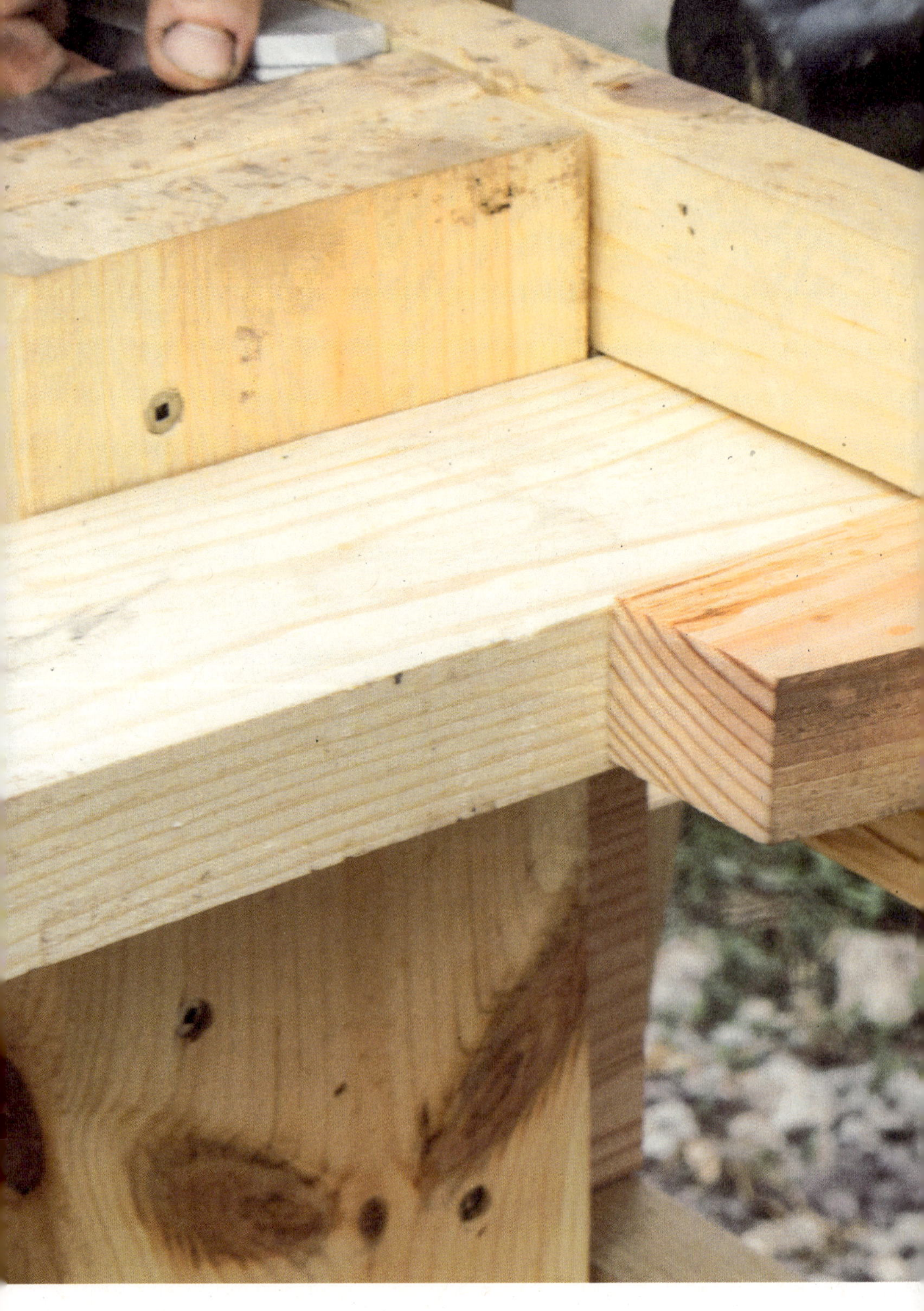

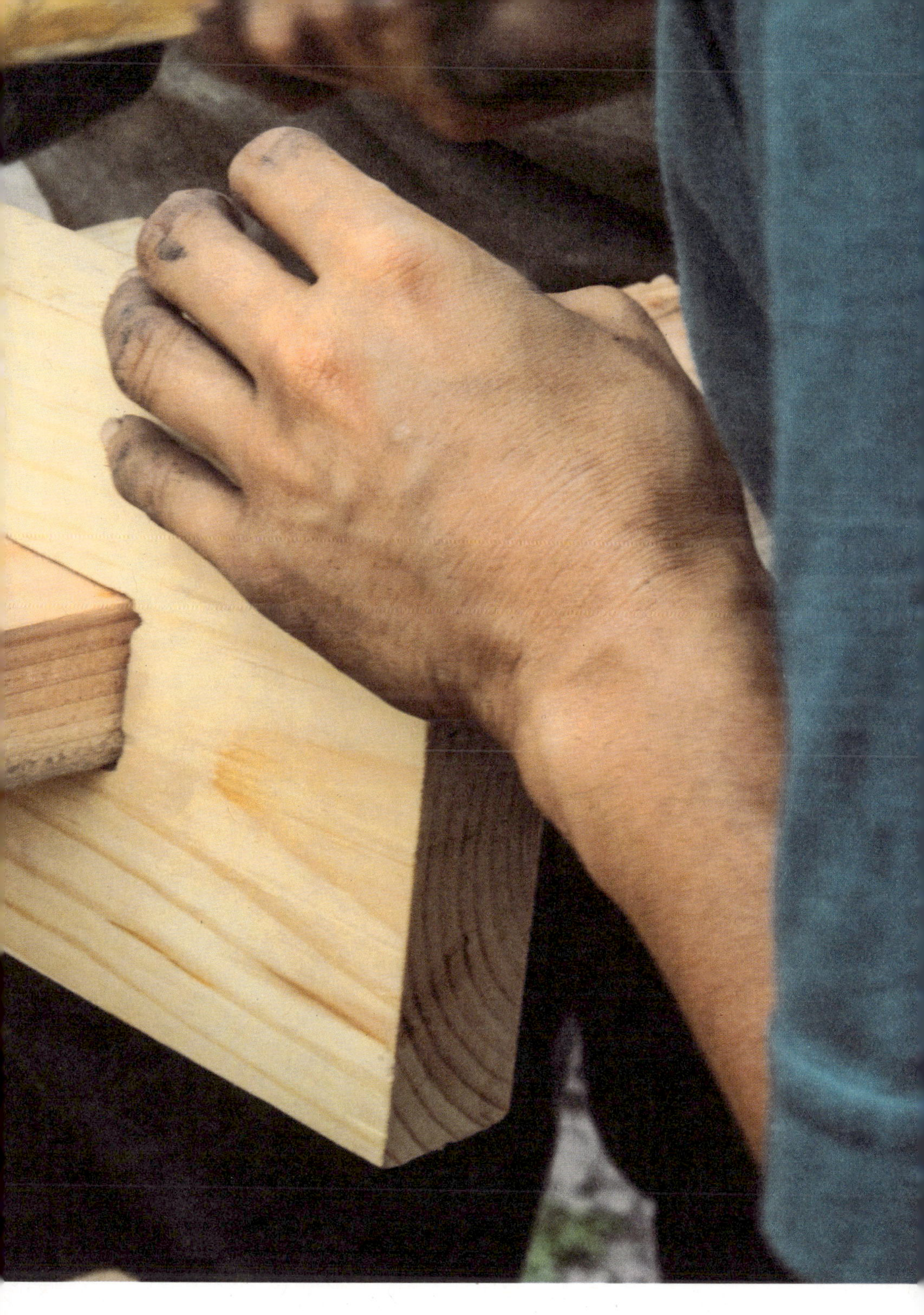

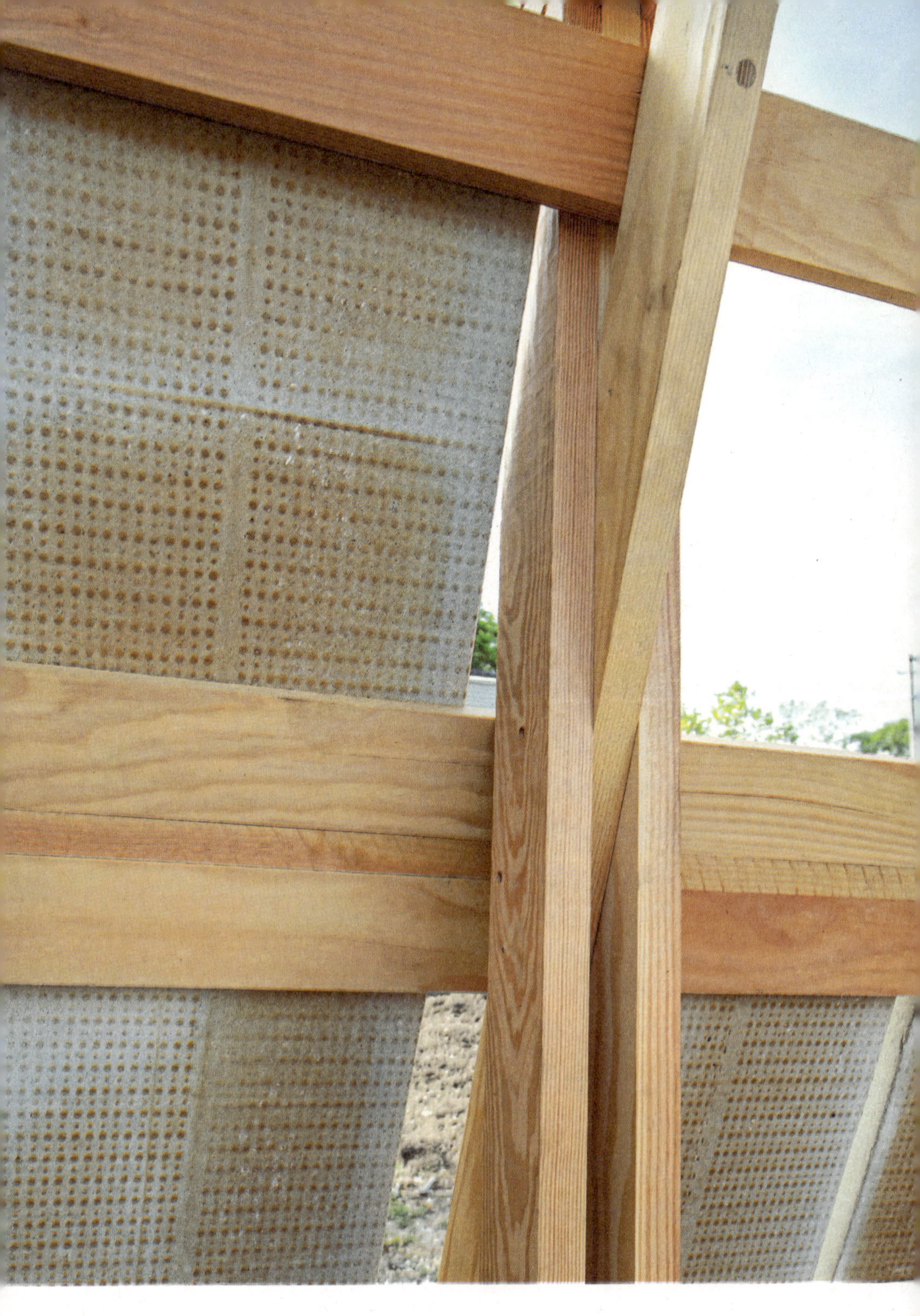

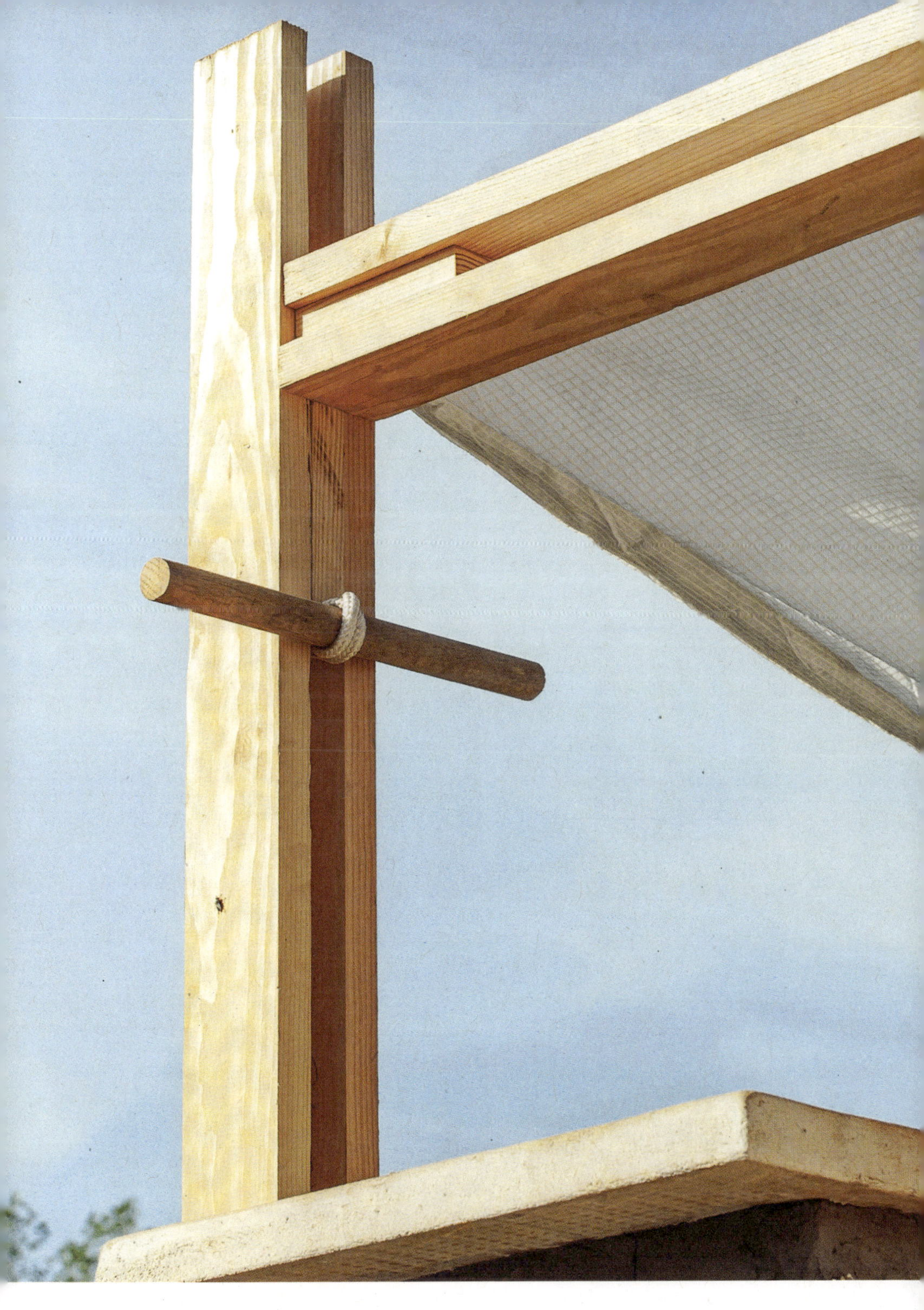

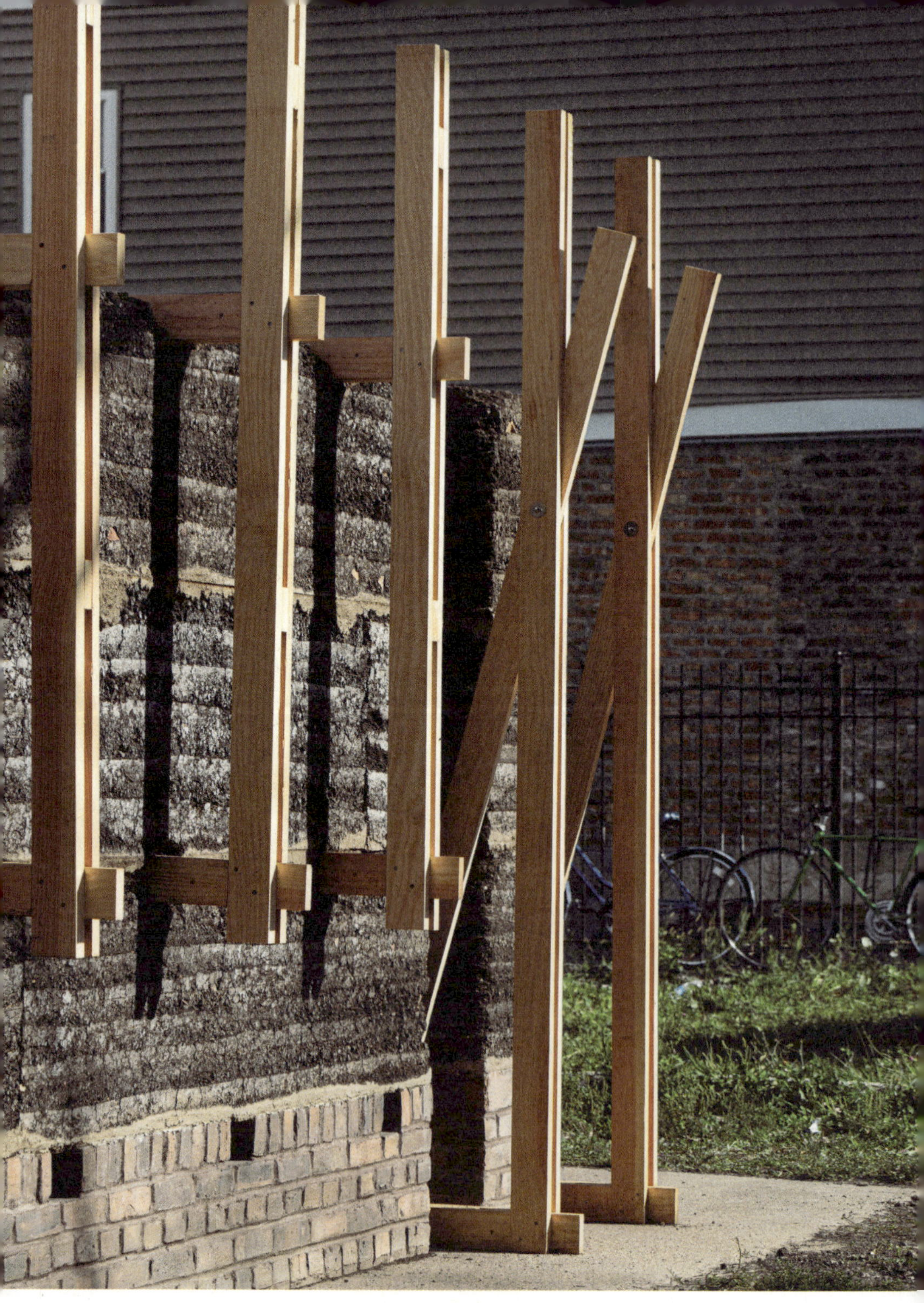

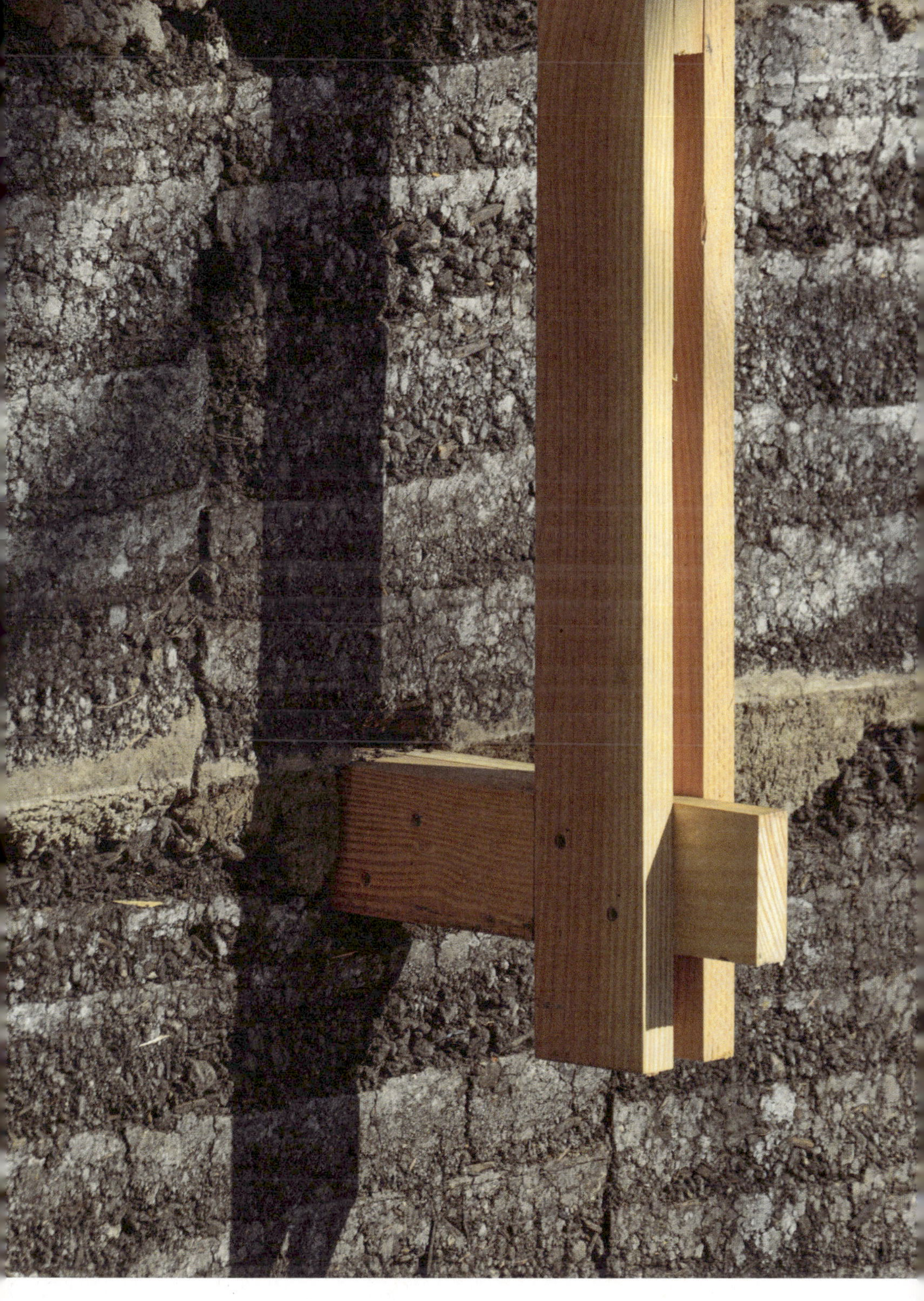

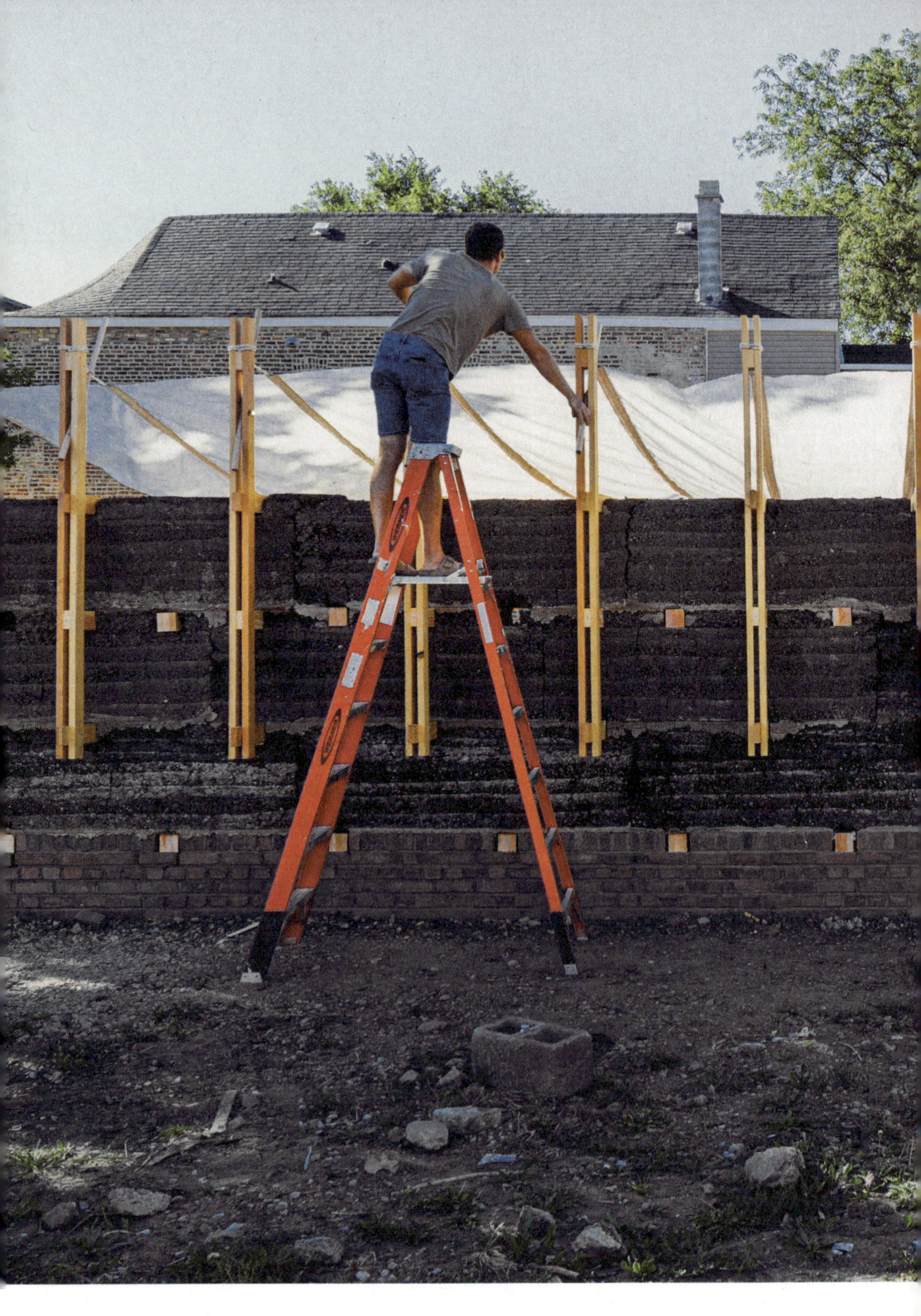

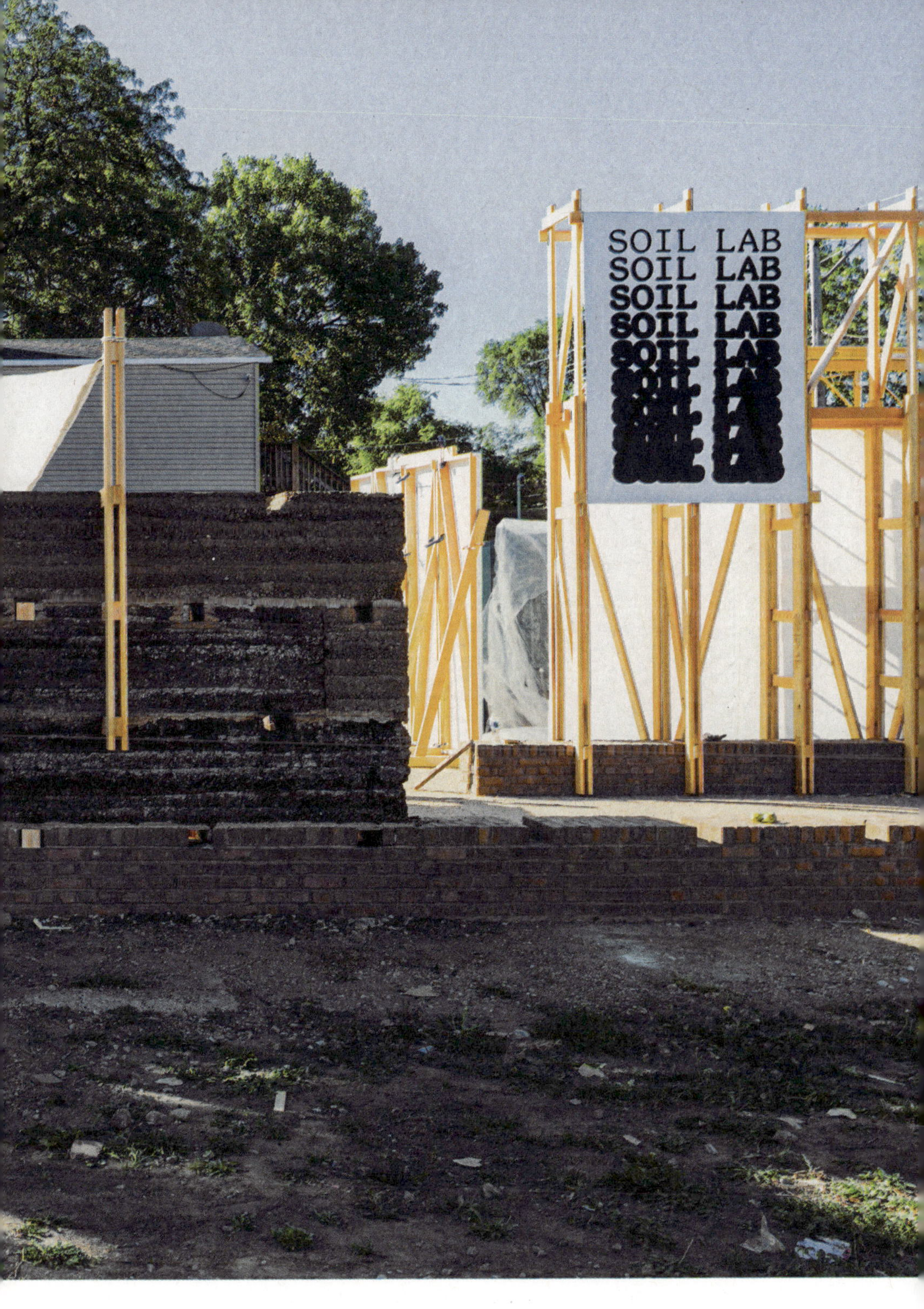
SOIL LAB
SOIL LAB
SOIL LAB
SOIL LAB

Emmett Scanlon

AFTER THE EVENT

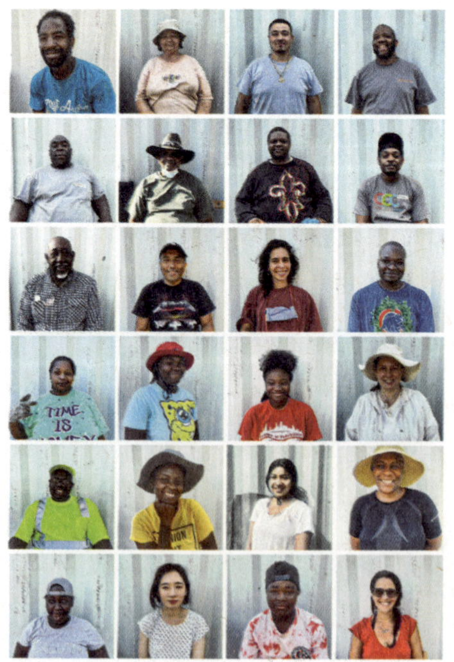

Emmett Scanlon is an architect, curator, editor and broadcaster based in Dublin in Ireland. He is the creator of the architecture podcast *What Buildings Do*, and hosted a conversation with us shortly after the Soil Lab opening event. Emmett's questions and insight brought to the surface themes and ideas deeply embedded in the project, as well as obstacles we faced both from afar and on the ground, in the making of the community structure. Emmett's text in this publication is a continuation of a conversation initiated by this podcast.

I never visited this built thing. I did not make it to Chicago to see it; indeed, I have never been to Chicago at all. I have never discovered it as all mine, as I wandered across the city to find it. As is the way, implicit in their very nature and written in the DNA of these biennials, this timber and mud pavilion, home to a kiln, a site of activity for a period of 19 weeks, is gone, over, lost, complete. It is no longer possible to visit, even if I wanted to.

Architecture, when it finds built form as it did for Soil Lab in Chicago, is a material, spatial thing; it is not abstract. When it comes to a built thing of architecture, you need to experience it to know it, to linger in its company to meaningfully understand it. I know from the drawings and images I have seen of the project, and my knowledge of the team who worked on it, this built thing was intended to be experienced both as it was made and as it was used. It was not built to fulfil some preassigned need or a brief, but rather it emerged as a device to enable gathering, action and making, and through these actions, the built thing—conceptually at least—was intended to dig and ram deeper into local histories, politics, and social and community structures.

The project was built by more people than the Soil Lab team. I recall the phrase "many hands make light work." It is not that the wider community team who built the pavilion made it necessarily easier or quicker to build, but more that, despite its anchoring, there appears to be a lightness to the pavilion that has emerged only through the process of open and evolving construction, from those outside formal architecture or design training. It takes courage to invite this productive uncertainty into an architecture building project, and tenacity to sustain it.

There is much visual evidence of all this: process shots of soil being mixed, timber joints being assembled and hands busy at work together, and posters about workshops and public events. This was an active and activated architecture. A single page of 24 headshots is included in the documentation of the pavilion. The caption confirms these are the *Rammed earth workshop participants, August – September*. Perhaps these portraits should be read as equivalent to, and as vital as, the more traditional representations of the architecture. Before Soil Lab existed, perhaps some of the *Rammed earth workshop participants* had already wandered by, waited on the corner and wondered what next for that land, never imagining they would, for a time, have an active role in its material making and later become a fundamental footnote in its ongoing social, political and architectural history. The inclusion of the portraits is enough to indicate that architecture as a process and a practice, even when applied to a specific built thing on an empty lot in Chicago, does not start on one day and stop on another. The Soil Lab members started this work before they were aware it would happen, before it ever crossed their minds, in other projects in Copenhagen or Ireland, together as a team or while working in other offices. All the time this empty lot stood there, latent.

At some moment, the curator of the Chicago Architecture Biennial and the team decided this would be a place suitable for their 2021 edition and that process began. In a room somewhere, someone probably talked about this land, perhaps presented a PDF or a PowerPoint, and narrated its history and outlined some of its potential. Snow came and went, trees leaved and the sun and political administrations rose and fell, according to the cycles. An application was made in Denmark by an Irish and Danish team. They won, they worked, they waited and wondered from afar. Covid hit. Two moved, two detoured and landed. In so many ways the project started all over again. A Soil Lab team rehearsal in Copenhagen to build timber prototypes and kiln-fire bricks could not prepare entirely for realities on the ground. The soil was contaminated; it lingered longer beneath nails; there was no water to mix soil save that borrowed each morning in buckets from the car wash. The idea of community involvement, first managed and discussed from some distance and in advance, became a complex matrix of human endeavour, care and potential frailty. Work on site progressed not according to any Excel schedule planned in an office but in accordance with the physical capacities of those building it. A day's work was made manifest in the line of soil which showed where ramming had ended, people learning the limits of their bodies. If the schedule slipped, it was because that was all that was possible for someone to do that day. The contractual formality of architect-contractor-community productively blurred. A casual "hello" from a passer-by, at first encouraged and curious and even anxious about sudden activity on the ground, later expanded into more talking, teaching and learning, appropriating, making and remaking the site as found, and finally a portrait photograph.

In the end, there is a quality in this piece of work that is remarkable in that it seems to declare a high level of architectural refinement and detail, yet feels open, ready to be made and remade toward some point of undefined completion. This dance between certainty and specificity—no part of this design is casual in intent or detail—and openness and willingness to deviate according to the capacities of the hands and hearts of the individuals who turn up on any given day, point to an architecture of appropriate social ambition. It is an ambition that much of architecture discourse today still identifies as marginal and fascinating, and not the essential and urgent benchmark needed to meet the needs of societies and the communities that form them.

In such work, the "transformative effect of participation" is often cited as an outcome for a "community" involved. Here, the Soil Lab team, through their inclusion in their press material of that photograph of 24 portraits, perhaps knowingly and cautiously steps back from this rhetoric, choosing instead to not differentiate the people from the project. They are all—person, people, sticks and mud—embedded in that built thing, fired up forever. They are *all* architecture.

The Soil Lab team are now transformed. Somehow that team, once made, was remade. Across the weeks and months, new connections formed, old ones deepened and some broke down. Individually their conceptual and physical capacities were questioned, expanded and burnished. There is change. You hear it now as they talk; it can be seen in the depth of their eyes. It is felt there in their hands, somehow now forever in touch with that dark, rich, sticky soil. Its weight can be felt in how they each carry themselves out into the world, architecture in their bags, now with added pockets and room inside for more than before. Architecture does not start or end; I think it might simply reside in our imagination, waiting. Sometimes, with luck, like in Chicago, architecture finds potent form in the most unlikely of places. When everyone acts, everything changes, and architecture is made to endure.

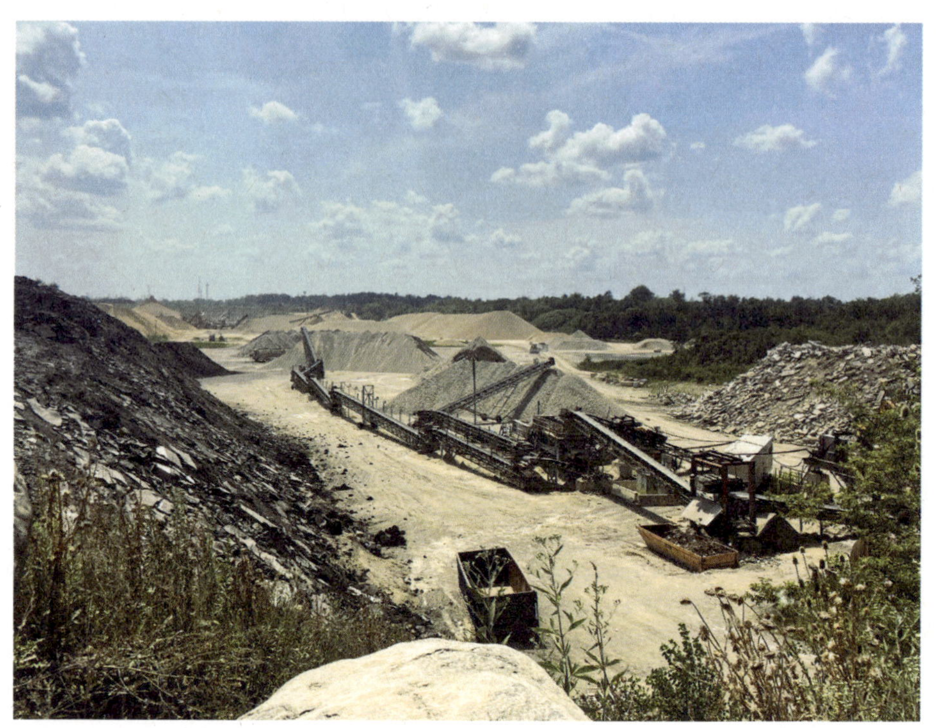

Soil Lab

EXPANDING **GROUND**

Soil Lab unearthed a complex relationship between social disadvantage and the site of North Lawndale. Counter to our initial proposal we were unable to use the soil from the site as it contained toxic elements. Through collaborative workshops with residents and local ecologists, Social Ecologies, we discovered the ground contained the history of its community.

In the 19th century, Chicago was almost level with Lake Michigan; the city's surface didn't naturally drain. A decision was made to elevate the city in an effort to solve the poor drainage of the low-lying swampy ground. Buildings were physically raised on jackscrews, and streets and sidewalks were covered with several feet of soil. Below street level sit myriad props, piles and retaining walls, creating an elevated section that sets the ground rules of the city. The city of Chicago navigates level changes with ease: elevated trains move between buildings above existing infrastructure and bridges span, swing and lift above the river.

After the Great Chicago Fire in 1871, the city looked to noncombustible building materials to comply with new fireproof building codes. Naturally occurring clay deposits along the riverbed, 1.5 to 2 feet beneath the topsoil, provided an ideal raw material for making bricks. This time excavated ground offered a new solution for raising the city. Huge, deep clay pits were dug to harvest the material that would go on to make Chicago common bricks.

As a consequence of the city's industrial legacy, the ground remains a fundamental concern for new construction. In response to Chicago Architectural Biennial's *The Available City*, we wished to hone in on both available material and available resources. Our ambition was to build with earth—the most widely available and venerated material in human history.

Biennials are, by their very nature, temporary: a defined period of time where an event takes place. In contrast, earthen walls are constructed with a permanence in mind. We proposed to play with this dichotomy by building a rammed earth structure for just the duration of the biennial, using local untreated earth to be recycled again after the event.

Only after winning the competition did we learn that access to our site—a vacant lot—came with significant stipulations from the city. Counter to our proposal, soil from the site could not be used due to a high risk it contained toxic elements, and we were told that the lot would need to be covered in protective barriers and 18 inches of wood chip.

We negotiated a change of site to a neighboring vacant lot with an existing concrete slab—a remnant of former habitation—but not being permitted to penetrate the ground unearthed something much richer in the project: the explicit understanding that embedded in the site, written into its ground, was a socio-political geography of the city—one that was fraught with contention and disadvantage.

We introduced ourselves and the ideas behind our project to the local community through a series of online roundtable meetings, and it became clear that the topic of soil was loaded. We wondered what message it would send if we could not use local soil and instead needed to purchase "clean soil" to make our structure. Had the project failed even before it had begun?

The ambition was to equip local people with the skills to construct small interventions that might benefit themselves and the community. In the absence of available soil on-site, this provoked a further question to those involved: for some participants it was the first time they understood that the soil was contaminated, raising an existential question of how they could live in this place. To get people involved in shaping their surrounding environment and embracing the archaic power of building with earth, we searched for a community of makers.

While we were not able to incorporate soil remediation as part of our build, we felt a responsibility to include this discussion as part of the process. Depending on the amount of contamination, it could take several years for the soil to be remediated; the first step was to analyze the existing condition. Originally looking only at soil composition, the focus had now shifted to include chemistry tests to ensure the purchased soil would not include a high percentage of heavy metals. We engaged with Nance Klehm, a local soil ecologist, to help carry out soil tests and help source custom soil for the job. Along with Maxwell Rodencal, a rammed earth enthusiast and graduate architecture student at Cornell University, they formed our soil team. Their research led us to Green Soils Management,

WALLACE LABS	SOILS REPORT	Print Date	Aug. 3, 2021	Receive Date	8/2/21
365 Coral Circle	Location	1312 S. Pulaski			
El Segundo, CA 90245	Requester	Nance Klehm, Social Ecologies			
(310) 615-0116	graphic interpretation: * very low, ** low, *** moderate				
		**** high, ***** very high			

ammonium bicarbonate/DTPA

extractable - mg/kg soil	Sample ID Number	21-215-18	
Interpretation of data	Sample Description	Soil Sample Received 08/02/2021	
low medium high	**elements**		graphic
0 - 7 8-15 over 15	phosphorus	8.80	***
0-60 60 -120 121-180	potassium	253.09	*****
0 - 4 4 - 10 over 10	iron	28.75	*****
0- 0.5 0.6- 1 over 1	manganese	5.83	****
0 - 1 1 - 1.5 over 1.5	zinc	103.74	*****
0- 0.2 0.3- 0.5 over 0.5	copper	62.98	*****
0- 0.2 0.2- 0.5 over 1	boron	0.25	***
	calcium	325.50	***
	magnesium	49.68	**
	sodium	157.77	***
	sulfur	14.20	*
	molybdenum	0.30	****
	nickel	1.17	**
The following trace elements may be toxic The degree of toxicity depends upon the pH of the soil, soil texture, organic matter, and the concentrations of the individual elements as well as to their interactions.	aluminum	n d	*
	arsenic	0.45	*
	barium	0.91	*
	cadmium	1.18	**
	chromium	0.12	*
	cobalt	0.05	*
	lead	167.95	*****
	lithium	0.18	*
	mercury	n d	*
The pH optimum depends upon soil organic matter and clay content- for clay and loam soils: under 5.2 is too acidic 6.5 to 7 is ideal over 8.0 is too alkaline	selenium	n d	*
	silver	n d	*
	strontium	0.53	*
	tin	n d	*
	vanadium	0.32	*

	Saturation Extract			
	pH value	8.05	****	
The ECe is a measure of the soil salinity: 1-2 affects a few plants 2-4 affects some plants, > 4 affects many plants.	ECe (milli-mbo/cm)	0.61	**	
				millieq/l
	calcium	29.9		1.5
	magnesium	6.3		0.5
	sodium	88.7		3.9
	potassium	21.0		0.5
	cation sum			6.4
problems over 150 ppm	chloride	22		0.6
good 20 - 30 ppm	nitrate as N	18		1.3
	phosphorus as P	0.5		0.0
toxic over 800	sulfate as S	13.1		0.8
	anion sum			2.7
toxic over 1 for many plants	boron as B	0.18	*	
increasing problems start at 3	SAR	3.8	***	
est. gypsum requirement-lbs./1000 sq. ft.		27		
	relative infiltration rate	slow/fair		
	estimated soil texture	sandy loam		
	lime (calcium carbonate)	yes		
	organic matter	low/fair	hydrophobic	
	moisture content of soil	6.0%		
	half saturation percentage	23.4%		

Elements are expressed as mg/kg dry soil or mg/l for saturation extract.
pH and ECe are measured in a saturation paste extract. nd means not detected.
Analytical data determined on soil fraction passing a 2 mm sieve.

a 68-hectare landscape waste and composting facility in Dundee, Illinois, 40 miles northwest of our site. It is an enormous site where megatonnes of soil from the Illinois area are dumped, screened, sorted and moved daily before being collected and shipped off to other parts of the city. The speed at which ground here is moved and mixed before being sold and sent off to new locations stands in stark contrast to the time it takes for clay deposits to form. The exchange of soil is a commercial economy.

As interlopers in an underemployed, under-served and disinvested context, we asked basic questions afresh. Why couldn't we touch the ground? Why couldn't the site have temporary access to water and electricity? Why should biennials be predicated on volunteerism? What if the investment in this post-industrial landscape we found ourselves in could be in the people?

Soil Lab sought to engage with these issues in a meaningful way within the framework of a biennial. Building materials, tools and equipment were sourced locally where possible and remained in the community after the biennial. The remainder of Soil Lab's resources was spent on investing in local people and labor, both skilled and unskilled; everyone who engaged with the project was paid an hourly wage for their time and effort, from local craftspeople and tradespeople to community participants.

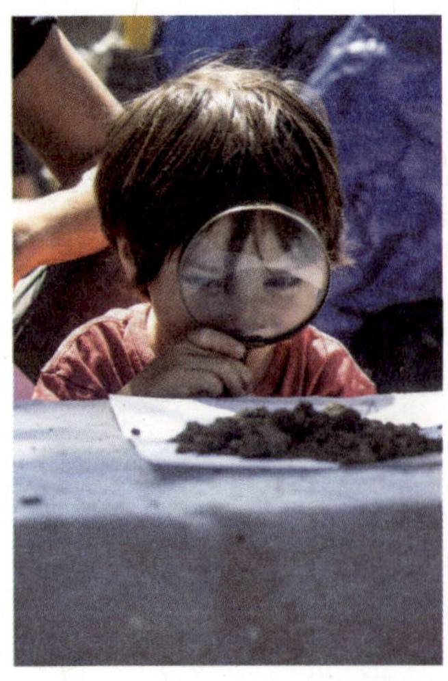

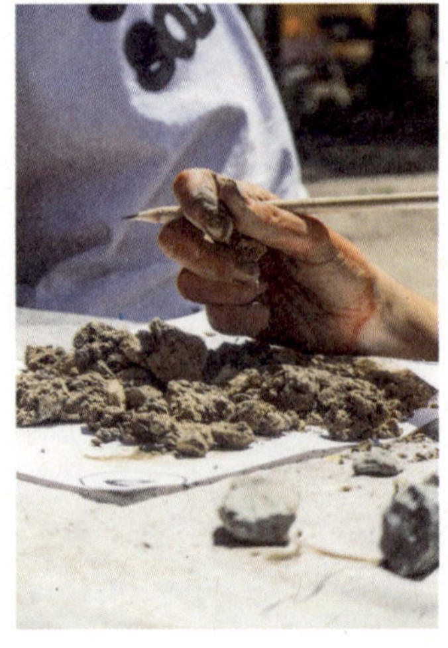

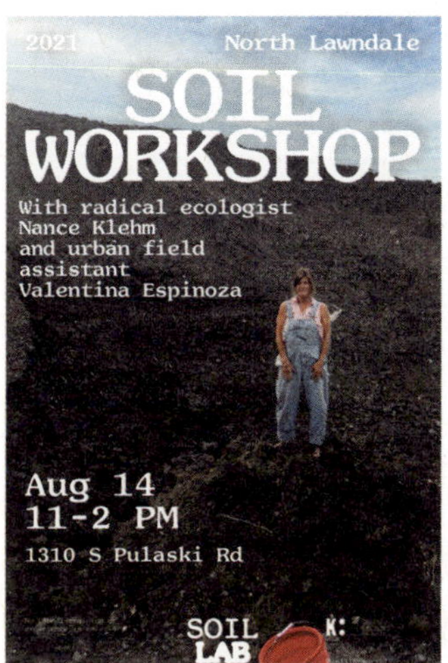

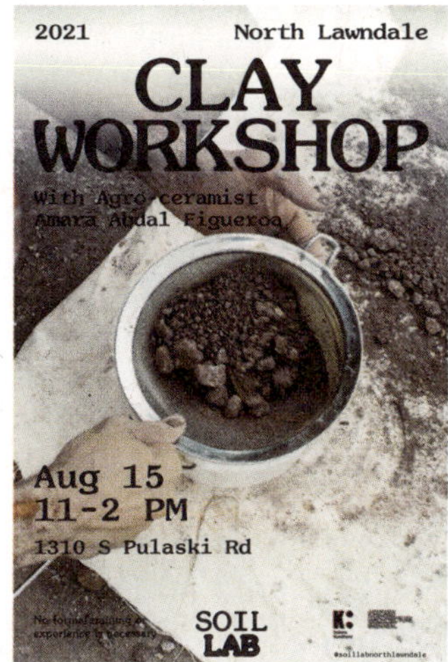

Soil was the medium that brought us together. Three different construction methods were introduced in our workshops, each a different expression of soil: rammed earth, bricks and ceramics. We sought to ask questions of permanence, investment, time, energy and legacy through our soil laboratory. The walls of the pavilion, made of unfired earth, were in place for only four months. It took six weeks of ramming manpower to raise them. It was through the making of these walls that we built our community. While the walls were demolished and material recycled, the investment and time was in the people. The clay in bricks and ceramic tiles change state when fired to become permanent; we too changed state in the making of the temporary pavilion through the generosity of the community.

The success of the project was in the conversations. Together, we discovered the ground contained the history of its community. The toxins in the soil revealed systemic racism and the reasons for social upheaval: riots, white flight, unjust planning legislation and the demolition of the community's heritage. At a time when the world was emerging from a global pandemic, the most we could aim to achieve was to inhabit the space and engage with the community through building and discussion. Though the walls began to crack before the biennial's end, the success of the project was not undermined; ultimately, like any building, the project was bigger than its physical construction.

Sami Akkach

ARCHITECTURE FOR THE MORE

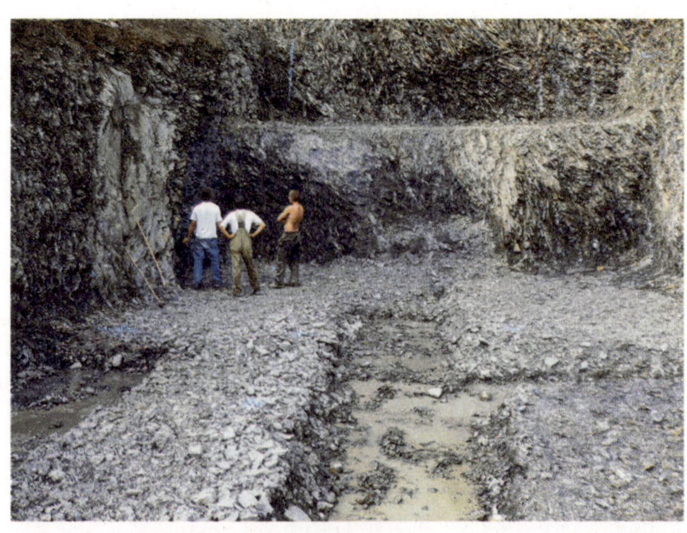

The pit that became Haus Rauch. Turning this “waste” into walls saved about 14,000 euros in disposal fees

In November 2021, two months after the biennial had opened and three months after we had first begun ramming, we reached out to Martin Rauch's studio in Schlins, Austria. We were novices in rammed earth construction before this project and wished to reflect critically on the construction of our walls so we could learn from our mistakes. Our rammed earth endeavours were received with genuine interest and curiosity by both the local community and further afield, and we felt that we owed it to the project to continue our investigations, analyzing lessons learned in an open conversation. Sami graciously responded to our email: "Regarding the technical execution of the build, there is room for improvement, and we could certainly offer some advice." He suggested we begin with a video call.

I often receive a typical enquiry that asks: "We have a sustainable project we are developing and we want to build it out of rammed earth. Can we use the earth from our site? And how much will it cost per square meter?" It is an innocuous request that reveals a lot about the current state of the building sector. Usually, the enquiry is from an architect and after the concept design has been made. I'm looking at a render already. The design almost always features a rammed earth facade, and the structural system is yet to be confirmed. The designer has applied a beautifully textured rammed earth skin with a swift click of the mouse. If only it were so easy.

Rammed earth is experiencing a renaissance: the climate crisis and growing awareness of the impacts of the building industry have spurred a search for alternative materials. A huge slice of the credit for the invigorated interest in contemporary rammed earth has to go to Martin Rauch. The recent laureate of the Global Award for Sustainable Architecture is not an architect, not by training at least. He is a ceramicist and builder who, through his expert craftsman's knowledge of clay, has experimented and innovated with earth as a building material for so long and to such a degree of quality that his output has become an example to established architects in their transition to ecologically sensible design.

Rauch started the company Lehm Ton Erde Baukunst ("Loam Clay Earth Building Art") some 30 years ago in his provincial Austrian hometown of Schlins. The office and factory remain here, but requests for work come from all corners of the world. The most ubiquitous of materials—earth—somehow requires the most specialized knowledge. Most architects do not start with a material, asking what they can build with it. Once a concept has been translated into three dimensions, often the material palette is eye-dropped onto various tectonic elements. The making of the building is very much a subsequent process. Our industrialized building materials cater to this: designers are used to specifying a cladding system, ordering it at a predetermined price per square meter, having it delivered to the building site, and the contractor knowing how to assemble it. This process doesn't work for rammed earth.

During the first video call with the enquiring architect, we discuss the process of turning the ground of their site into their building. I sometimes ask: "What else could you build your project with using only the material on-site?" Invariably, there is no other material. Even if the plot features a forest, those trees still need to be felled, dried and then processed into workable timber. With earthen construction, however, the thread between raw material and finished wall is less understood. To design and build a rammed earth building requires a more integrated approach between the designer and maker than methods more conventional in the west.

To realize a rammed earth building, the enquiring architect needs to know it will be a journey for them and their client. As the veil of hopefulness begins to lift to reveal the deflated expression of understanding, the logistical questions begin to amass. How deep do we need to dig? Where do we store the material? Where do we mix the material? What equipment do we need? Where do we get that equipment? Who will build it? Who knows how to build it? How do we train them? These challenges are not insurmountable, but they do require patience and money. We, Lehm Ton Erde, have also reached a point where we need to see a desire to carry on the technique into future projects. Like morale on the battlefield, motivation on the building site is an unquantifiable factor that affects the quality of the walls. Unfortunately, on some projects on which we have taught, the fever didn't grip. After a long, yet usually profitable, journey, the contractor finds repeating the process too daunting, laying that transferred know-how to rest.

To determine if the material on-site is worthy of wall-building requires an experienced hand. "It is simpler than a recipe for making bread: the sun is the only cooker required," William Facey wrote in 1997 in reference to adobe brick production in vernacular Najdi architecture. The domestic analogy holds, even if it is not quite so straightforward. A rammed earth mixture requires a recipe, and the recipe includes the method and the ingredients. The mixing method is adapted to the site situation, the quantity needed and the contractor's available infrastructure. The ingredients are gravel, sand and silt as the aggregates, and clay as the binder. In our experience, any site-won material can make up at least half of a rammed earth mix; it is a matter of course for us to maximize the amount of excavated site material in the mix. In the case of Haus Rauch, completed by Lehm Ton Erde in 2008, the mix was 100 percent site material. What constituents can't be found in the excavation must be sourced locally—it is the transport of this material which usually has the largest impact on lifecycle emissions of rammed earth walls. What is commonly referred to as rammed earth, with its wavy pigmented layers, is more like rammed concrete and will contain anywhere from 5 to 12 percent Portland cement as a stabilizer, making it behave like a completely different material. In this text, I only refer to unstabilized rammed earth, meaning no cement or lime is added to the mixture.

Rammed earth is not a standardized product: every project varies as much as the geology beneath it. This custom-fit process, coupled with a labor-intensive production technique, makes rammed earth a costly material to implement in countries with high wages. In his 1969 book *Architecture for the Poor*, the Egyptian architect Hassan Fathy wrote, "A house is essentially a communal production: one man cannot build one house, but a hundred men can easily build a hundred houses." This was not only a reflection on the organisation of labor in rural communities; it was also a quantification of the effort needed to produce a house.

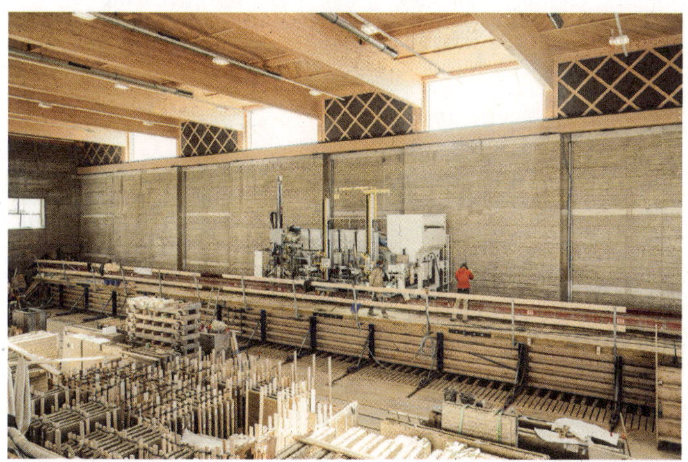

The ERDEN Werkhalle with Roberta, the prefabricating robot, running along its track, ramming 40m² of earth, layer by layer. In the foreground, 7cm-thick rammed earth interior lining panels dry on their pallets

As a technique, rammed earth has changed little over thousands of years, requiring many man-hours for mixing, formwork and ramming.

In bygone times, local labor was adept at using local materials. In Egypt, it was the knowledge of adobe makers that produced houses. In the province of Vorarlberg, where Lehm Ton Erde is based, it was the Walser craftsmen using timber. Skip forward an age and industrialized materials reduced the need for so many experts. Instead of each village having its own mud-brick expert, a whole region could have a single brick factory as long as transportation was available. Distribution of know-how gave way to distribution of off-the-shelf building materials. Specialized knowledge gave way to a standardized product. There is now a need for industrialized, premixed raw earthen materials, and prefabricated rammed earth building elements, as produced by Lehm Ton Erde.

When Lehm Ton Erde started, all projects were produced in situ; mixing was done on-site because the earth was already there. This had the obvious advantage of lower embodied energy due to a lack of transportation. It also maintained the poetic narrative of a building made of its place. Since then, with the development of prefabrication and the difficulty of mixing on-site on many projects, we have centralized our operations. Our factory prepares waste material: excavated earth from groundworks partners,

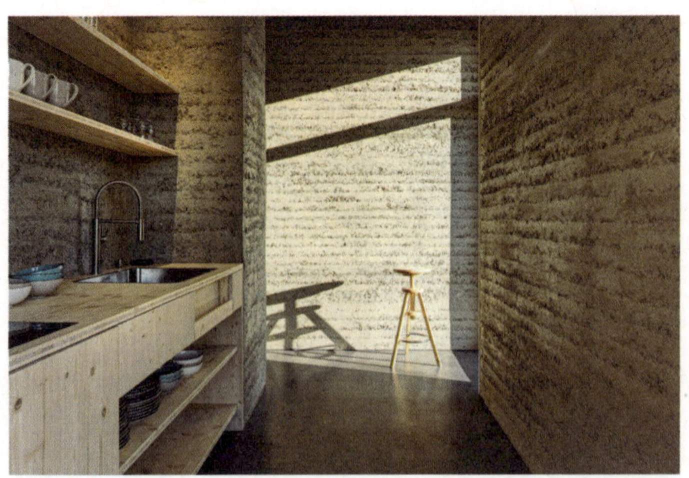

A close collaboration between architect and maker, the Atelier AHA is a "Scandinavian kasbah" as the designer Sven Patrick Krecl puts it, where materiality was key to evoking atmospheres from the clients' cross-cultural experiences

trucked in from underground parking lots and roadworks from the Walgau, our valley in the Alps. We produce bespoke rammed earth elements in a controlled manner, planned well in advance, to reduce time and cost on-site.

Some have critiqued that centralizing production increases the embodied carbon of rammed earth by increasing transportation. This is true, and we consider this when we choose projects to execute. It doesn't make sense to freight heavy earthen blocks halfway across Europe, as the logistical emissions begin to stack up. This simple observation needs to be put into perspective, however. Concrete requires huge energy input: cement produces 1kg of CO_2 per 1kg output and requires large-scale limestone mining. Concrete's other constituents—sand and gravel—are the most extracted group of minerals and are often sourced from different quarries. These components all need to get to the batching plant which mixes them, and then the concrete needs to be transported to site. And that is before we get to the end-of-life and pollution part of the discussion. There is no comparison between concrete and prefabricated rammed earth when it comes to their logistical impacts.

A building is the terminus of the vast, geophysical processes through which modern architecture is extracted. Our cities are made of stuff mined and processed off-site and out of sight, often leaving behind landscapes and communities in ruin. A modern steel and concrete structure is made of materials chosen for their resistance to gravity and wind loads, not their load to the planet. But environmental and social loads constitute the architecture: the design of a building is inseparable from them. To reduce the immense impact of a building's resources—material, labor, energy—we need to return to locally sourced and produced building matter. We need more earth builders everywhere to facilitate growing demand, whether it takes the form of centralized prefabrication facilities and industrialized premixed suppliers of earthen materials, or a universal trade with small earth-building companies as ubiquitous as carpenters, able to turn a plot to *pisé*. Both are occurring across Europe, and as rammed earth and its practitioners spread, more equipment will be available. Shortages in skilled labor will be filled. Infrastructure and regulations will catch up. Projects will become more feasible.

Fundamentally, the impetus for this discussion is the climate crisis: bioclimatic design, aesthetics, economics, energy costs, livelihoods or a return to craftsmanship are all secondary. From post-war Germany to Afghan refugee camps today, earth has always been used during crisis. It is omnipresent, requires no fossil energy, is independent of transportation, and can be produced with the most rudimentary tools and infrastructure. With its origins in every ancient civilisation, its time earth was used to rebuild ours.

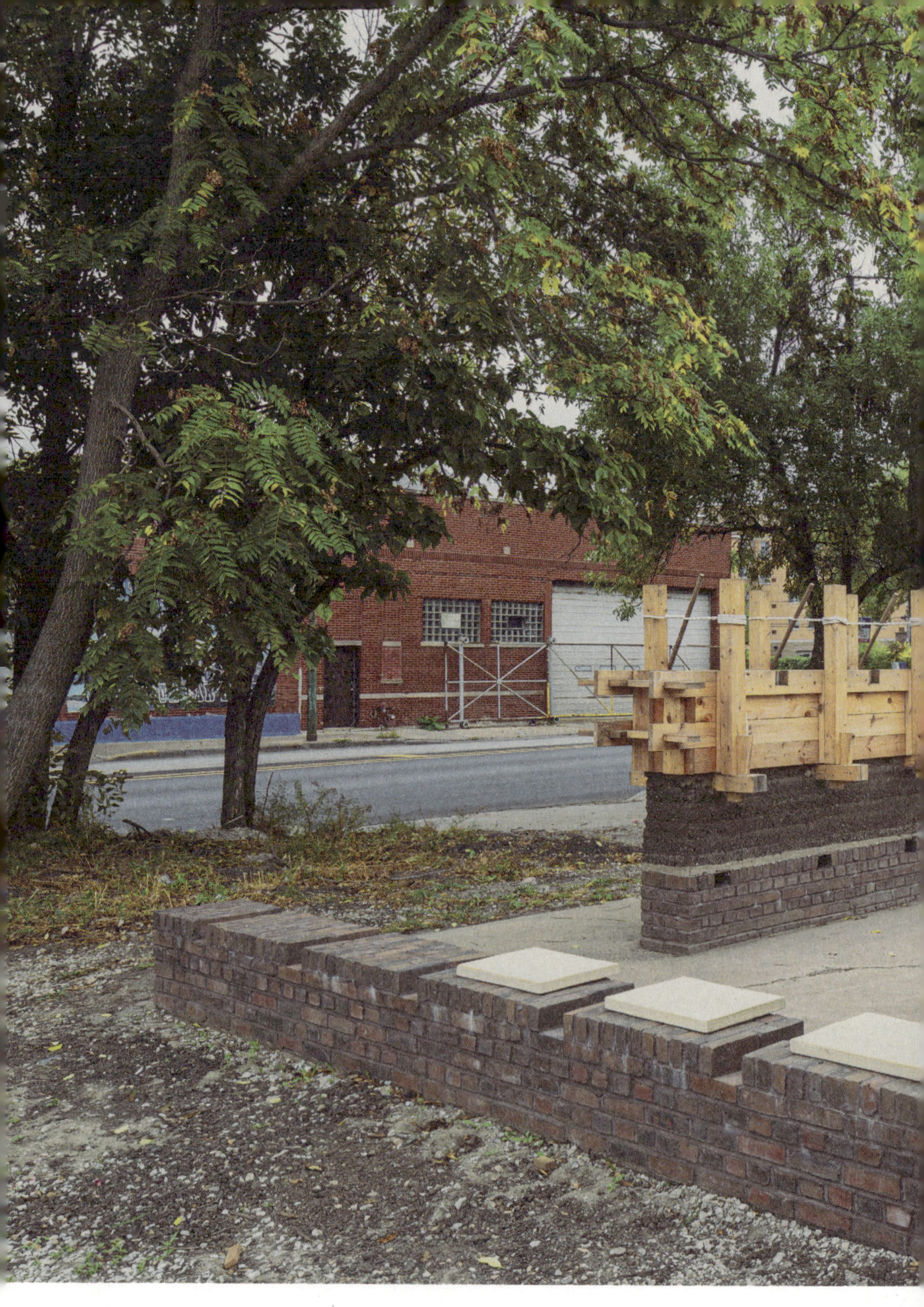

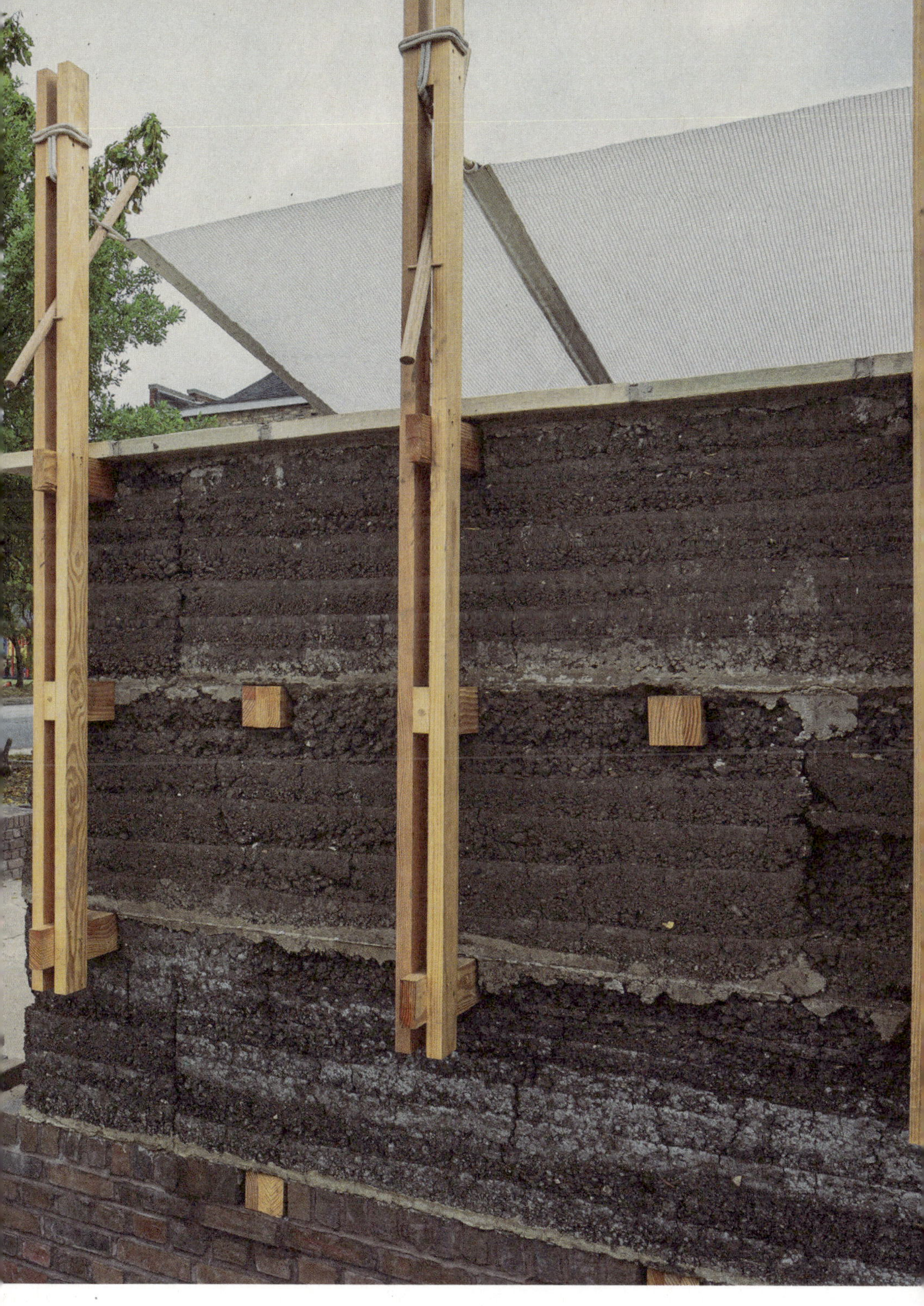

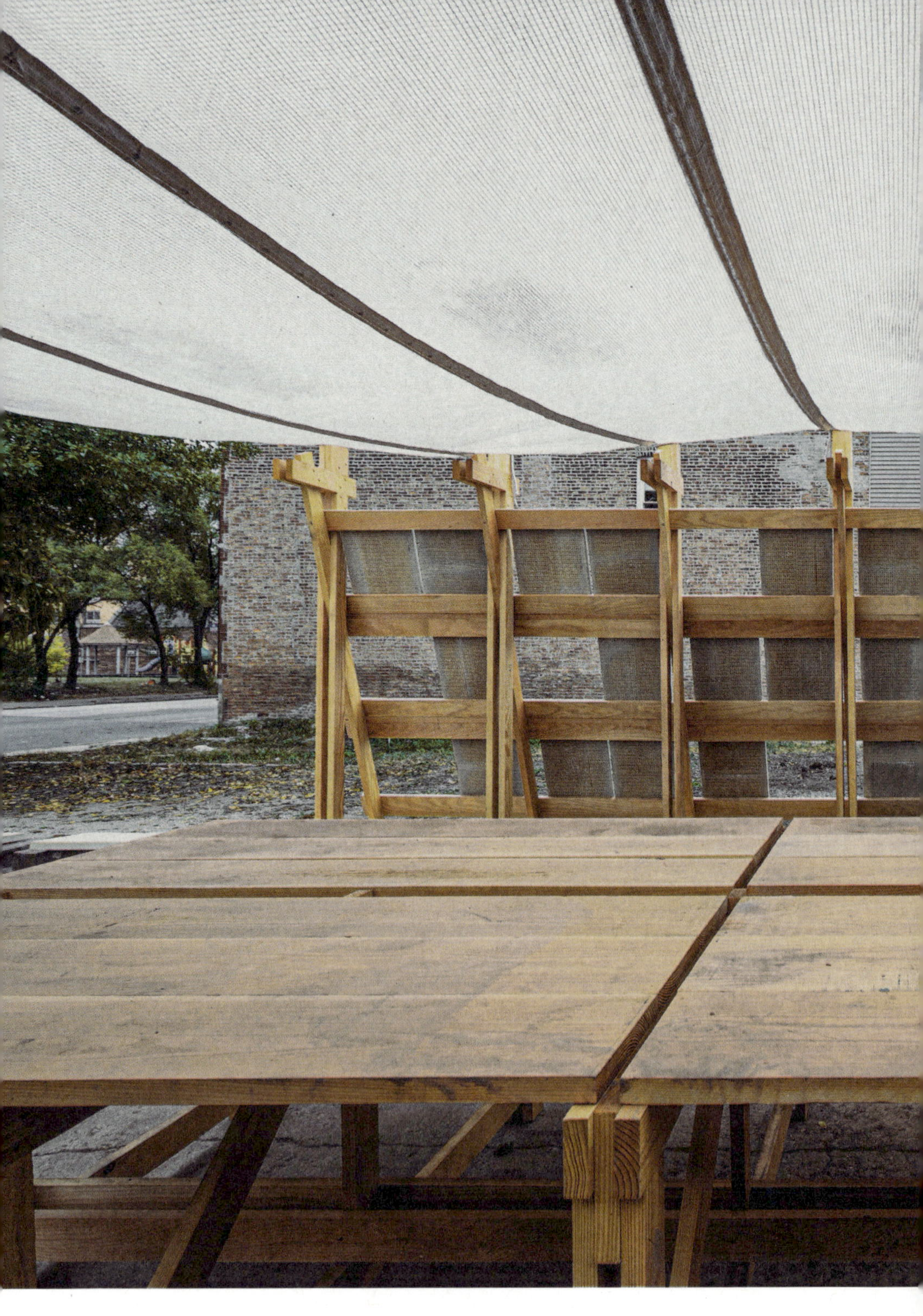

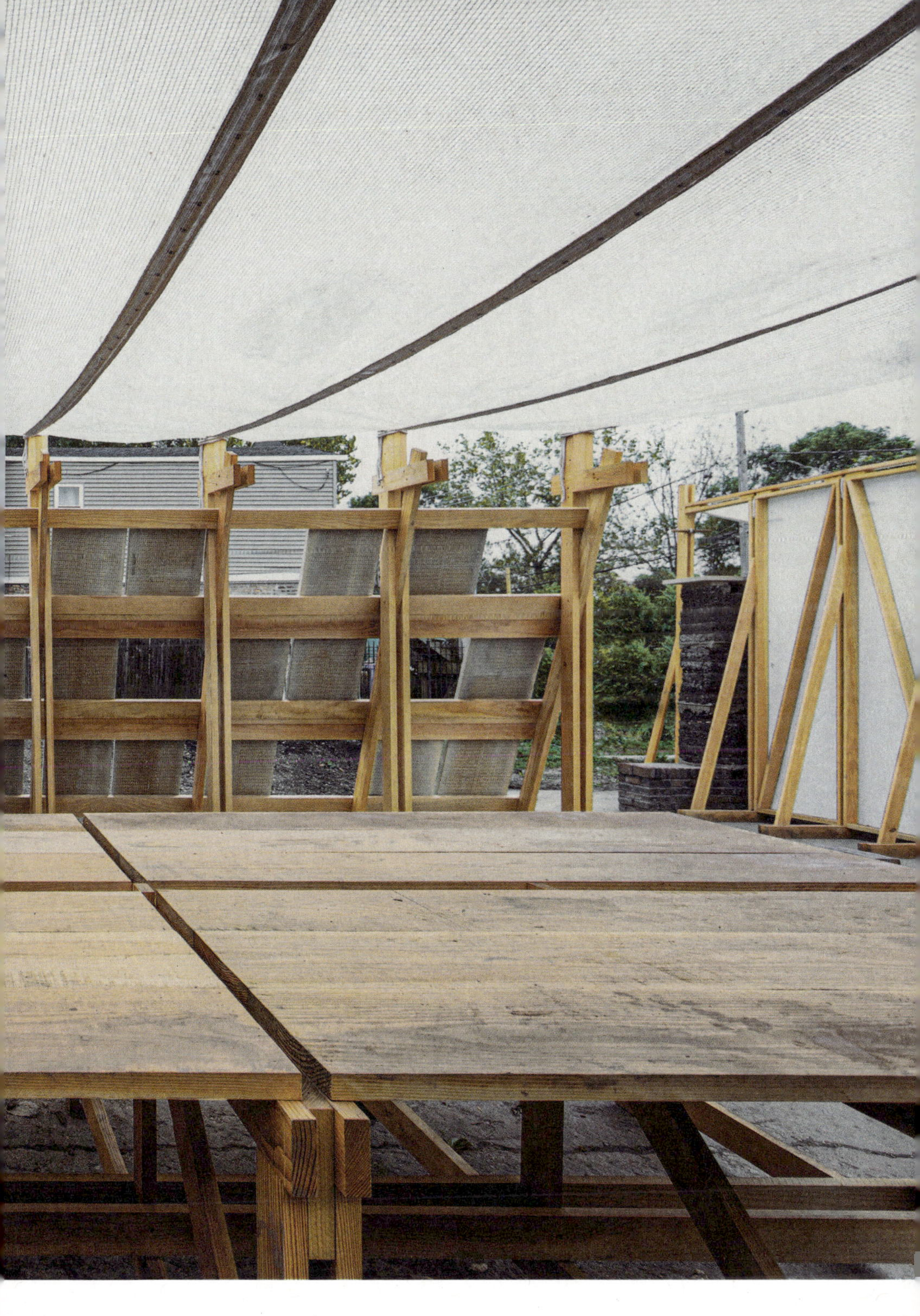

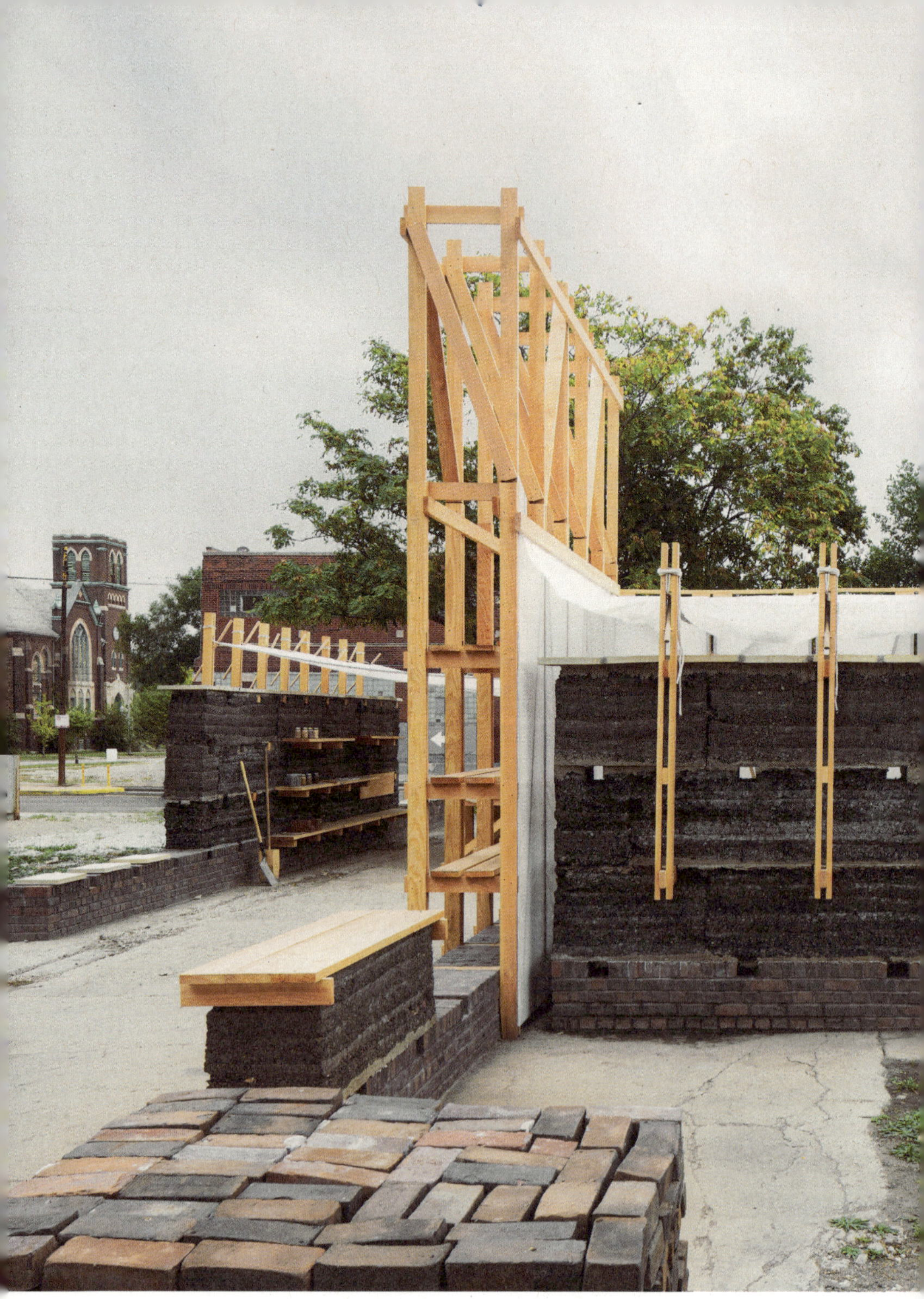

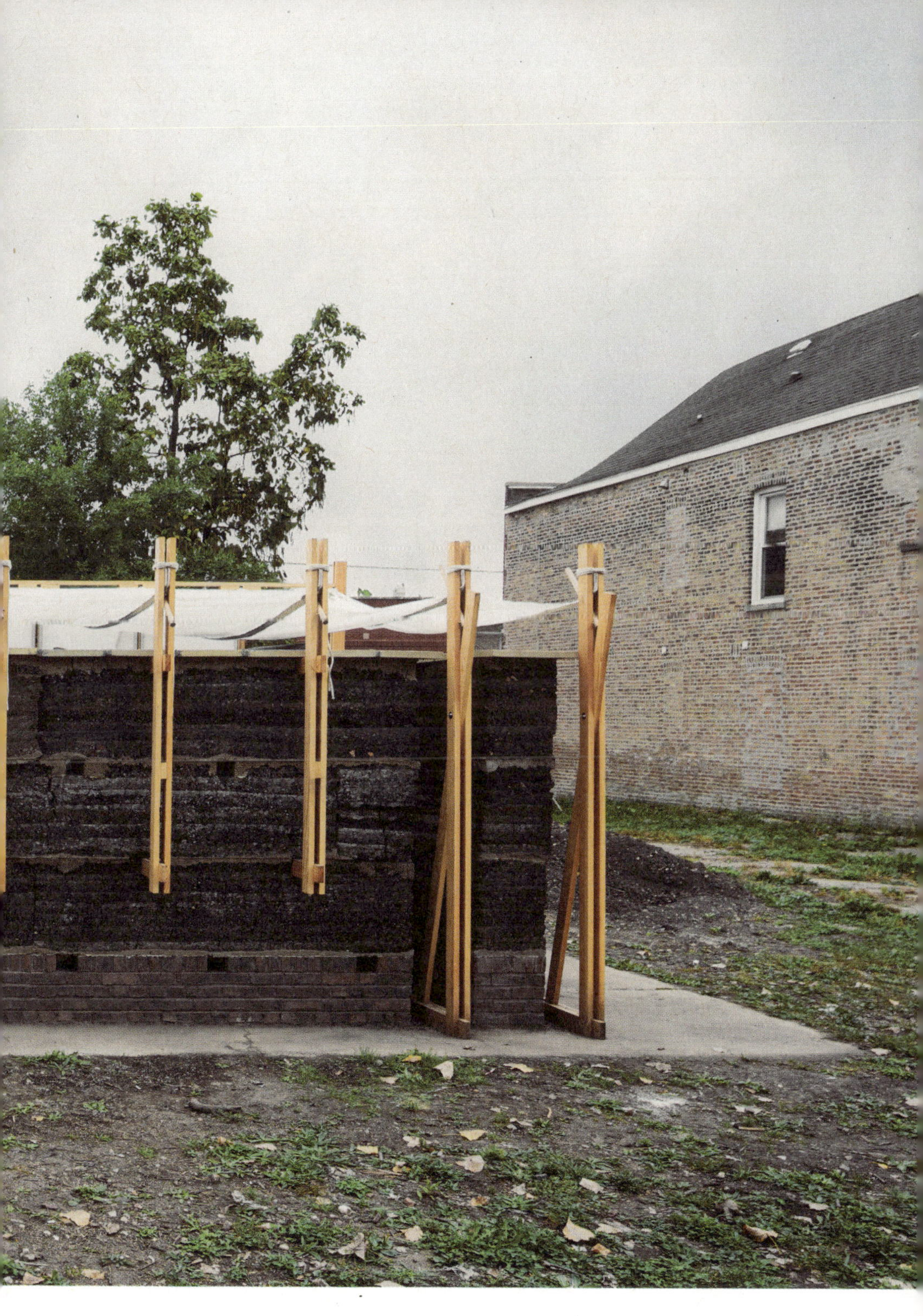

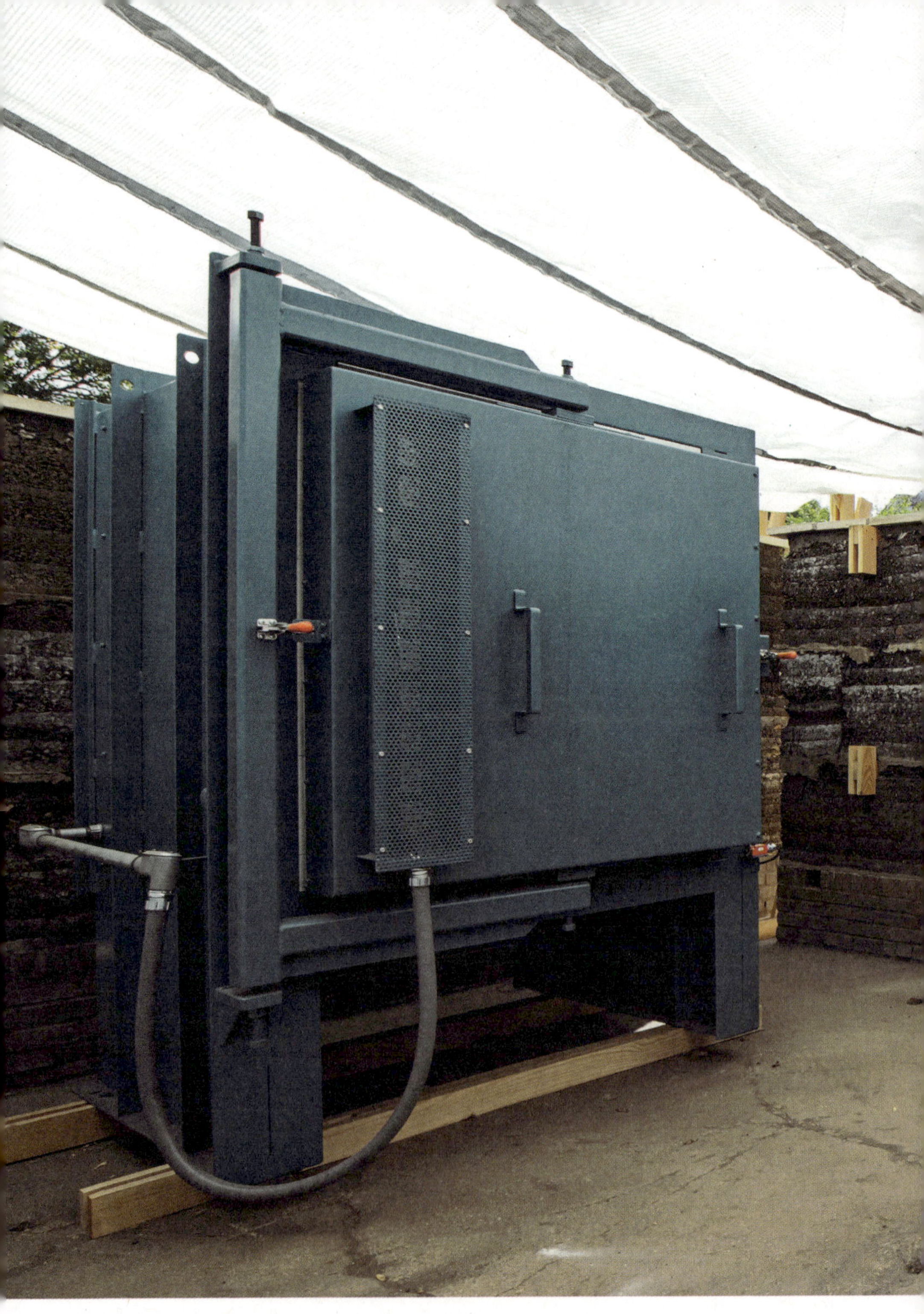

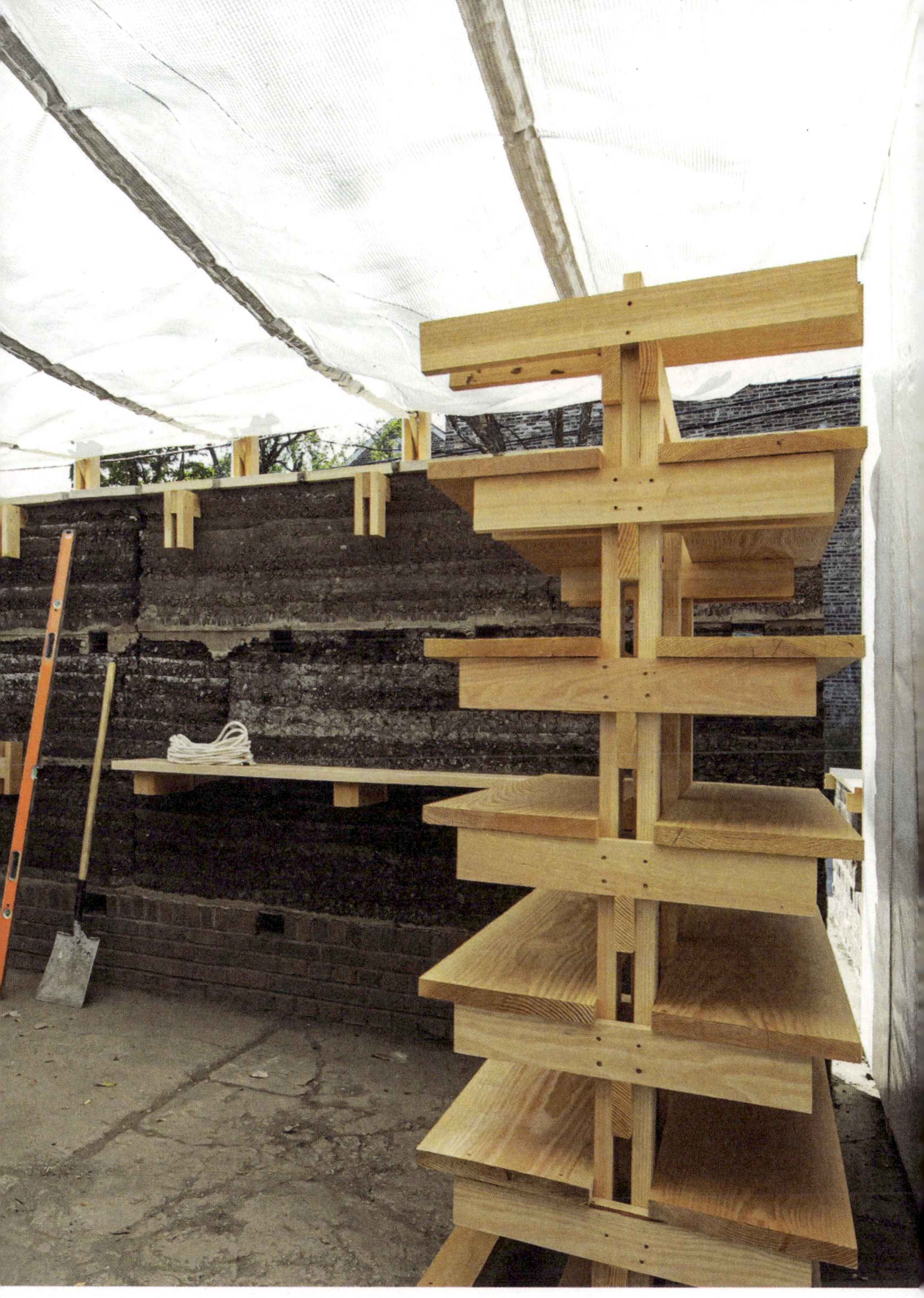

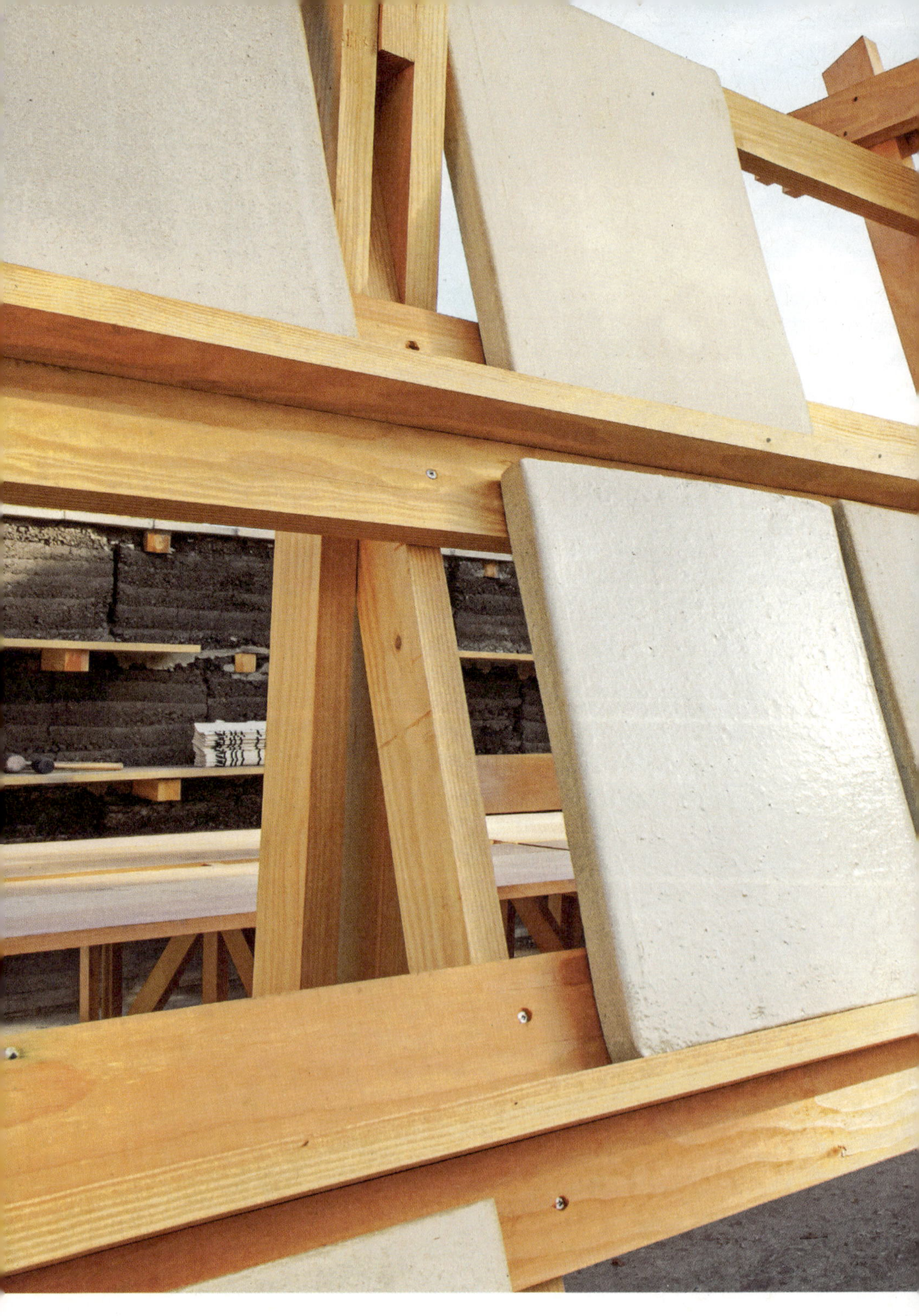

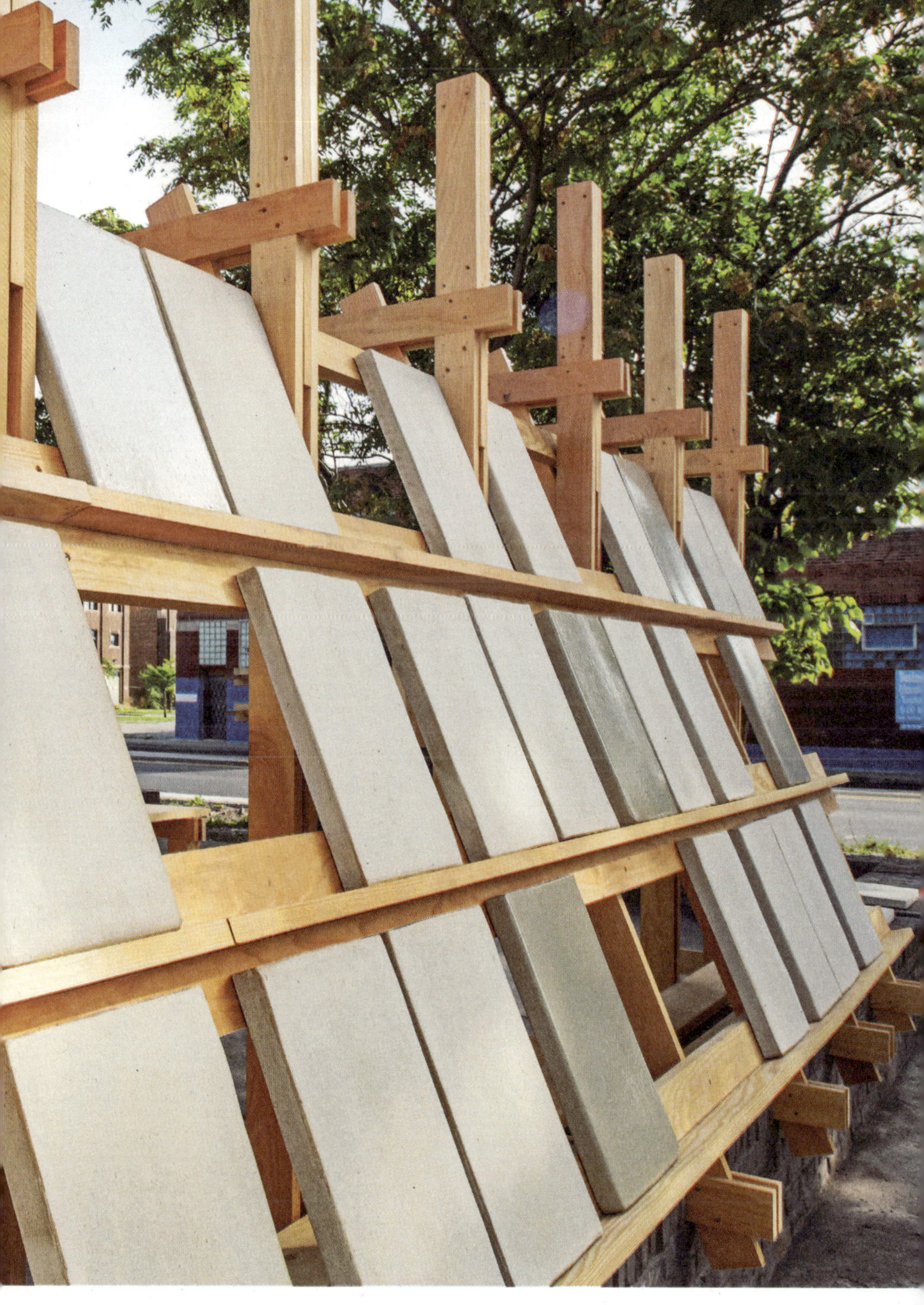

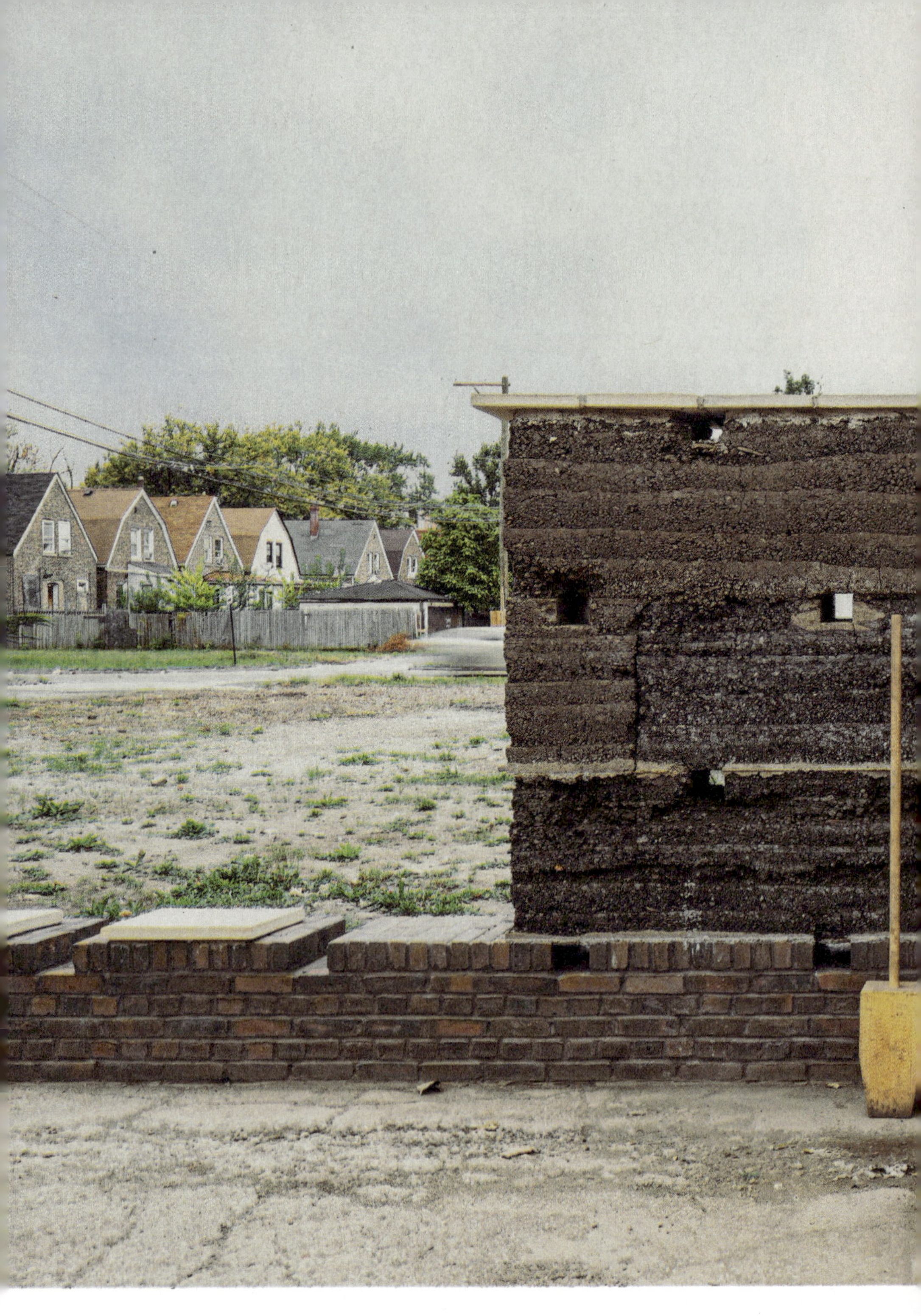

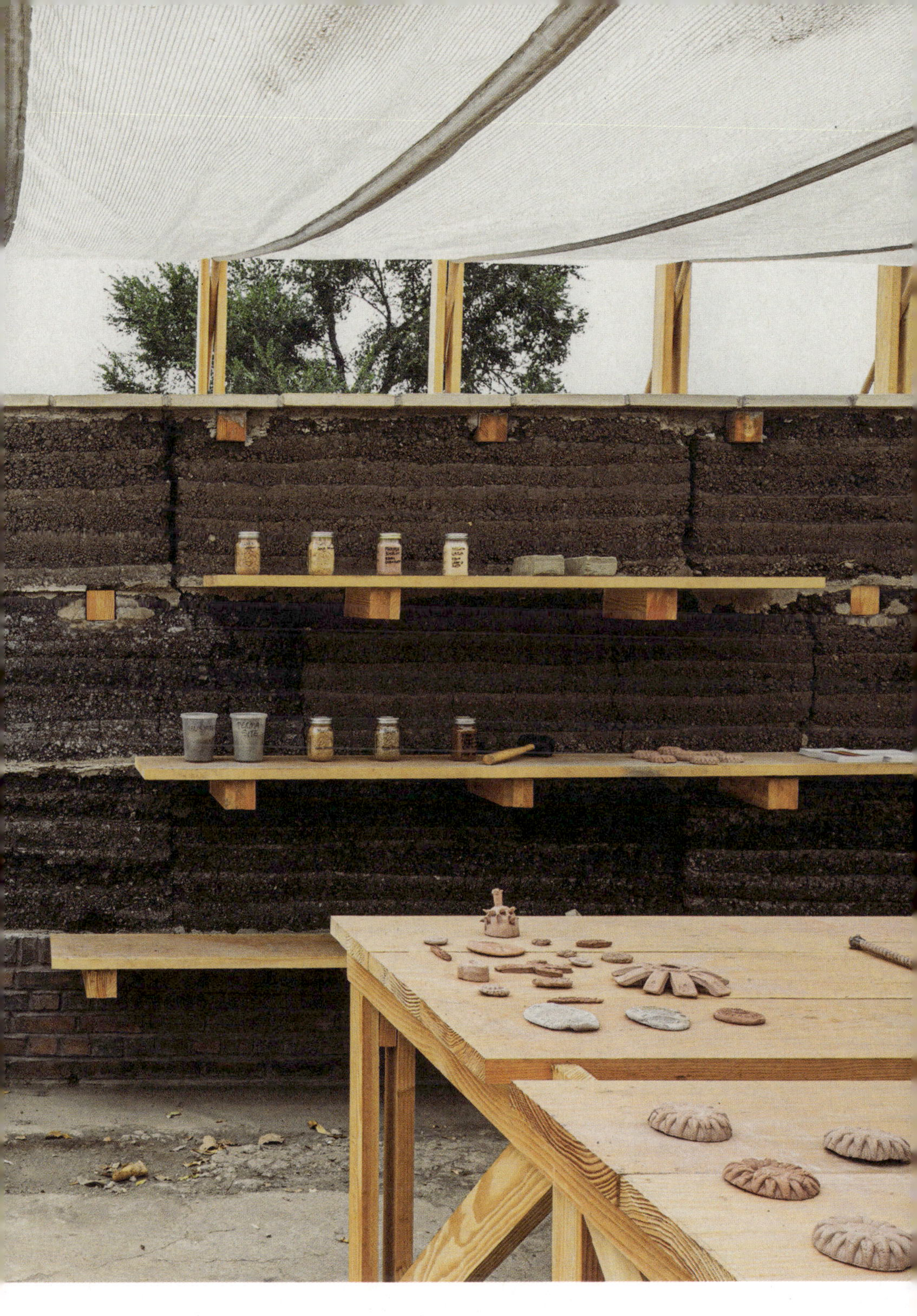

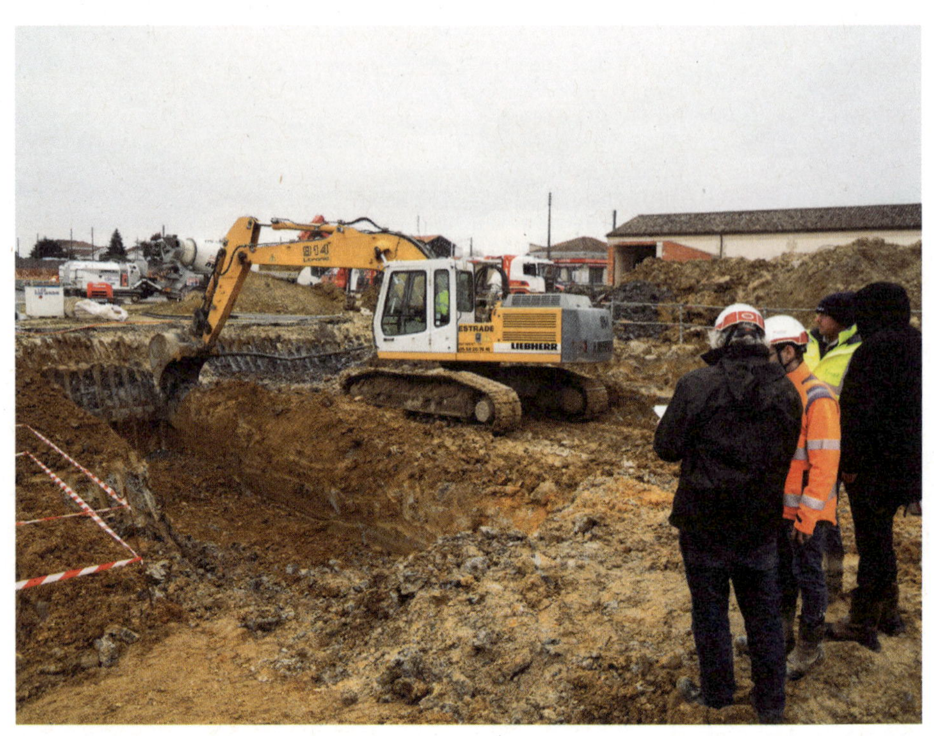

Sami Akkach

STIRRED NOT TUMBLED: A RECIPE FOR RAMMED EARTH

In June 2021, while based in Copenhagen testing soil ratios, we searched naively for the magic ratio of silt, sand, clay and aggregate. Ratios ranged from source to source. When the eight big bags of clay soil ordered from waste-processing company Solum arrived, we queried why they had delivered sand: the soil from Roskilde, on the north of Zealand, was yellow, grainy and sandy to touch. This was our first introduction to the richness and variety of soil types across the world. Many failed tests later we understood that the clay content of this Danish soil was low. We learnt the ratio would depend on the makeup of the local found ground. Below is a step by step guide, the kind of recipe we searched for when starting out.

Every rammed earth building is as unique as the geology beneath it. Turning that geology into architecture requires a recipe: the ingredients and the method that allow one to build consistently with a non-standardized material to modern standards. The ingredients—silt, sand and gravel as the compressive constituents and clay as the binding matter—are universally available. The challenge is finding them in the right ratios. This method describes how the ingredients from a building site can be prepared into ready-to-ram loose earthen material.

Developing a rammed earth recipe is a process that adapts with each new project. There is no one-size-fits-all approach. The ever-changing subsoil composition, construction type, local infrastructure, labor force, project size and timeline all influence the design of the recipe. In bygone times, the range of earth that was built with was broader. Legal and reputational risks now dictate a more precise and standard specification of the recipe, and this can mean more adaptation to the local excavation material.

Developed over 35 years, the steps given here are a general outline of the workflow Lehm Ton Erde follows when creating a new recipe. Gaining understanding through experimentation—tacit learning by feeling

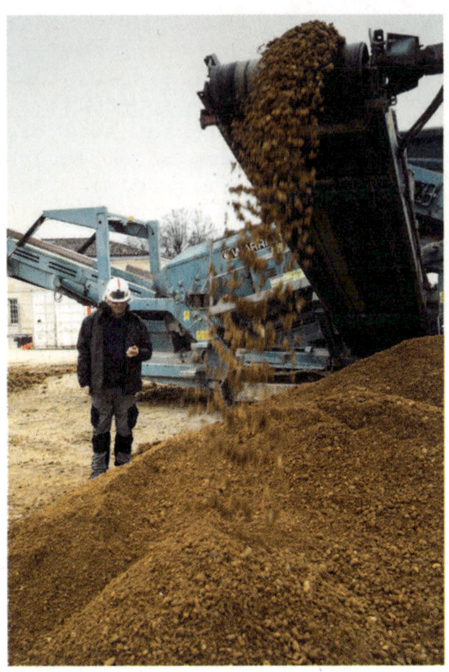

the material—is an irreplaceable part of grasping the rammed earth recipe process. The best approach is to just play in the mud.

Step 1: collecting a sample

It is essential that the material for building comes from beneath the topsoil. A rammed earth mix must contain almost no organic material, such as humus. This usually means digging down about half a meter to reach the subsoil layer. Often, some sort of earthworks have already taken place on-site and a heaped mound of dirt is perfect for sampling. The collected material must be representative, so a number of samples from across the plot is most useful. To ensure the final mix is homogeneous, the excavated material available should be enough for the entire project. Excavation works dig through several sedimentary layers—earth from different geological periods—but material should be collected and grouped from a single depth. This helps ensure minerals are of the same type and color.

Step 2: sample assessment

Often, a geotechnical report is already available for review. This is a good starting place for understanding the soil composition. This alone is not enough, though, and collecting a physical sample is unavoidable.

Get a good sniff of the loam sample: organic material from topsoil usually produces an odour, so its absence is a good sign. If the loam contains rocks and gravel, the makeup can be judged by sieving it, trying to separate the larger constituents from the fines: particles below a few millimeters in diameter. The fines—clay, silt and sand—are inseparable in a practical sense, so they are categorized as "binding and compressive" material. The sieved-out rock is purely "compressive." Taking a handful of earth-moist loam and compressing it in the palm of the hand offers a quick indication of the binding capacity and therefore clay content of the material. The stickier, the higher the clay content. By separating the constituents and getting a feel for the clay content in a sample, it is possible to predict which ingredients need to be increased or decreased.

Step 3: systematic documentation

As the material is assessed and the recipe begins to develop, document findings systematically. For each constituent, the type of material, grain size, color, bulk density, source and distance to site should be recorded. This final piece of information helps determine the logistical impact of additional off-site material. When trialling mixtures, the parts added can be recorded like a cocktail recipe. For example, two parts site loam, one part sharp sand, two parts gravel, stirred not tumbled.

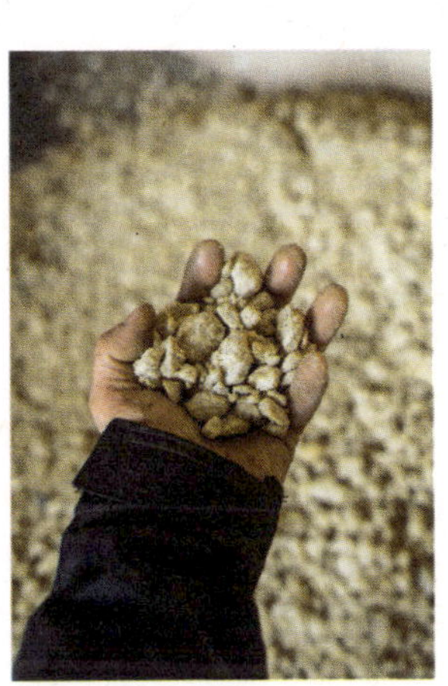

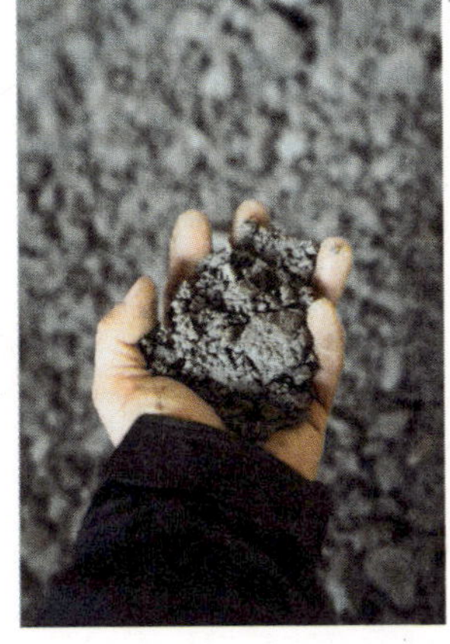

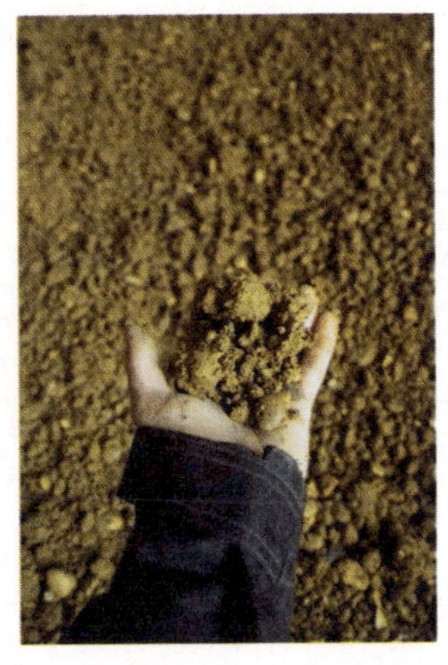

Apart from controlling quality, batches of mixes with slightly varying constituents or from different excavation sites can result in obvious tonal changes in finished walls. Clay gives rammed earth its color, for the most part. However, in cases where the walls are exposed to weathering, after some years of erosion, the fine clay washes out of the surface exposing more aggregate. This results in the weather-facing walls changing tone and texture to the predominant appearance of the aggregate content. This does not happen uniformly on a building and should be considered during recipe development.

Step 4: recipe development

An even distribution of small to large grain sizes of aggregate is important for good compressive strength. A grain size analysis of a sample can be conducted by a lab which graphs the different particle sizes and their distribution on a curve and can inform the development of a recipe. However, a range of curves work, so it is faster and more pragmatic to make several mixes and develop the best recipe through trial and error. If mixing is to be done by hand, the excavated loam should be dried in order to pulverize it and accurately introduce water content into a mix. Aggregate must be angular in geometry rather than rounded and mixing two different clayey materials can achieve better results.

As batches of earth are mixed, with slightly differing ratios of ingredients, many criteria must be satisfied at once. Adjusting one component of the recipe to meet one criterion can have effects on other criteria. Experience is the only way to learn this. Some criteria can't be assessed until after samples have been rammed and dried. Criteria to consider when creating a mixture include:

- Compressive strength
- Sustainability of mix
- Erosion resistance
- Workability of material
- Availability of material components
- Cost of material components
- Ease of replicability
- Resistance to cracking
- Expression of horizontal texture
- Tonality
- Mineral deposition on surface

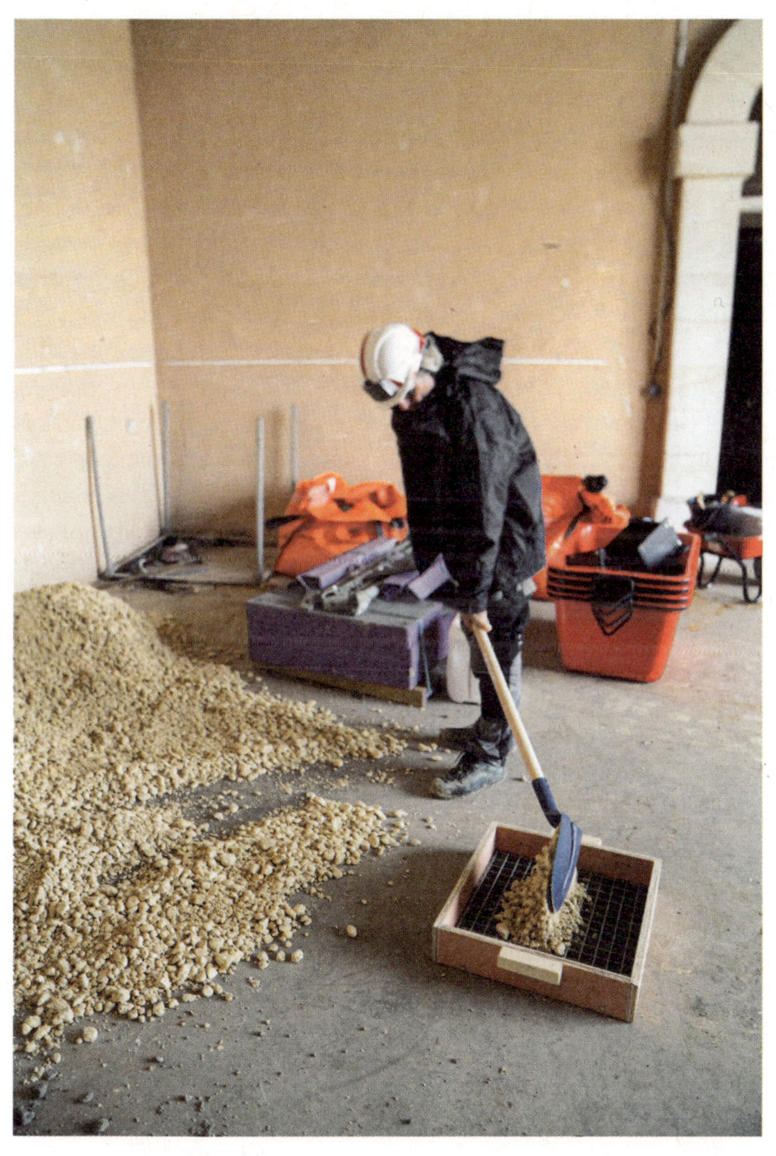

Step 5: mixing procedure

The mixing procedure has as much impact on the strength and quality of the rammed earth as does its makeup. The aim is to coat each larger grain of gravel in a surface of smaller grains bound by the clay. Start with a dry mix, which includes all the constituents turned together in a dry state. It is sometimes helpful to wet the gravel before combining with the rest of the ingredients to ensure a good coating of loam covers the aggregate. When possible, this dry mix can be made in a large enough quantity to supply the entire project and stored under cover.

A day before ramming is scheduled, moisten the dry mix with a hose, adding between 5 and 6.5 percent water by mass to produce a wet mix. This is estimated and judged by feel, as measuring the exact amount of water is difficult in practice when handling large volumes. The mixing cannot take place in a tumble mixer, as with concrete, because this causes balling of the clay and results in a non-homogenous mix. The highest quality mix is produced in a forced-action mixer, also called a vertical axis mixer. Otherwise, the traditional method of turning and spreading the material on a slab works well too, albeit with a wheel loader to save on labor. The moist mixed material should then be stored and allowed to cure, at least overnight if not a whole day, to allow the moisture to permeate throughout the mix. The wet mix should be stored with a tarpaulin cover to contain its moisture.

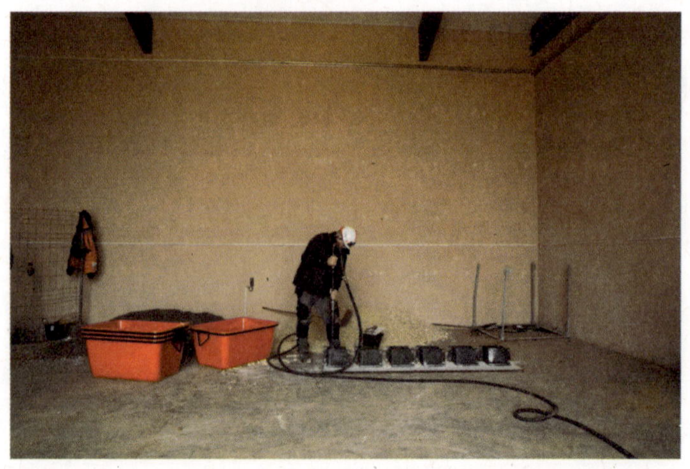

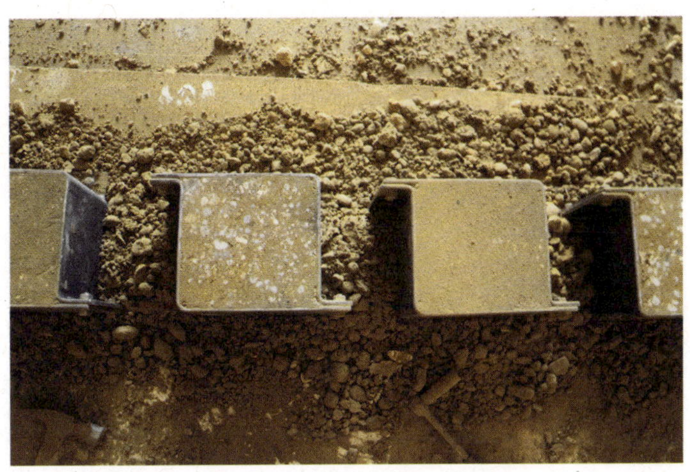

Step 6: ramming samples

After curing, produce rammed samples. Cubes of 20cm are a practical size and allow for three compacted layers. The size and geometry of the sample may also be defined by the lab conducting the compression tests. Make four samples of each mix and dry for at least two weeks. Multiple samples allow the averaging of the results. It is possible to gain a feeling for the behaviour of the material while ramming the samples: if it's too wet or contains too much silt, the material can be very plastic and move around within the formwork while tamping; too dry or not enough clay and the gravel will bounce around and not interlock into position. The samples are also the first visual confirmation that designers and clients will have of the rammed earth's appearance: the color, texture and horizontal striation that give rammed earth its distinctive appearance. Hone down the tops of the samples with a diamond cup wheel and abrasive pads to level the surface and reveal the composition of the mix.

Step 7: documenting results

A recipe developed by an experienced hand will perform well and be easily repeatable. But in a litigious western context, choosing a mix will ultimately be influenced most by the result of compressive tests. There are many factors that affect compressive strength, making accurate

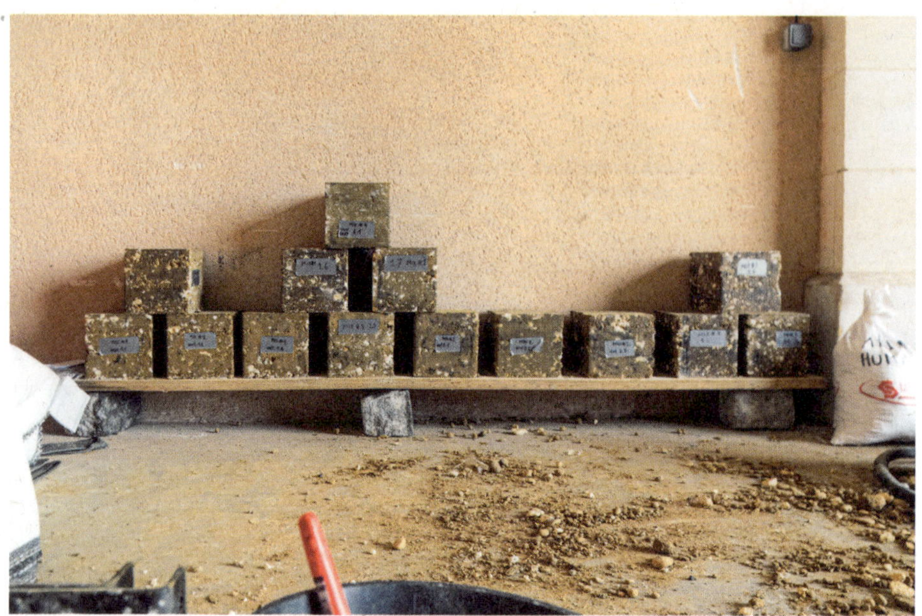

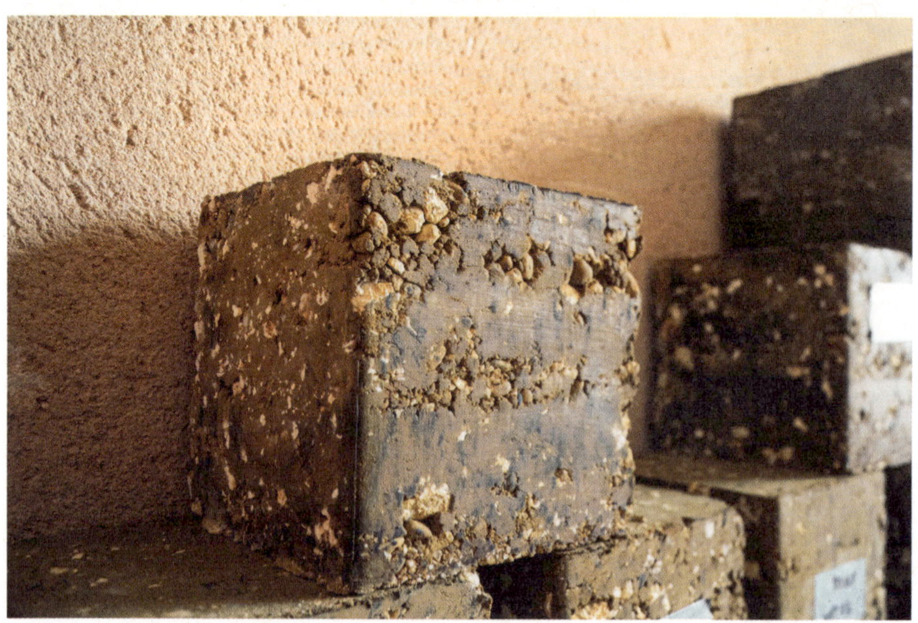

recording important. Water content, clay type, aggregate distribution, compaction equipment, mixing method and layer thickness are some of the key factors.

Once rammed and removed from its formwork, weigh the test cube. It can then be left to air dry or put in an oven. When dry after two to three weeks, weigh again, and the moisture of the mix can be determined by the weight lost. This method also works on loose mix before it is rammed. The compaction ratio of loose to fully compacted material can be calculated and should be roughly 50 percent reduction in height.

If the compressive strength of a recipe meets the specified benchmark, larger sample walls or mockups can be produced. Understanding the compaction ratio and the mixing method then informs production planning later down the line.

Traci Wile and
Craig Stevenson

PARTICIPANT
INTERVIEWS

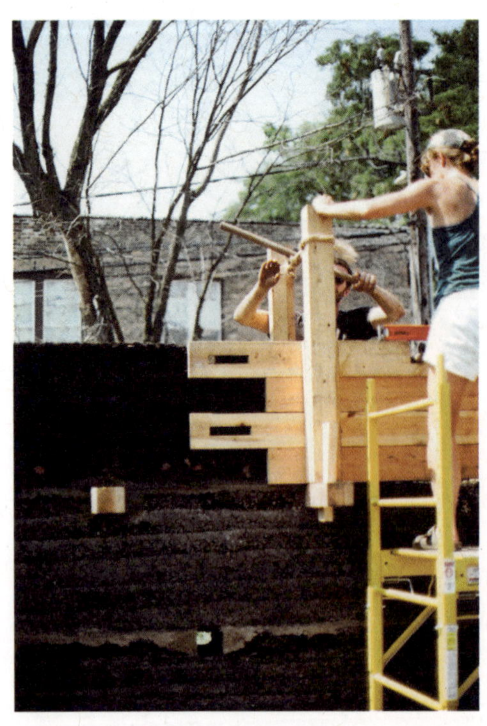

The days working on-site were punctuated by questions from passers-by. While we were anxious to keep momentum, we appreciated that these conversations formed the foundation of our community building. As the pavilion of rammed earth took shape, the nature of the open structure continued to encourage and invite the members of the public to stop, approach and appropriate the project on their own terms. The project took on different meanings to different people and it was all of these things at once.

The project allowed for different levels of engagement and a day's work was the product of the rise and fall of the group's energy; our collective strength was manifest in the layers of compacted soil. Each building block acted as a stepping stone, a learning curve, together a library of different tamping techniques and mixing methods, a product of our collective spirit and experience together.

Each day started out with a discussion, an assessment of the walls in front of us, the strains of our muscles, and hopes for the day ahead. Each day concluded with a lunch enjoyed together in the shade of the trees in the neighbouring Perma Park. Throughout, as we shared stories, we formed friendships and made a community, a community of makers: Soil Lab.

In the following interviews conducted by Traci Wile on-site and Craig Stevenson retrospectively, we would like to introduce you to some of the participants with whom we share this project.

Susana Core

My name is Susana and I am originally from Argentina. I learnt about this project through an ad that I saw in the local library. Since my childhood, I have always tried to reconnect with the earth, and I have always thought that it is wonderful to learn another skill, and that's what brings me here.

I live here in North Lawndale where this project is being built. I think it is fabulous that we can make this neighborhood better with something that is participatory, something that is educational, and in that way leaves a legacy here. That's important.

I learnt that there are a lot of things that we have forgotten about our ancestors—things they were very good at—and this project is a revival of these good things they did, a revival of their construction techniques improved with new knowledge: a combination of old and new. And I think that is fabulous.

Antwan Fipps
I'm Anwan Fipps from Chicago, Illinois. I heard about this project through James and my sister, Nini. When they told me about the project, I was like, "I'm game."

I was really interested in the material and the pile of dirt that we patted down and molded—we transformed it into layers like bricks. That's the thing that really amazed and surprised me: that you can shape dirt or clay into a wall or any type of pottery, if need be.

I'm excited that it's here in the neighborhood. This project we're building is going to be a workshop, where people can get hands-on training, get an insight into something they never knew about, something they can learn about—like a trade. Everybody here needs something to occupy their time. Everybody needs something to get away from the harshness of life. Everybody needs something that's different, instead of doing the same thing over and over. But even though there are times of strife and despair here, people still stick together. People still have love for one another. That's what I love about my neighborhood.

Gregory Davis
My name is Gregory Davis and I'm from Chicago's West Side. I live here just across from the site. One of the days, I was just looking out the back door and I saw people working. I went to say hello and I ended up joining.

I don't have any building experience. None, this is all learning. I've had fun too, I've made some friends and I'm coming back every day until it's done.

Sheila Holmes
I'm Sheila Holmes from North Lawndale. I had the opportunity to work at the Soil Lab for a week this summer. It was a great experience: I learned a lot about soil and the different things you mix together to make sure it sticks.

Soil Lab brought this global community to North Lawndale. There's folks out there from

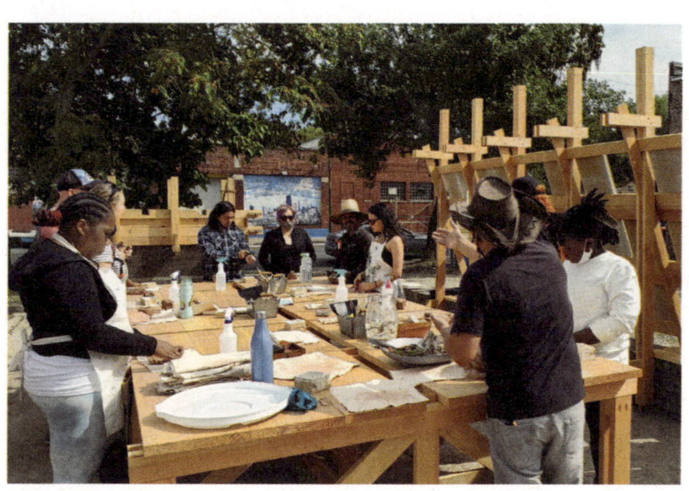

2021 North Lawndale

COMMUNITY BRICKMAKING WORKSHOP

with Will Quam, Bricks of Chicago

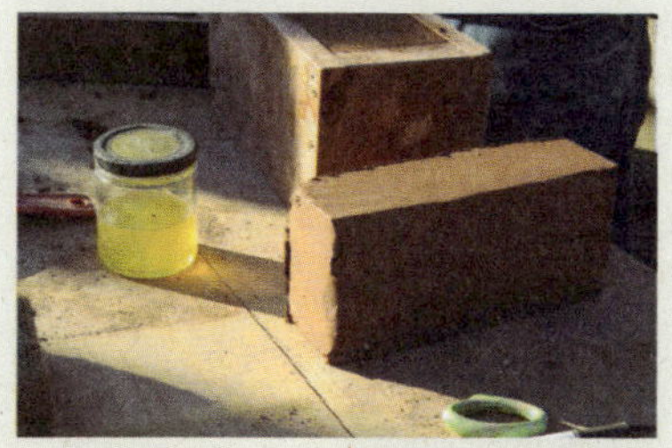

November 2
November 20
November 13
December 4

2:00-4:00 pm

A creative and participatory workshop to explore ideas for the design of a North Lawndale Brick. **Bring a personal artifact that is important to you.** The workshop will be facilitated by Soil Lab, Odile Compagnon and Traci Wile

Register here:
bit.ly/soil-lab-brickmaking

1310 S. Pulaski Road
@soillabnorthlawndale

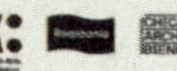

around the country, and I met someone from Ireland and Denmark and Argentina. It was such a great show of how everybody—all groups, nationalities, it doesn't matter about color—everybody can work together. I love that.

Sheila Holmes
My name also is Sheila Holmes and I live in the North Lawndale area. This is where I grew up. What Soil Lab has taught me is teamwork: that you can't do anything without a team because you can't really do it by yourself. And in a team, you get to bond with new people, you get to meet new people and you get to see their personality as you work together. I learnt also that you need to be around people who are going to work and that you know are not going to be like, "I'm tired of this." I feel like the more that you work together, the more it's going to pay off.

Amorianne Allen
My name is Amorianne Allen and I go to North Lawndale College Prep High School. I heard about the Soil Lab through my sister and my mother. It's a lot of fun when you actually do the work. It gets easier day by day as you start where you left off, and you just keep going up and up. The best part about it was that you got to work with people that you never met before. You come together to do positive things in the community instead of just protesting against police brutality all the time. It was fun for me to have that experience in the community.

HC Warfield
My name is HC Warfield. I was born in Panther Burn, Mississippi in 1949. I came up here because of the prejudice and the wages. I didn't come to the South Side; I came to the West Side. I got a chance to get into a Christian home, because I got saved and I started going to church and this church opened up a ministry for men coming out of the penitentiary, men coming out of drugs and just ordinary men that didn't have anything to do. We had a home for 15 guys.

That's how I got connected with Lawndale. I go to school four days a week and one evening after I got out I passed by Pulaski Road and saw these people working over there. I met James and I started talking to him and I asked him, "What's going on?" I live in the community and I like to know what's going on because I like to come and tell the seniors some of the things that are happening, because I get around a little more than the rest of them.

That Friday I came back and started working, and I worked for three weeks. It didn't take me too long to catch on. I remember when I was down South we used to make stuff up in buckets with a certain kind of clay and when it set we would make little houses and things. So it was interesting to make this huge structure.

And then to discover that we were building a brick workshop, a place where we could create bricks—that was just crazy interesting. My son got interested and he came over too. I like to create things, I like to put things together. And I thought, "Wow, maybe I could create a brick."

And it was for the community. That's what really had my heart and mind in it. We really do need something in this community to help these young men: some of them walking around ain't doing anything.

You don't get to know someone until you meet them. I got a chance to meet and make friends here. I don't know how far y'all gonna go, but I always thought it was something nice to do. And whatever y'all do after this is over, I sure want to be a part of it. I really would.

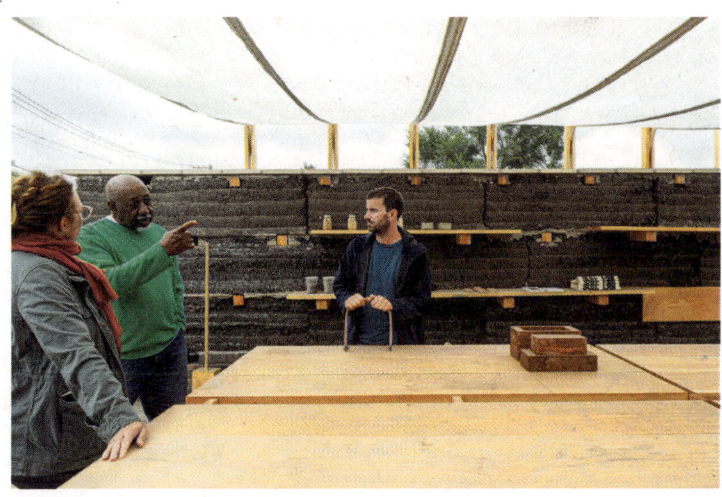

Calvanita Fipps
aka Nini

SOIL LAB RAP

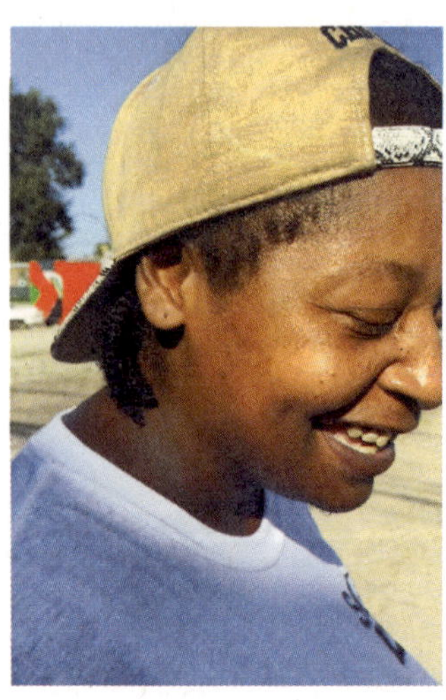

Nini was one of the first people we met on-site, stopping by the vacant lot on her way home from work one evening: inquisitive and welcoming with dancing eyes, eager to find out who we were, where we were from and what we were doing in her neighborhood. These evening visits became a regular thing we looked forward to. There was always good humor and song when Nini was around. She was curious about the dirt walls rising, playing with the sounds and rhythms of our construction techniques, riffing on the process, lifting our energies and rhyming in time as we tamped in the evening sun. We commissioned Nini to write this rap about da soil lab, which she performed at the opening.

da soil lab is a place to participate
and create
and use your mind to elevate

wake up and get ready for da soil lab
grind hard work hard at da soil lab
learn create be great at da soil lab
learn a new trade at da soil lab

wake up get ready for da soil lab
grind hard work hard at da soil lab
learn create be great at da soil lab
learn a new trade at da soil lab

welcome to da soil lab where we come to build and grow
we learned how to build a wall out of dirt you know
we used clean dirt, meaning we learned the difference between soil

da soil lab taught us how to work as a team
we used wheelbarrows of dirt
filled with buckets
transferred it to open compartments
stamped it down
with a ram
made sure it was even

the last touches were silt lime sand mixed with water
it creates an old-fashioned concrete mix
that helps hold the walls up
we used shovels gloves chisels
and a 15 and a half center block of wood
and metal ramps to stand on and keep us level with the wall

we also learned the basics of it all
how to make clay out of water and dirt
we also have an oven to make ceramics
and create our own ideas in a machine that makes clay
and turns it into the size of a brick

to help with this
we had some great workers who learned something new,
we all learned something new
and got to meet a host of great people
from other areas and communities

da soil lab is all about building creating
connecting with the community
what about the unity?
we got unity
that's why they in our community.
get it

Anjulie Rao

REVALUING EMPTINESS IN CHICAGO

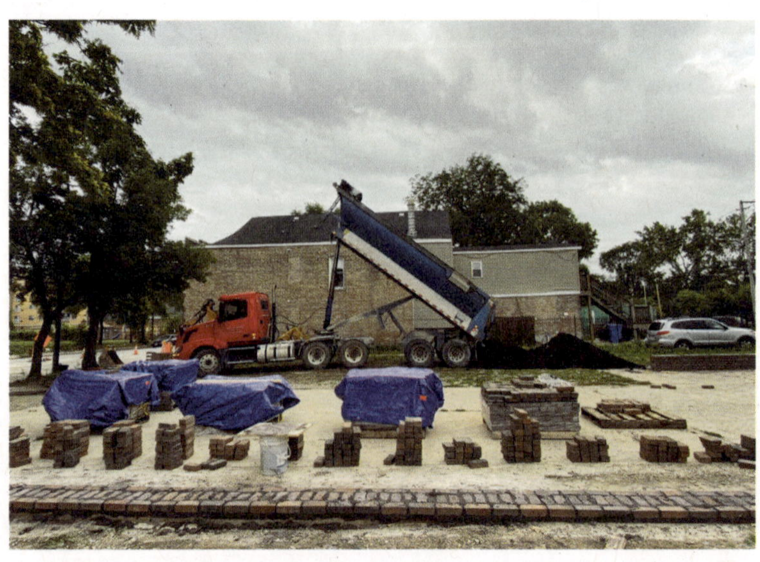

Shortly after the opening of the biennial, Anjulie Rao wrote a critical article for *Architects' Magazine* about the true availability of the sites used during *The Available City*. The article captured our attention as we too had faced obstacles like the ones she described. She is a journalist and critic based in Chicago, covering the built environment.

In 2019, Andrea Yarbrough, a furniture designer and founder of nonprofit design group *in c/o: Black women*, wanted to acquire a vacant lot in Chicago's South Side neighborhood of Englewood. The lot was available, listed among the thousands of empty lots and abandoned properties on the Cook County Land Bank Authority website. She applied to obtain the land, but the Land Bank declined her application, stating the reason that Yarbrough was not building a structure on the land and had no history of development.

Yarbrough wanted to acquire the lot, not to build a house or a business, but because the lot had sentimental value to her personally. "It was very close to the elementary school that I graduated from," she explained. "My little brother's best friend was killed in front of it." Yarbrough planned to use the lot to "really think about the schools that have been closed down, and how we can think about the legacies of the people who were here."

Yarbrough's idea of how to deal with cultural memory—and the results of policies that dispossessed communities, leading to violence and abandonment—were central to the Chicago Architecture Biennial's (CAB) 2021 theme *The Available City*. The theme directly addressed the 16,000 city-owned vacant lots in Chicago that were strategically made vacant by ongoing disinvestment. Under CAB's directive—to create new ways of utilizing this vacant land—participants were confronting the legacies of a decades-old machine that systematically demolished structures in Black and Brown neighborhoods. But what several groups encountered instead was a machine of a different sort: one of bureaucratic mechanisms designed to manage liability. Participants quickly discovered that land made "available" by disinvestment was not, in fact, readily available.

The problem of vacant land has been a burden for the City of Chicago for decades; the Cook County Land Bank Authority was formed in 2013 to help manage the number of vacant and abandoned parcels across the city in an effort to help sell or redevelop those properties. Through a series of programs and initiatives—such as Large Lots and the Adjacent Neighbors Land Acquisition Program, which sought to sell those properties to residents and developers at costs as low as one dollar—the county attempts to move land into private hands. But these lots are still slow to sell: according to Steven Vance, urban planner and founder of Chicago Cityscape, a website that maps and tracks city-related property data, these efforts have left only a small dent in the amount of vacancy. "There are around 14,000 city-owned lots, and another 16,000 privately owned vacant lots," Vance confirms. "At the pace of selling of them or redeveloping them, it would take until 2050 to complete."

In 2018, City Open Workshop, a now-defunct alliance of city-minded volunteers, decided to investigate the vacant lot problem. Vance, alongside urban planner Paola Aguirre of urban design practice Borderless Studio and a group of volunteers, studied the challenges of managing the amount of vacancy in the city. They were able to identify three main issues: the scale is too large, the pace of stewardship is too slow, and acquisition processes are unclear, opaque or incomplete.

The group proposed a new city agency—the Office of Land Stewardship—which would be in charge of providing resources, processes and tools for everyday Chicagoans who wanted to become land stewards. They based their proposal on Detroit Future City's *Field Guide to Working with Lots*, "a pattern book" Aguirre explains, "designed very well in a way that is very accessible." The *Field Guide* includes information on plantings to create a pollinator garden, resources for funding, and even space to draw a map of the plot. "They were building this bridge between the policy idea and what it looks like on the ground for the people that get to implement and live with the consequences or impact of this intervention," Aguirre continues.

Chicago has no such toolkit, and acquiring access to vacant city-owned land is still deeply opaque, according to Ben Helphand, executive director of NeighborSpace, a nonprofit that works to build community green spaces on Chicago's vacant lots. His organization works as an intermediary between neighborhood groups that want to acquire a vacant parcel for a garden or green space, and helps them get access to the land, water and electricity if needed. A Right of Entry or lease is needed to access this land which most community groups find difficult to obtain, so, as Helphand explains "more and more people are looking to NeighborSpace or other entities to hold the lease or get the Right of Entry, but it still takes months and months."

Right of Entry is a form that CAB 2021 participants used to access city-owned land for their installations. Helphand explains that the Right of Entry "wasn't made for what people are trying to do with it in this context" but instead is "intended for the City's law departments to give an entity permission to use city-owned land for a very specific purpose, usually very short term." He notes that, for CAB, it was "likely the best possible tool," but comments that "the temporary is not what the City is built to do."

The requirements for temporary installations were daunting: 18 inches of wood chips were required to be placed on a piece of city-owned vacant land to protect visitors from possible soil contaminants—ironic considering that Soil Lab hoped to build their installation using the site soil. As a result, Soil Lab chose to move to a nearby lot to make use of an existing concrete foundation, and trucked in soil from a soil management facility in Dundee, Illinois, 40 miles from the site. When Yarbrough was planning to build a skatepark in Englewood as her contribution to CAB 2021, she encountered another issue. The lot they planned to activate had two components: grass at the front owned by the city, and a concrete pad at the back owned by the private neighborhood redevelopment company Community Investment Corporation (CIC). Though the lot seemed perfect, with space for furniture on the grass and skating on the pad, Yarbrough explains that CIC were unwilling to insure the lot for skating, and they were not allowed to pour additional concrete on the city-owned grass.

Yarbrough hit a liability wall. "No one wanted to take on the liability of getting the insurance for it." The biennial told them that their partner, Natty Bwoy—a group of three brothers who do pop-up skate classes—had to get the insurance, which they weren't in a position to do. Regardless, Yarbrough searched for quotes, receiving one for $10,000: far outside her price range.

The challenges result from issues surrounding land ownership. Private entities—individuals or organizations—who own their own lots are able to provide insurance and therefore don't need to comply with some liability measures such as ground contamination protection. There is greater flexibility in how land is used, as long as any design work is code-compliant; owners also have final say over use based on liability, as Yarbrough discovered. Privately-owned lots allow groups and individuals, like CAB participants, to build temporary structures—a use that the City of Chicago currently doesn't have a process for on their land—and work with the land in the way that they might need. Accessing infrastructure becomes simpler, insurance is less burdensome and questions of liability can be answered straightforwardly. City-owned lots, simply, aren't available.

"Everything's built around ownership," Aguirre insists. "No one has thought about what the policies and regulations around stewardship are." Stewardship, she continues, implies that an individual or group activates a lot, not because they have stakes or financial incentives, but that, "it just has to be done." Aguirre believes that "we need to redefine availability to mean having the knowledge, the resources, and support" and asks "how does it make me feel as a regular resident of the city that I can have access to the land, whether it's private or public?"

Perhaps, she recommends, we might think about the differences between "available"—a term most often used to speak about property in the context of real estate to describe a piece of land that is "available" for ownership—and "accessible." Making land "accessible" might suggest a different way of structuring city programs, resource allocation and even bureaucratic processes, to encourage a way of thinking about city-owned land outside capital-driven ownership. Accessible land stewardship could present new opportunities or city structures to help residents and neighborhood groups collectively or cooperatively own this land in the future.

"What the biennial edition ultimately revealed," admits Rachel Kaplan, executive director of the Chicago Architecture Biennial, "was that making a permanent change to how vacant land is used, or changes to processes needed to ensure that city residents feel like they can make an impact upon their own neighborhoods, is difficult and necessary." Since CAB 2021 closed, the City of Chicago has released a new program intended to expedite the sale of city-owned lots, called ChiBlockBuilder. The program is more nimble than Large Lots—the City of Chicago claims the revamped process will eliminate six to eight months of processing time—and allows individuals to purchase lots with the intention of doing activations like gardens or green spaces. Importantly, interested buyers must provide information about their plans for longer-term maintenance, which helps to ensure that purchased lots don't sit empty and unprogrammed for decades, replicating the same disinvestment-to-vacancy pipeline Chicagoans are all-too familiar with.

"The way we try to address how vacant land can be transformatively programmed or activated must also attend to the time it took to create the problem of vacancy—which was decades," Kaplan continues. "It needs to be met with resources given to groups and individuals who want to activate these spaces, but also to maintain them continuously."

However, ChiBlockBuilder is still focused on ownership, and like past programs, still favors developers, Yarbrough explains. She has still pressed on; in 2021, she went under contract with Cook County Land Bank Authority to acquire an abandoned building, which she hopes to transform into an artist's collective. She has come to understand that temporary interventions aren't resourced, and that her community needs more than just a three-month activation stint. "It's not fair to put something in a community just to have it snatched away."

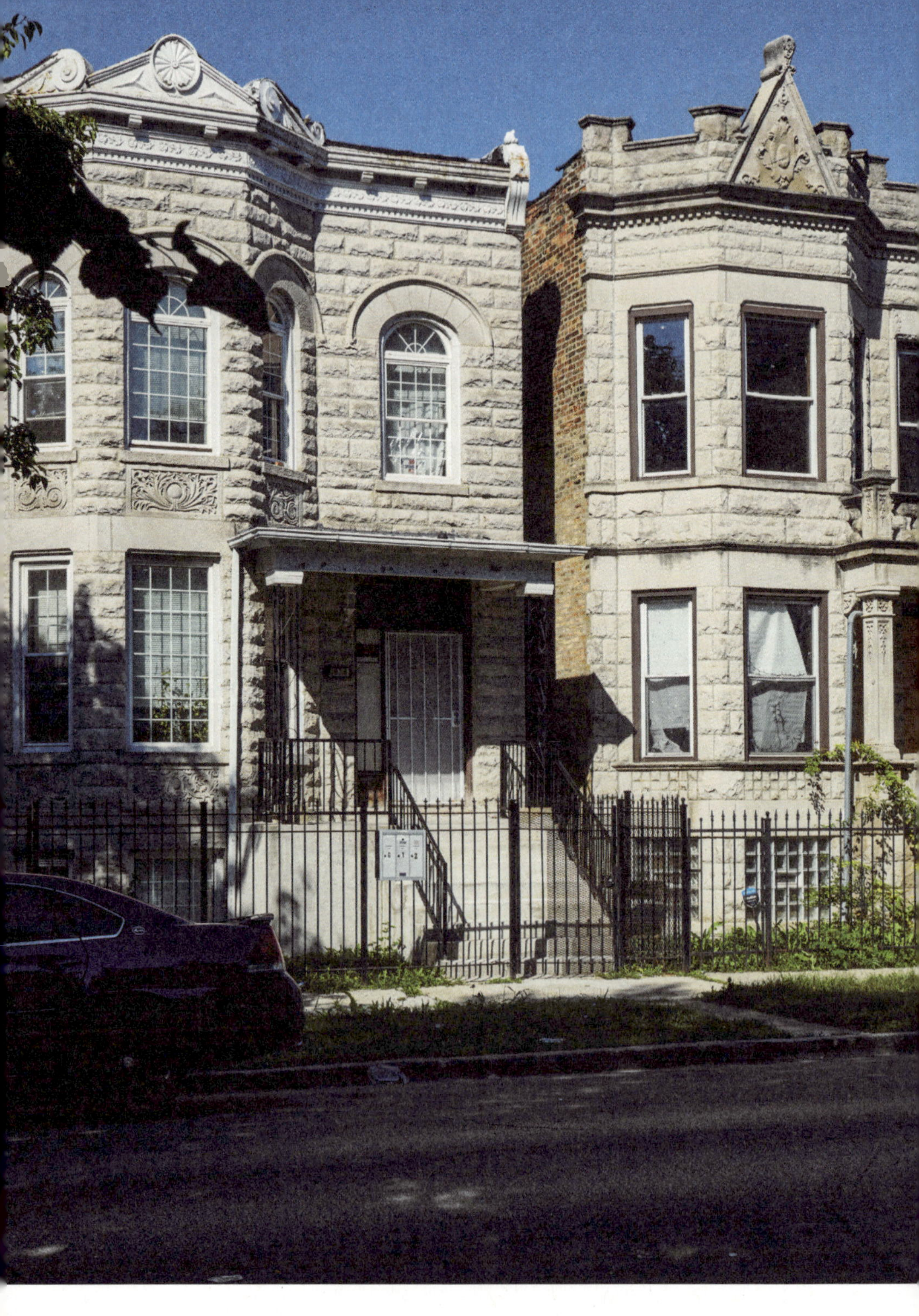

South Hamlin Avenue

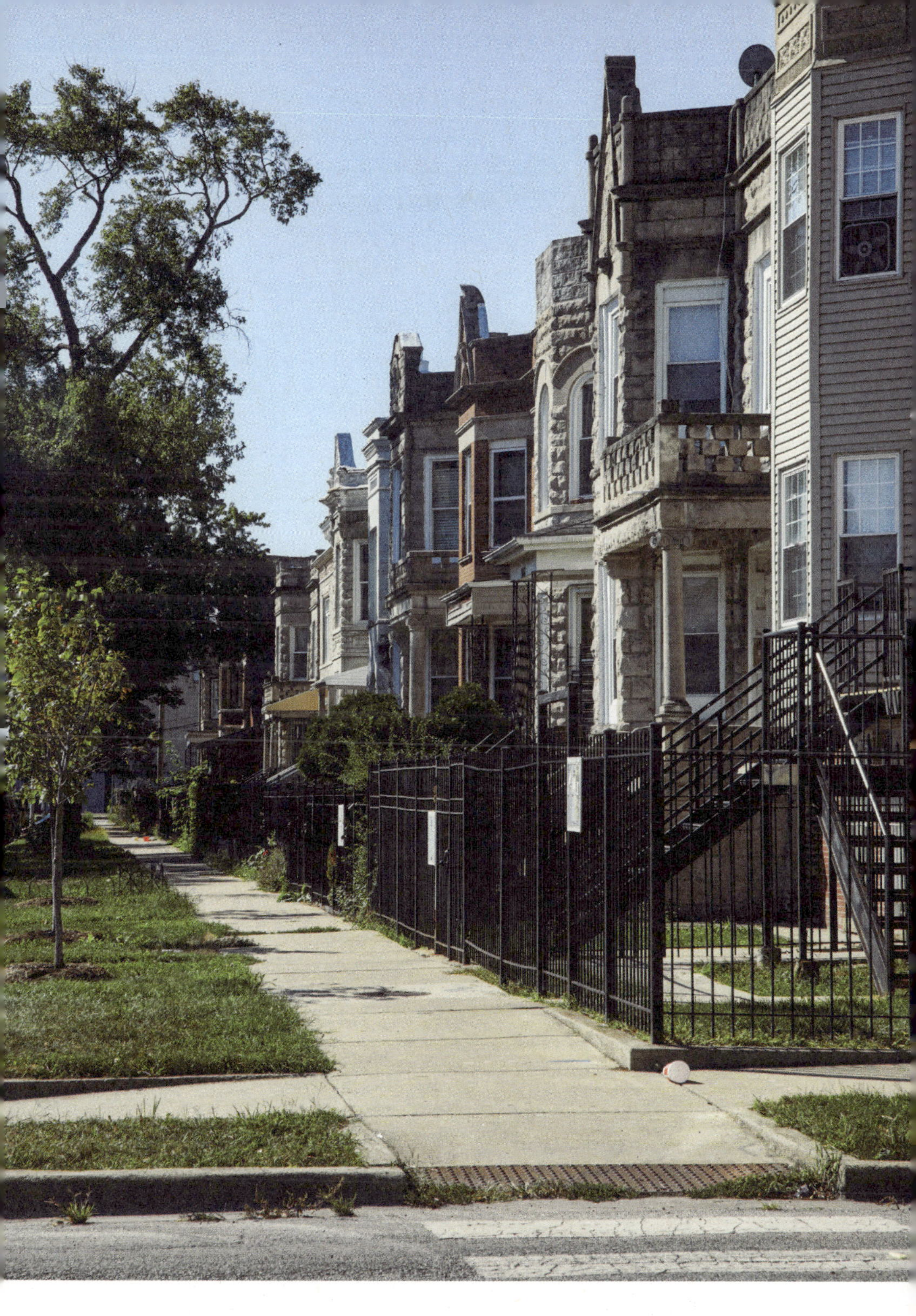

South Hamlin Avenue

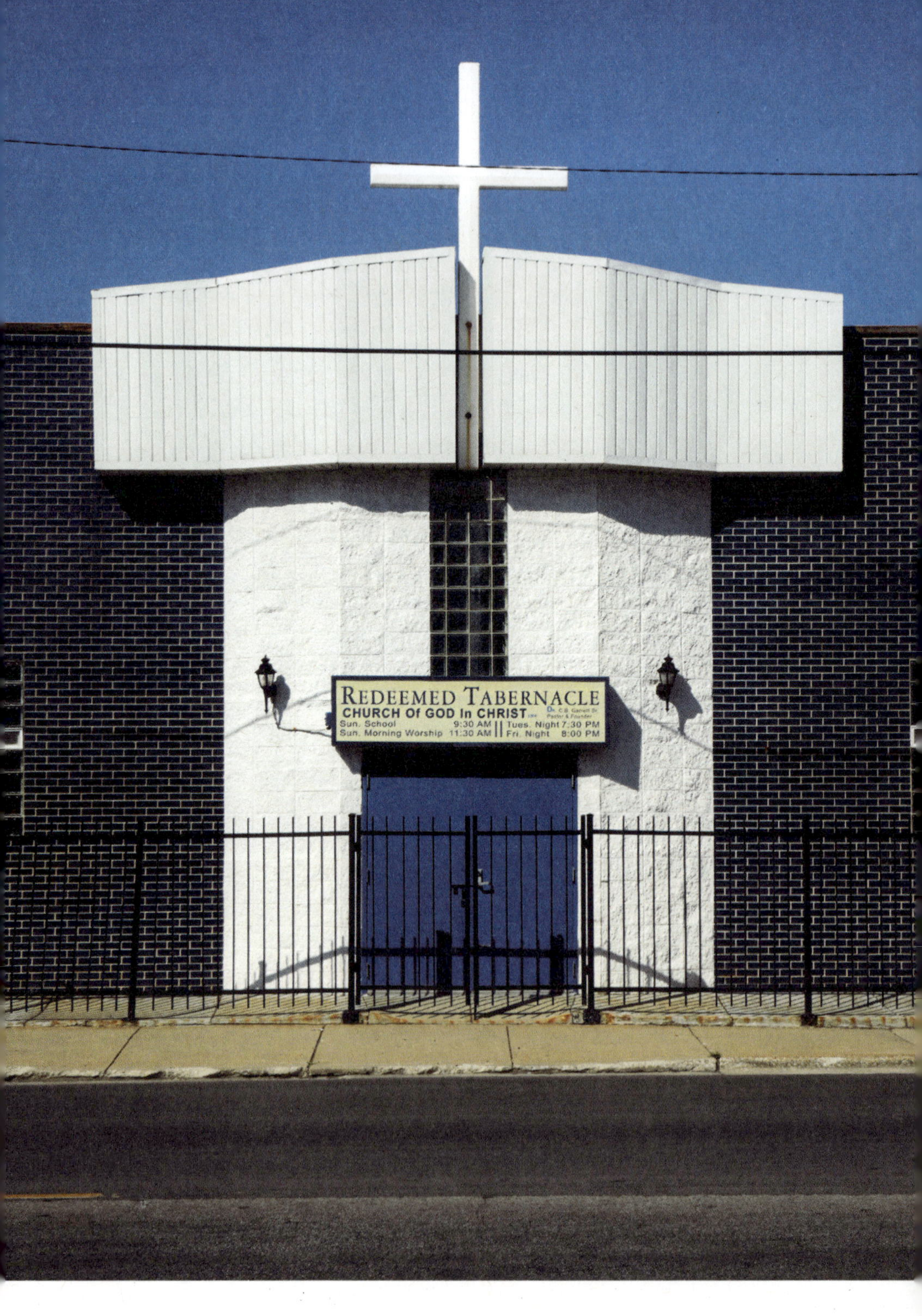

 Redeem Tabernacle Church South Pulaski Road

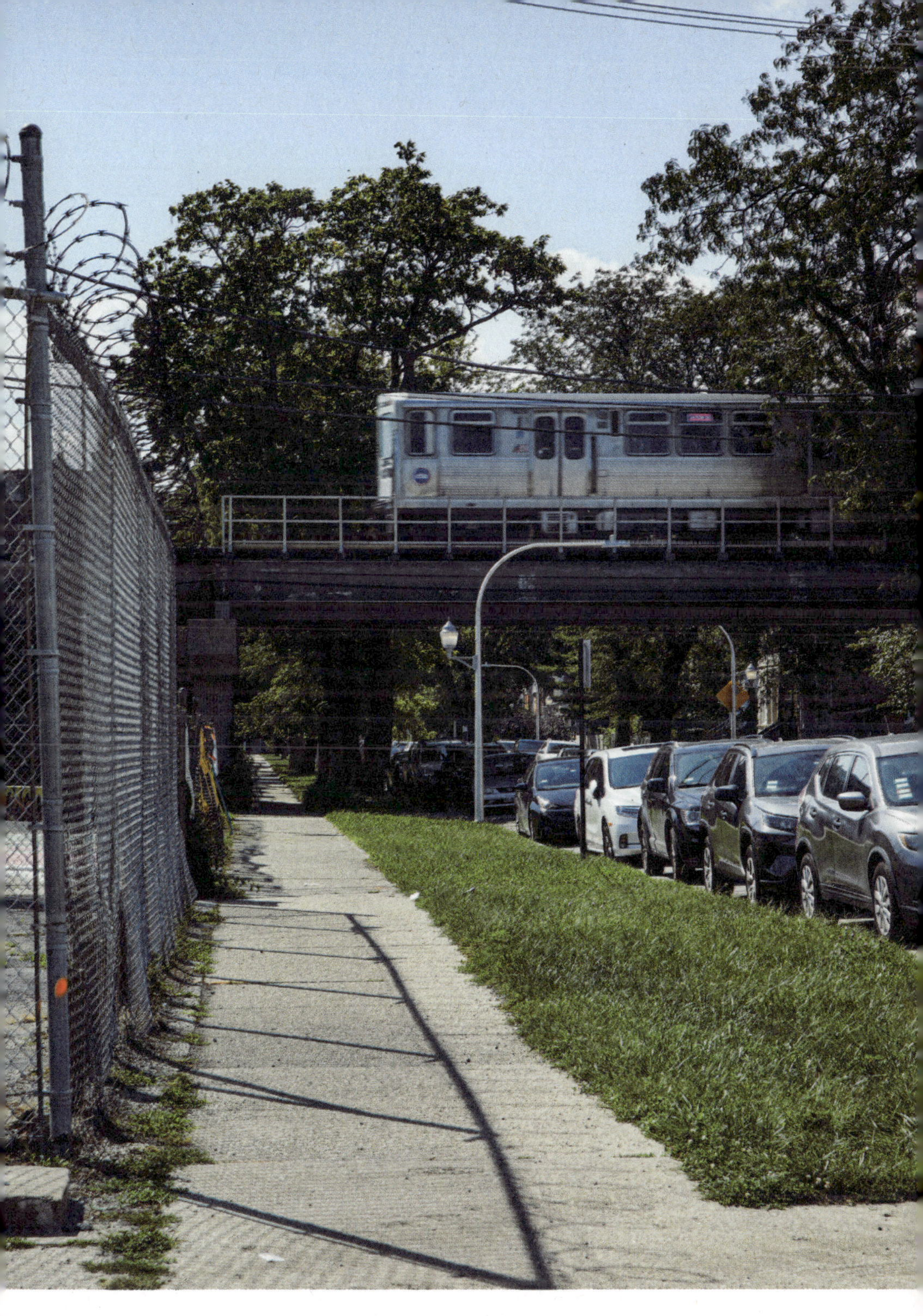

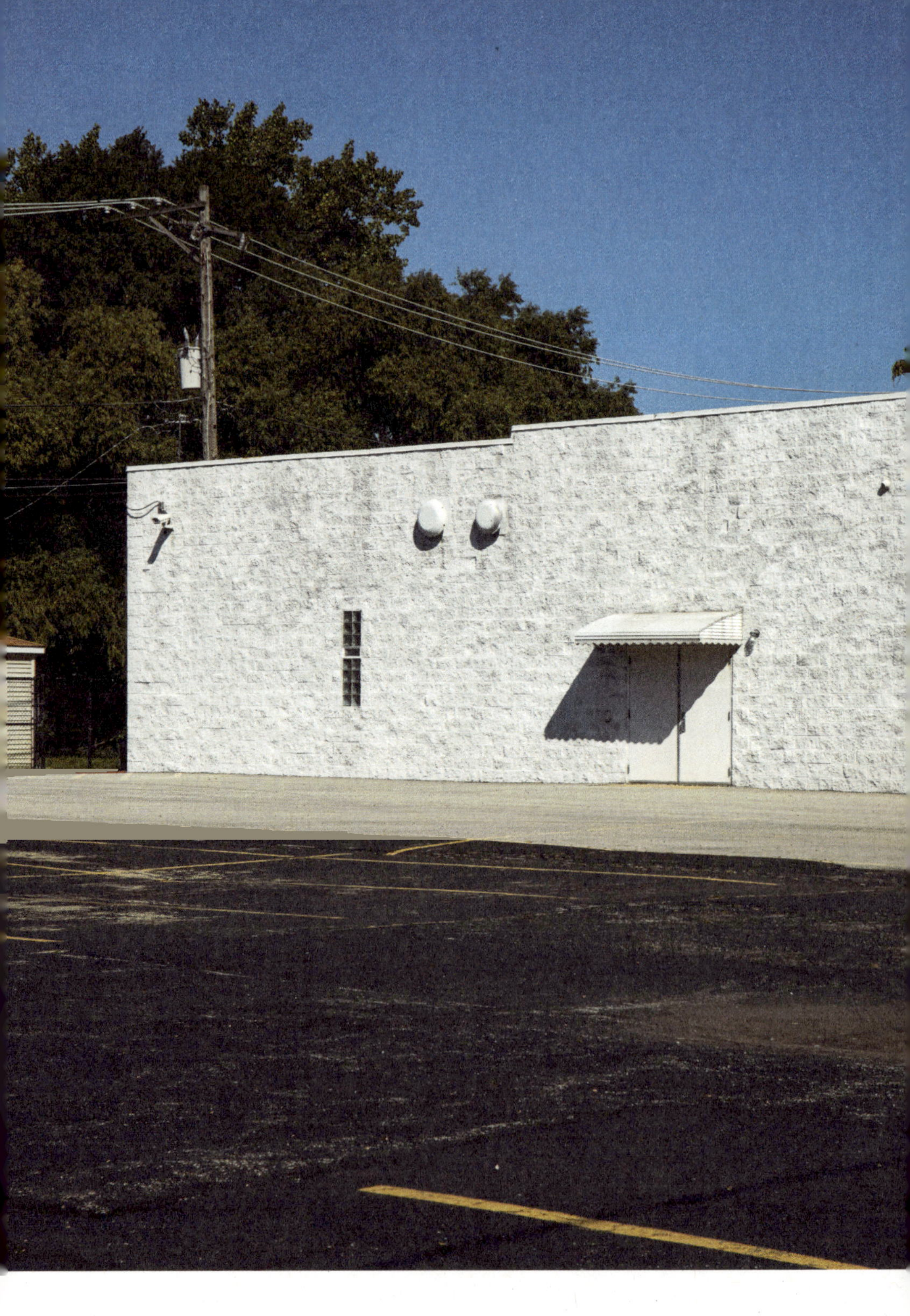

 Redeem Tabernacle Church South Pulaski Road

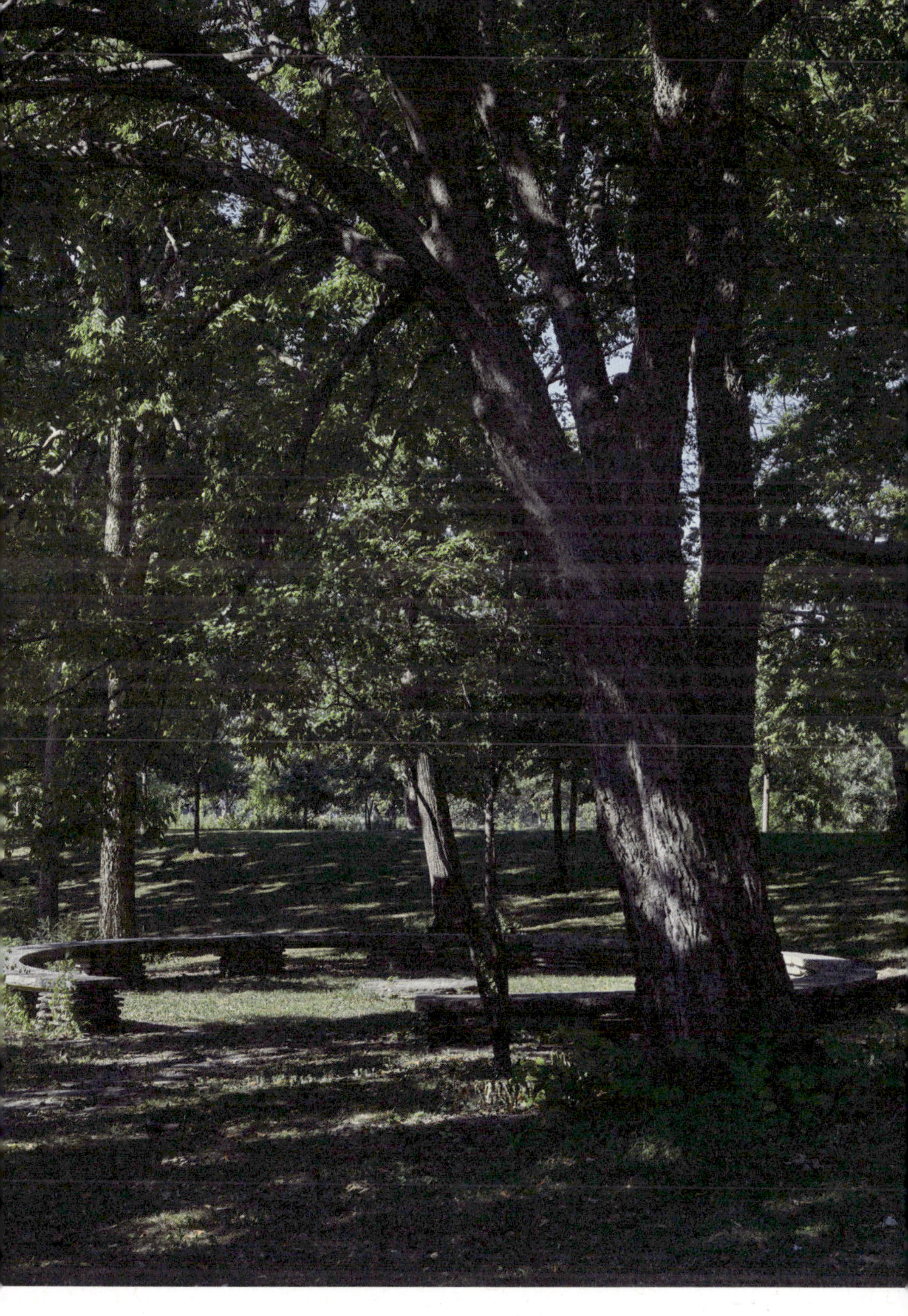

Jens Jensen Columbus park Council Ring

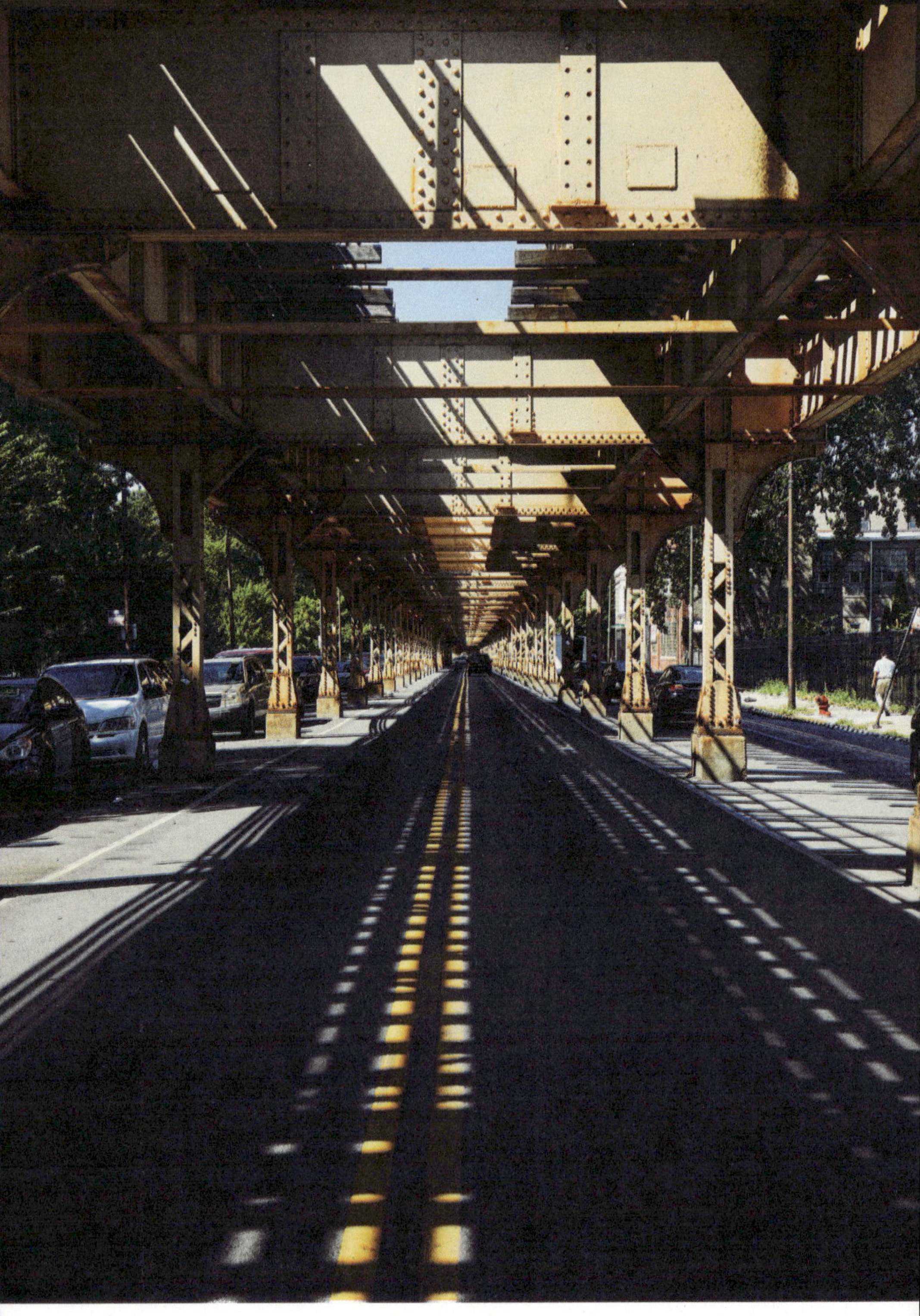

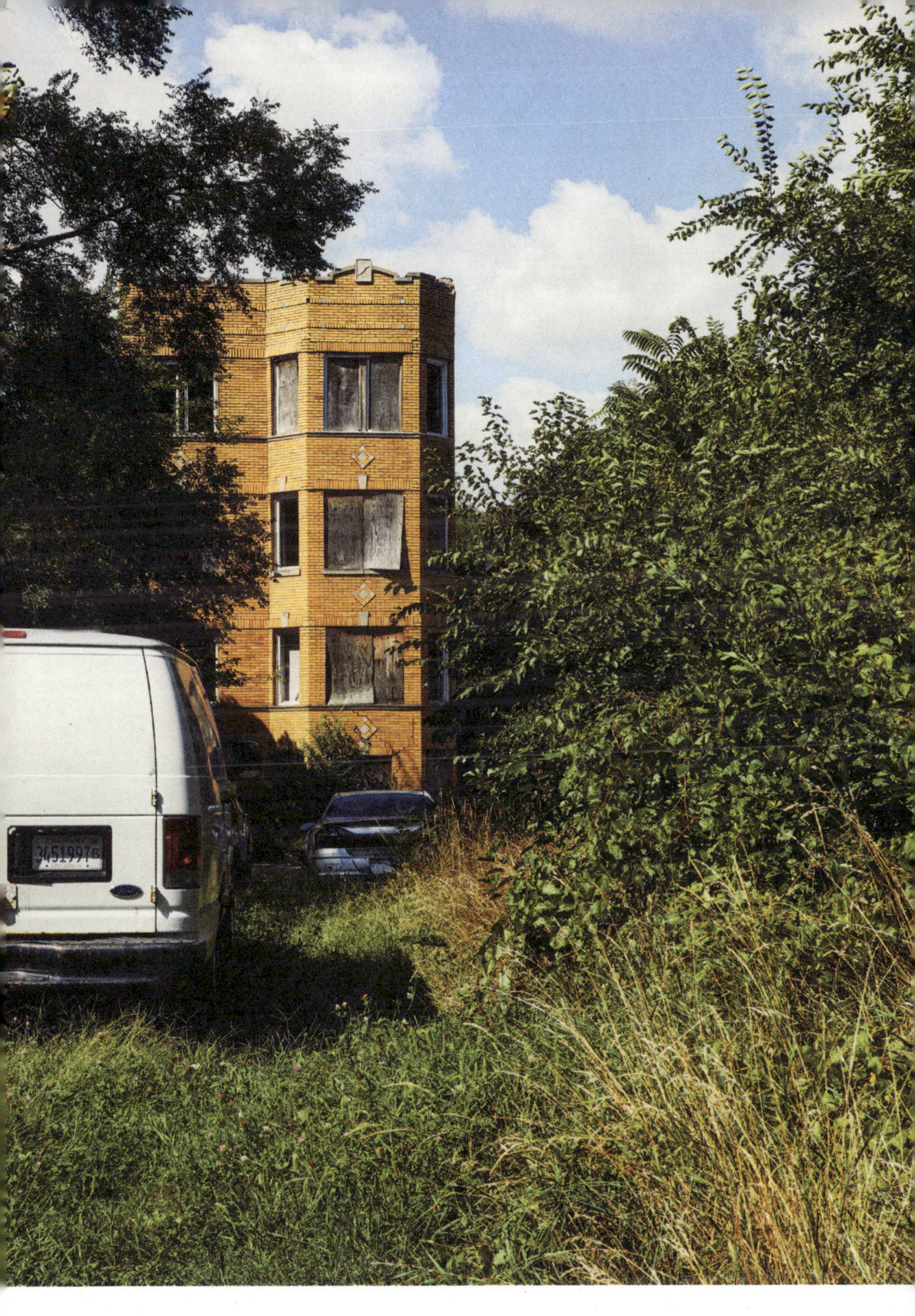

1331 South Komensky Ave

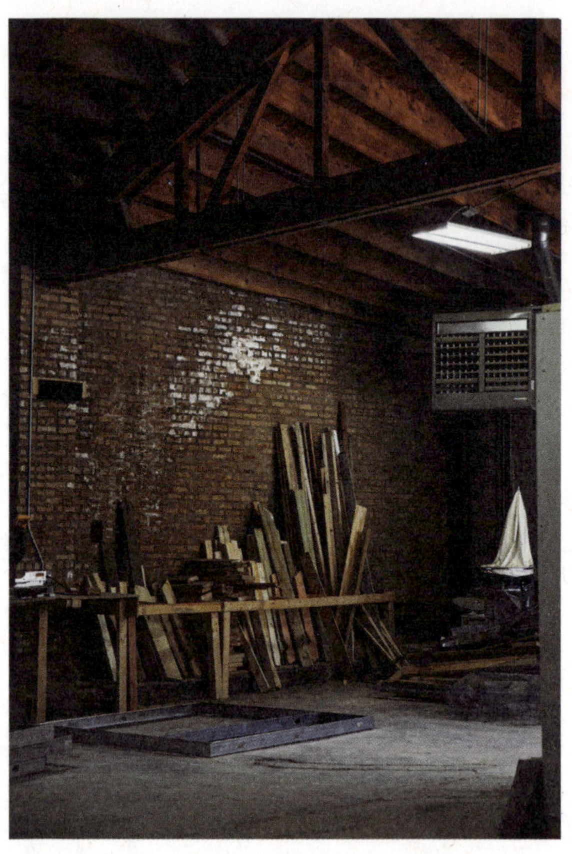

Craig Stevenson and
Benita Marcussen

COMMUNITY INTERVIEWS

Early in the process, it became very clear that in North Lawndale there already existed many passionate people and local forces who worked tirelessly to strengthen the social and physical infrastructure of the area. Through our work, we crossed paths with many initiatives and here it became clear that we had to listen, learn and stand on the shoulders of this enormous local commitment, in order to succeed in involving the local community. Through these interviews we get to know individuals who all showed courage, skill and loyalty in their collaboration with Soil Lab.

Revolution Workshop
My name is Chad Hagedorn and I am the production manager here at Revolution Workshop, a nonprofit social enterprise workshop. I remember when the Soil Lab team first got in touch with me, they sent a picture of the formwork they built in Copenhagen for their initial rammed earth experiments. I remember it had all these wedges and tensioning ropes and it looked like some weird medieval contraption. I knew I wanted to be involved.

In an early Zoom call, we discussed at length how this formwork should look. There was a lot of aesthetic consideration which I appreciated. You want to build a box, but you want to talk to me about it for six hours. I was like, "I am on board for this!" That was how it started.

First, we built the formwork, and then we were hired to do all the rest of the project's woodwork. It was great to have the trainees from the workshop on it because it was not a conventional project. We spent a whole month in the workshop making all the pieces, and when we went to do the install on-site, the Soil Lab team had already started building the rammed earth walls.

Those weeks of installation felt pretty cool. They had hired a bunch of local folks from North Lawndale who needed some day work. There was a big age diversity: there were some young people, people who were not from the community who were still in school, there were older folks, there were veterans, there were old construction workers who were just curious about what people were doing and they were coming by. And then there were people from Europe and some artist folks stopping by too. It was an interesting mix of people who didn't know each other.

From Revolution Workshop we had six trainees working on-site with me for the install, and by chance three or four of them lived within a five-block radius. About 80 to 90 percent of our trainees are from the West or South Side so it was a happy coincidence that it worked out like that. I think that added something.

Most of the time, people who come through this program are commuting big distances to get to work. They often commute all the way to the North Side, to the suburbs, so it was rare that they would be like, "I only have to go down the block to go to work?" It was good for them to be able to say, "I am working on a project in my own neighborhood."

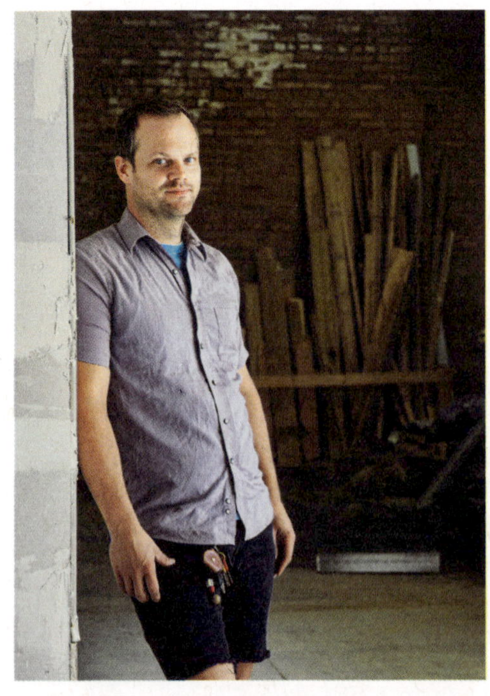

Lawndale Pop-Up Spot

My name is Jonathan Kelley and I'm the co-founder of the Lawndale Pop-Up Spot. It's a community museum in a shipping container in North Lawndale. I started getting involved in North Lawndale in 2016 when my colleague and graduate school friend, Chelsea Ridley, and I started working on the idea of a community museum that would be of, by and for the community of North Lawndale. It was a project that started with some residents and stakeholders who invited us in, and from there we've done a number of art and placemaking engagements—exhibitions with photography, art, history, social issues, literacy—and we are now located at Love Blooms Here Plaza, right on the corner of Central Park Avenue and Douglas Boulevard.

I heard rumblings about Soil Lab relatively early in the process as I was following the work of the biennial, and then, through Zoom meetings and phone calls, I continued to follow as plans started to take form and blossom.

The materiality of the project was definitely among the most interesting things for me. Watching the entire process as it developed, through the use of materials from the neighborhood to build things, was really interesting, and though I'm more of an ideas guy than a making person, getting involved and making a brick on my own was fascinating. I went away with the belief and the commitment that, regardless of issues of disinvestment, of inequity and inequality, we do have the capacity at a local and community level to be stewards of growth, to be stewards of creativity, to invest in development and invigoration of communities in really fundamental and elemental ways. And my hope is that this spirit continues in other forms of placemaking and community service—human interventions and sustainable practices—in North Lawndale.

CCA Academy

My name is Ida Harden. I recently started working at the CCA Academy in North Lawndale, and as a Chicago native, I love to see any effort that supports green and sustainable initiatives. I believe the efforts to make more community gardens that the locals can interact with is very important. So I'm very happy to be here.

Perma Park is a Permaculture Food Forest. It is permanent agriculture, and while there are others in the city, it's our attempt to get our youth to work and interact with nature. In doing so, they understand that supportive communities are what make communities strong, what make families strong, and what make a school strong. And permaculture is that: it's a representation of how nature works together. The different plants and insects, the whole ecology and ecosystem, work together to create a stronger structure which makes it possible for the many different plants, animals and insects to be successful. We started it with the staff and students of the School of the Art Institute, and it's been six years now that CCA has been developing it.

My name is Nancy Zook and I've been working here at the CCA Academy for 15 years now. Our school was also involved in the Chicago Architecture Biennial. *The Available City* was something that we were very interested in: the idea that you could work with community groups and find vacant unused land and reactivate it as community space, for gatherings, growing and building community. That's how we got involved in *The Available City*. And Soil Lab was another

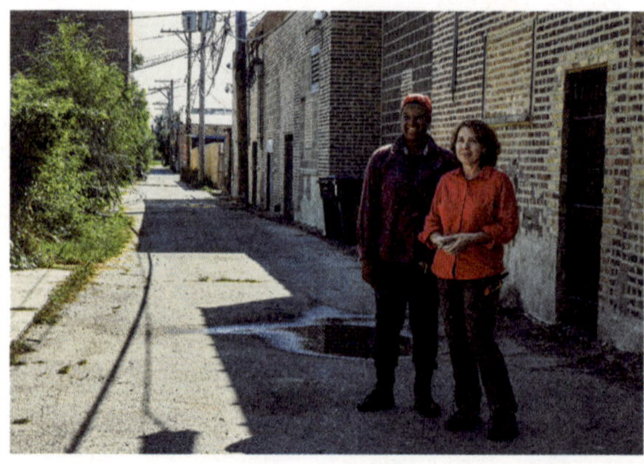

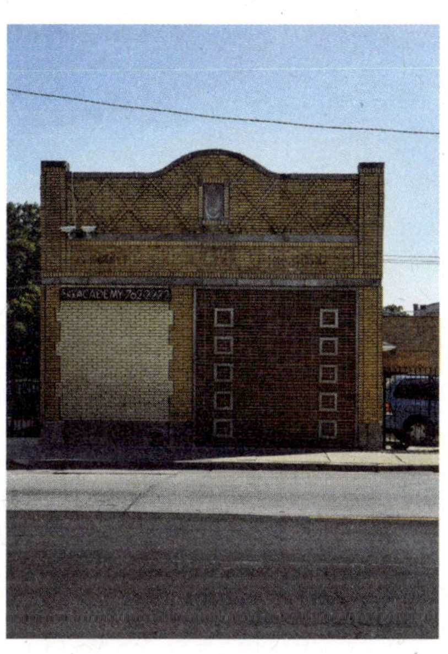

Available City site, another piece of vacant land next to our Perma Park, so we got to know each other very well over the summer months as they were building. I think it's really interesting that, because we were so close to each other, we really helped each other quite a lot to be more successful. There were a lot more people interested in coming by to learn about what we were doing and got involved because we were so close. The Young Men's Educational Network (YMEN) is another organization that worked with the biennial and was located on the other side of the Soil Lab site. Having these different community groups working together on the different projects in unison made it something very special.

What I experienced was an expression of something that I knew and I've always been excited about: the creative power that comes about when people collaborate. You can still have your own space and your own goals, but lifting others up makes you stronger, makes your goals stronger, and makes things work better for your organization as well. It was exciting to see that through the course of the summer we could all work together and collaborate and were all the better for it. It was permaculture.

Stone Temple Baptist Church

Hi, my name is Reshorna Fitzpatrick, and I am the executive pastor of the historic Stone Temple Baptist Church, located in North Lawndale. The senior pastor, Bishop Derrick Milas Fitzpatrick, happens to be my husband. We're standing in a sanctuary, a place that I come to, to worship every Sunday, and one that I'm so happy with and proud of. This podium that I preach from is the same podium that Dr King spoke from when he was here in the 1960s fighting for equality for our people or for anybody that was experiencing social injustices. And before this became our church this was a Jewish synagogue. In 1926, when the building was finished, the Queen of Romania came over to inaugurate it. So this place has been graced by a king and a queen, and when you come in here,

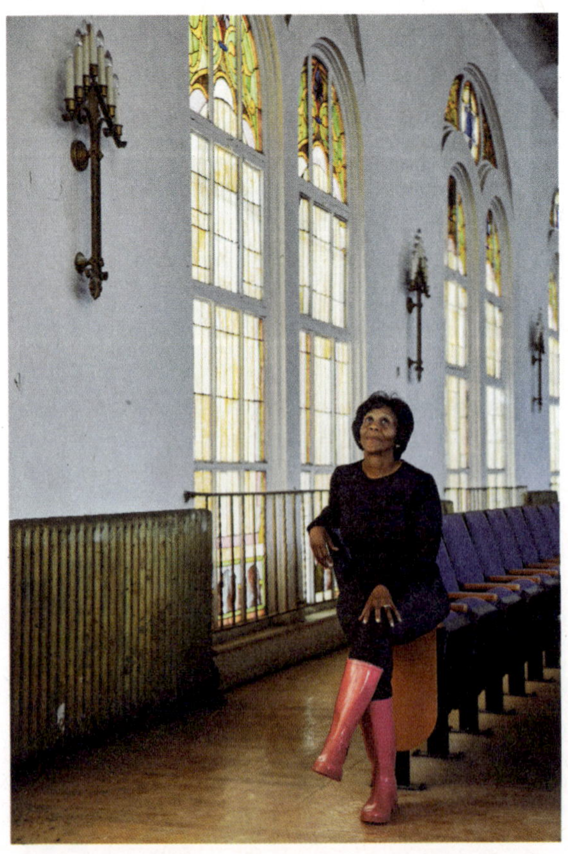

whether you are male or female, you automatically know that you are royalty.

North Lawndale is where I went to elementary school, and this boulevard is where I played with my siblings. I'm 58 years old now and I chair the North Lawndale GROWSS (Greening, Open space, Water, Soil and Sustainability) committee. It's through this that I learned about the Soil Lab project. I immediately got very excited thinking about how many things we could make with bricks: I thought about a pizza oven, I thought about an outdoor kitchen, I thought about all these beautiful pavers that could be made by the people in the community.

And I learned that people from different countries can come together and create something amazing. I also learned that there is a process to creating beauty. I learned that things take time: developing relationships, building a community. I learned that you can do so many different things with soil. I knew I could plant in it, I knew I could grow in it. But to create those beautiful bricks and plaques and pavers, to be able to do that, to be able to garner that skill, was just awesome and amazing.

I think brick making could actually be a social enterprise for this community. The machinery is here and people need to be mindful of what they can do with their hands if they have the right training and the right equipment. This could be a real opportunity for people in the community to do something amazing.

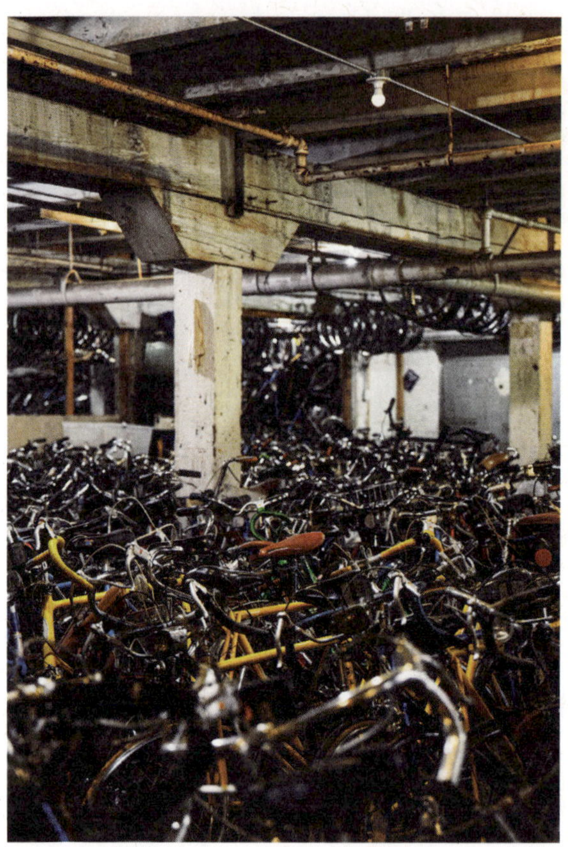

Working Bikes

I'm Colette Balas and I'm from the Kansas City area. I moved here for college and got really interested in the city's biking culture, especially during Covid when you couldn't really use public transportation. I really loved how accessible a lot of things were on the North Side, which is where I live, but as I started coming to the South and Southwest Sides of Chicago, I realized how poor the cycling infrastructure is here. Finding Working Bikes and seeing the impact this organization makes in the North Lawndale, Little Village and surrounding Pilsen communities really inspired me, and I've continued to run the local donation program as well as the volunteer program here.

Our main goal of the program is to get more bikes out into the community and specifically to use bikes as a tool of empowerment for folks. Our main Cycle of Power and Cycle of Peace programs are geared towards getting folks rolling: those who need bikes for transportation purposes and can't afford one otherwise. We are entirely volunteer-based here, but we get about a thousand people rolling in the community each year.

The Working Bikes volunteer sessions are open to everyone and include folks from all over Chicago, including our neighbors in North Lawndale. It was with Marcus Thorne, one of the attendees, that we developed the idea for the Young Men's Educational Network (YMEN) North Lawndale Bike Box. The Bike Box is located next to the Soil Lab site, and is a community space where residents can borrow bikes (free of charge), fix bikes, and even purchase bikes. It is a bicycle resource in a bicycle shop desert. The Bike Box is a partnership of many community organizations and managed by both YMEN and Working Bikes. The network of individuals and organizations living and doing good work in the neighborhood is incredible, and we're excited to get more folks in the community using bikes. It's a beautiful place to ride!

Ta-Nehisi Coates

THE CASE FOR REPARATIONS

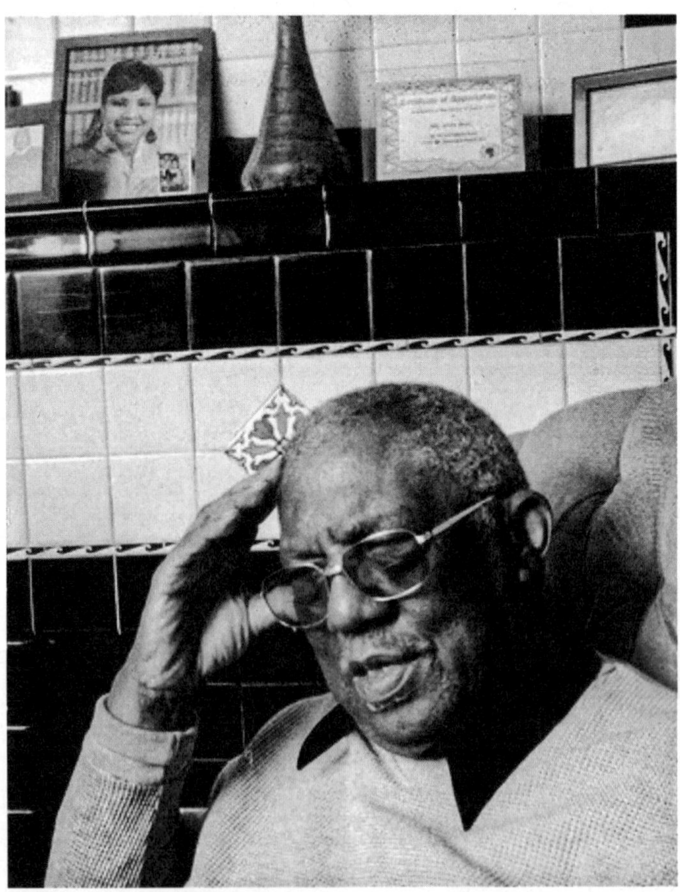

Clyde Ross, photographed in November 2013 in his home in the North Lawndale neighborhood of Chicago, where he has lived for more than fifty years. When he first tried to get a legitimate mortgage, he was denied; mortgages were effectively not available to black people.

In the lead-up to the Chicago Architecture Biennial, we attempted to grapple with a place far away from where we were, a neighborhood on Chicago's West Side called North Lawndale. To familiarize ourselves with the context that we would act in and the place we would soon call home, we met with various community figures through online roundtable meetings. In these speed dating-style Zoom sessions, we sought out new friends and collaborators to share with us information about the place and relay their interests and concerns about our proposal. It was through these formative meetings that we were directed to this text by Ta-Nehisi Coates, originally published by *The Atlantic* in 2014 and available to read in full online. This text, of which an excerpt is reproduced here, was the wake-up call we needed.

Two hundred fifty years of slavery. Ninety years of Jim Crow. Sixty years of separate but equal. Thirty-five years of racist housing policy. Until we reckon with our compounding moral debts, America will never be whole.

[...] In 1961, [Clyde] Ross and his wife bought a house in North Lawndale, a bustling community on Chicago's West Side. North Lawndale had long been a predominantly Jewish neighborhood, but a handful of middle-class African Americans had lived there starting in the '40s. The community was anchored by the sprawling Sears, Roebuck headquarters. North Lawndale's Jewish People's Institute actively encouraged blacks to move into the neighborhood, seeking to make it a "pilot community for interracial living." In the battle for integration then being fought around the country, North Lawndale seemed to offer promising terrain. But out in the tall grass, highwaymen, nefarious as any Clarksdale kleptocrat, were lying in wait.

Three months after Clyde Ross moved into his house, the boiler blew out. This would normally be a homeowner's responsibility, but in fact, Ross was not really a homeowner. His payments were made to the seller, not the bank. And Ross had not signed a normal mortgage. He'd bought "on contract": a predatory agreement that combined all the responsibilities of homeownership with all the disadvantages of renting—while offering the benefits of neither. Ross had bought his house for $27,500. The seller, not the previous homeowner but a new kind of middleman, had bought it for only $12,000 six months before selling it to Ross. In a contract sale, the seller kept the deed until the contract was paid in full—and, unlike with a normal mortgage, Ross would acquire no equity in the meantime. If he missed a single payment, he would immediately forfeit his $1,000 down payment, all his monthly payments, and the property itself.

The men who peddled contracts in North Lawndale would sell homes at inflated prices and then evict families who could not pay—taking their down payment and their monthly installments as profit. Then they'd bring in another black family, rinse, and repeat. "He loads them up with payments they can't meet," an office secretary told *The Chicago Daily News* of her boss, the speculator Lou Fushanis, in 1963. "Then he takes the property away from them. He's sold some of the buildings three or four times."

Ross had tried to get a legitimate mortgage in another neighborhood, but was told by a loan officer that there was no financing available. The truth was that there was no financing for people like Clyde Ross. From the 1930s through the 1960s, black people across the country were largely cut out of the legitimate home-mortgage market through means both legal and extralegal. Chicago whites employed every measure, from "restrictive covenants" to bombings, to keep their neighborhoods segregated.

Their efforts were buttressed by the federal government. In 1934, Congress created the Federal Housing Administration. The FHA insured private mortgages, causing a drop in interest rates and a decline in the size of the down payment required to buy a house. But an insured mortgage was not a possibility for Clyde Ross. The FHA had adopted a system of maps that rated neighborhoods according to their perceived stability. On the maps, green areas, rated "A," indicated "in demand" neighborhoods that, as one appraiser put it, lacked "a single foreigner or Negro." These neighborhoods were considered excellent prospects for insurance. Neighborhoods where black people lived were rated "D" and were usually considered ineligible for FHA backing. They were colored in red. Neither the percentage of black people living there nor their social class mattered. Black people were viewed as a contagion. Redlining went beyond FHA-backed loans and spread to the entire mortgage industry, which was already rife with racism, excluding black people from most legitimate means of obtaining a mortgage.

"A government offering such bounty to builders and lenders could have required compliance with a nondiscrimination policy," Charles Abrams, the urban-studies expert who helped create the New York City

Housing Authority, wrote in 1955. "Instead, the FHA adopted a racial policy that could well have been culled from the Nuremberg laws."

The devastating effects are cogently outlined by Melvin L Oliver and Thomas M Shapiro in their 1995 book, *Black Wealth/White Wealth*: "Locked out of the greatest mass-based opportunity for wealth accumulation in American history, African Americans who desired and were able to afford home ownership found themselves consigned to central-city communities where their investments were affected by the 'self-fulfilling prophecies' of the FHA appraisers: cut off from sources of new investment[,] their homes and communities deteriorated and lost value in comparison to those homes and communities that FHA appraisers deemed desirable."

In Chicago and across the country, whites looking to achieve the American dream could rely on a legitimate credit system backed by the government. Blacks were herded into the sights of unscrupulous lenders who took them for money and for sport. "It was like people who like to go out and shoot lions in Africa. It was the same thrill," a housing attorney told the historian Beryl Satter in her 2009 book, *Family Properties*. "The thrill of the chase and the kill."

The kill was profitable. At the time of his death, Lou Fushanis owned more than 600 properties, many of them in North Lawndale, and his estate was estimated to be worth $3 million. He'd made much of this money by exploiting the frustrated hopes of black migrants like Clyde Ross. During this period, according to one estimate, 85 percent of all black home buyers who bought in Chicago bought on contract. "If anybody who is well established in this business in Chicago doesn't earn $100,000 a year," a contract seller told *The Saturday Evening Post* in 1962, "he is loafing."

Contract sellers became rich. North Lawndale became a ghetto.

Clyde Ross still lives there. He still owns his home. He is 91, and the emblems of survival are all around him—awards for service in his community, pictures of his children in cap and gown. But when I asked him about his home in North Lawndale, I heard only anarchy.

"We were ashamed. We did not want anyone to know that we were that ignorant," Ross told me. He was sitting at his dining-room table. His glasses were as thick as his Clarksdale drawl. "I'd come out of Mississippi where there was one mess, and come up here and got in another mess. So how dumb am I? I didn't want anyone to know how dumb I was.

"When I found myself caught up in it, I said, 'How? I just left this mess. I just left no laws. And no regard. And then I come here and get cheated wide open.' I would probably want to do some harm to some people, you know, if I had been violent like some of us. I thought, 'Man, I got caught up in this stuff. I can't even take care of my kids.' I didn't have enough for my kids. You could fall through the cracks easy fighting these white people. And no law."

But fight Clyde Ross did. In 1968 he joined the newly formed Contract Buyers League—a collection of black homeowners on Chicago's South and West Sides, all of whom had been locked into the same system of predation. There was Howell Collins, whose contract called for him to pay $25,500 for a house that a speculator had bought for $14,500. There was Ruth Wells, who'd managed to pay out half her contract, expecting a mortgage, only to suddenly see an insurance bill materialize out of thin air—a requirement the seller had added without Wells's knowledge. Contract sellers used every tool at their disposal to pilfer from their clients. They scared white residents into selling low. They lied about properties' compliance with building codes, then left the buyer responsible when city inspectors arrived. They presented themselves as real-estate brokers, when in fact they were the owners. They guided their clients to lawyers who were in on the scheme.

The Contract Buyers League fought back. Members—who would eventually number more than 500—went out to the posh suburbs where the speculators lived and embarrassed them by knocking on their neighbors' doors and informing them of the details of the contract-lending trade. They refused to pay their installments, instead holding monthly payments in an escrow account. Then they brought a suit against the contract sellers, accusing them of buying properties and reselling in such a manner "to reap from members of the Negro race large and unjust profits."

In return for the "deprivations of their rights and privileges under the Thirteenth and Fourteenth Amendments," the league demanded "prayers for relief"—payback of all moneys paid on contracts and all moneys paid for structural improvement of properties, at 6 percent interest minus a "fair, non-discriminatory" rental price for time of occupation. Moreover, the league asked the court to adjudge that the defendants had "acted willfully and maliciously and that malice is the gist of this action."

Ross and the Contract Buyers League were no longer appealing to the government simply for equality. They were no longer fleeing in hopes of a better deal elsewhere. They were charging society with a crime against their community. They wanted the crime publicly ruled as such. They wanted the crime's executors declared to be offensive to society. And they wanted restitution for the great injury brought upon them by said offenders. In 1968, Clyde Ross and the Contract Buyers League were no longer simply seeking the protection of the law. They were seeking reparations.

According to the most-recent statistics, North Lawndale is now on the wrong end of virtually every socioeconomic indicator. In 1930 its population was 112,000. Today it is 36,000. The halcyon talk of "interracial living" is dead. The neighborhood is 92 percent black. Its homicide rate is 45 per 100,000—triple the rate of the city as a whole. The infant-mortality rate is 14 per 1,000—more than twice the national average. Forty-three percent of the people in North Lawndale live below the poverty line—double Chicago's overall rate. Forty-five percent of all households are on food stamps—nearly three times the rate of the city at large. Sears, Roebuck left the neighborhood in 1987, taking 1,800 jobs with it. Kids in North Lawndale need not be confused about their prospects: Cook County's Juvenile Temporary Detention Center sits directly adjacent to the neighborhood.

North Lawndale is an extreme portrait of the trends that ail black Chicago. Such is the magnitude of these ailments that it can be said that

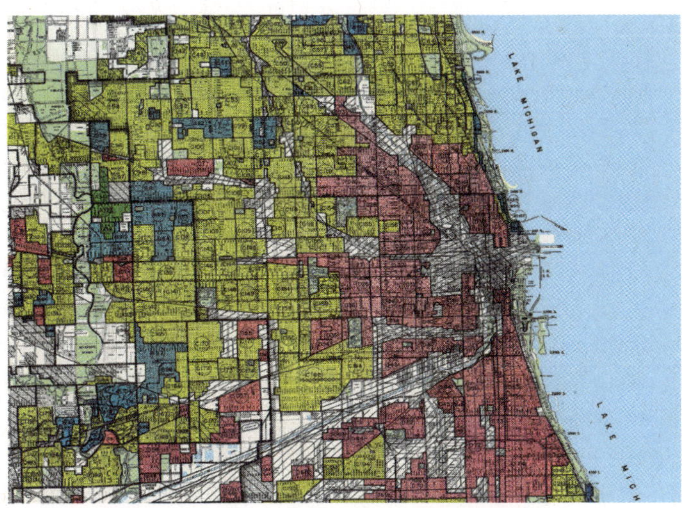

A 1939 Home Owners' Loan Corporation "Recidential Security Map" of Chicago shows discrimination against low-income and minority neighborhoods. The residents of the areas marked in red (representing "hazardous" real-estate markets) were denied FHA-backed mortgages

blacks and whites do not inhabit the same city. The average per capita income of Chicago's white neighborhoods is almost three times that of its black neighborhoods. When the Harvard sociologist Robert J Sampson examined incarceration rates in Chicago in his 2012 book, *Great American City*, he found that a black neighborhood with one of the highest incarceration rates (West Garfield Park) had a rate more than forty times as high as the white neighborhood with the highest rate (Clearing). "This is a staggering differential, even for community-level comparisons," Sampson writes. "A difference of kind, not degree."

In other words, Chicago's impoverished black neighborhoods—characterized by high unemployment and households headed by single parents—are not simply poor; they are "ecologically distinct." This "is not simply the same thing as low economic status," writes Sampson. "In this pattern Chicago is not alone."

The lives of black Americans are better than they were half a century ago. The humiliation of whites only signs are gone. Rates of black poverty have decreased. Black teen-pregnancy rates are at record lows—and the gap between black and white teen-pregnancy rates has shrunk significantly. But such progress rests on a shaky foundation, and fault lines are everywhere. The income gap between black and white households is roughly the same today as it was in 1970. Patrick Sharkey, a sociologist at New York University, studied children born from 1955 through 1970 and found that 4 percent of whites and 62 percent of blacks across America had been raised in poor neighborhoods. A generation later, the same study showed, virtually nothing had changed. And whereas whites born into affluent neighborhoods tended to remain in affluent neighborhoods, blacks tended to fall out of them.

This is not surprising. Black families, regardless of income, are significantly less wealthy than white families. The Pew Research Center estimates that white households are worth roughly 20 times as much as black households, and that whereas only 15 percent of whites have zero or negative wealth, more than a third of blacks do. Effectively, the black family in America is working without a safety net. When financial calamity strikes—a medical emergency, divorce, job loss—the fall is precipitous.

And just as black families of all incomes remain handicapped by a lack of wealth, so too do they remain handicapped by their restricted choice of neighborhood. Black people with upper-middle-class incomes do not generally live in upper-middle-class neighborhoods. Sharkey's research shows that black families making $100,000 typically live in the kinds of neighborhoods inhabited by white families making $30,000.

"Blacks and whites inhabit such different neighborhoods," Sharkey writes, "that it is not possible to compare the economic outcomes of black and white children." A national real-estate association advised not to sell to "a colored man of means who was giving his children a college education."

The implications are chilling. As a rule, poor black people do not work their way out of the ghetto—and those who do often face the horror of watching their children and grandchildren tumble back.

Even seeming evidence of progress withers under harsh light. In 2012, the Manhattan Institute cheerily noted that segregation had declined since the 1960s. And yet African Americans still remained—by far—the most segregated ethnic group in the country. With segregation, with the isolation of the injured and the robbed, comes the concentration of disadvantage. An unsegregated America might see poverty, and all its effects, spread across the country with no particular bias toward skin color. Instead, the concentration of poverty has been paired with a concentration of melanin. The resulting conflagration has been devastating.

One thread of thinking in the African American community holds that these depressing numbers partially stem from cultural pathologies that can be altered through individual grit and exceptionally good behavior. (In 2011, Philadelphia Mayor Michael Nutter, responding to violence among young black males, put the blame on the family: "Too many men making too many babies they don't want to take care of, and then we end up dealing with your children." Nutter turned to those presumably fatherless babies: "Pull your pants up and buy a belt, because no one wants to see your underwear or the crack of your butt.") The thread is as old as black politics itself. It is also wrong. The kind of trenchant racism to which black people have persistently been subjected can never be defeated by making its victims more respectable. The essence of American racism is disrespect. And in the wake of the grim numbers, we see the grim inheritance.

The Contract Buyers League's suit brought by Clyde Ross and his allies took direct aim at this inheritance. The suit was rooted in Chicago's long history of segregation, which had created two housing markets—one legitimate and backed by the government, the other lawless and patrolled by predators. The suit dragged on until 1976, when the league lost a jury trial. Securing the equal protection of the law proved hard; securing reparations proved impossible. [...]

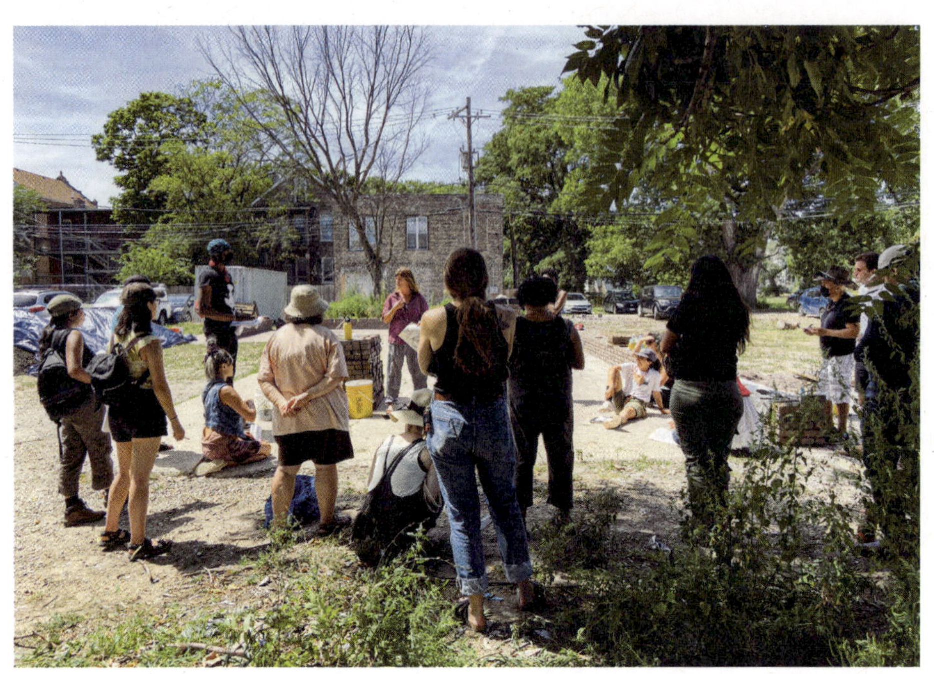

Annette Skov

BUILDING COMMUNITIES

How could we make a meaningful connection with the people of North Lawndale? How could we gain their trust, and how, as one safeguard asked, could we "avoid causing them harm after we left?" Throughout the project, Annette acted as our advisor in community engagement. Based in Copenhagen, she has worked for many years with art as a method to create communities. From her experience working as a visual artist, project manager, educator and former Head of Learning at Copenhagen Contemporary, Annette guided us to be present, to listen and be curious, and to reciprocate. Through these five short texts, Annette illustrates how art and architecture can create a space for sharing knowledge and a catalyst for change in, and alongside, a community.

The Apollo method

In the spring of 2001, my mother purchased an Apollo-branded trailer in Brønderslev in Denmark. It was orange and brown and it was from 1983. The original plan was to place it in the dunes in Tversted in North Jutland, so that she could enjoy being there, very close to the sea. A utopia, indeed—but nobody is allowed to camp in the dunes and my mother was already far too ill to be able to realize these plans. Regardless, she filled the Apollo with the best gear: special cups, dish towels, soft duvet covers, a bottle opener from the blacksmith in Aabybro. Bowls, plates and pillows. And the Apollo stood in my mother's garden, with the awning out, as the lush grass shot up and the warm summer gave rise to a record number of blackcurrants, which I picked. My mother walked across the lawn to sit inside the Apollo a few times, but it was too cold for her. She passed away in the fall of 2001. I inherited the Apollo and my uncle taught me how to handle it.

In the ensuing years, the Apollo traveled around Denmark to cities, towns and suburbs, and countless locations in Copenhagen. In all of these places, I—and often also a companion—welcomed guests into the Apollo in order to exchange stories. They visited the Apollo out of curiosity, out of need, because they were tired and were looking to find a place to rest, out of loneliness, or because they wanted to share some intense experience. And there something special happened in this secluded place: because we were exchanging stories, we got to know each other, our lives and ourselves. The room became a secret island of intimacy, a magical space for being. A place where we were able to exchange thoughts and stories, and could gather around life, for a moment.

The trailer became a container that bubbled with words and emotions. A womb. A corrective to all the hustle and bustle going on just outside the orange curtains. Back then, it felt very important to create a space where people could meet and share stories. The cities had been emptied of public meeting places that were not defined in advance or arranged with specific economic objectives in mind. The Danish philosopher KE Løgstrup explained, "An individual never deals with another human being, without holding some piece of their life in his own hand." In the meetings in the old Apollo we sensed just this: we felt that we took on importance for each other.

The Apollo also became a way of investigating places. Whenever we parked the trailer, the place was instantly transformed—and we became privy to knowledge connected to precisely that particular place. We created a place in order to investigate a place. Collecting the stories, dreams and hopes of those people who knew the places became our method of inquiry. Places take on their meaning from those who live there.

We can learn from friendships

I believe we form communities for the same reason that we build and cultivate friendships: because we want something together, because we have a need for it, because it generates value, meaning and joy for the individual, and because we want to build something larger than ourselves. Aristotle expressed it so well: "If an isolated person is no longer communicating, he languishes, he is consumed, and he feels that he alone does not exist."

If we want to work with somebody, it has to make sense for the individual to become part of the community and co-create the community. People take part for many different reasons, but we cannot know anything about those reasons if we are not in dialogue. We don't know what it is that makes sense to others until we ask, and we cannot succeed in building communities if we fail to build with the answers.

Start as locally and as personally as possible. Ask openly and curiously. Listen. Involve and get involved. Let what is complicated proliferate. Don't be too quick to reject. Pay attention and share energy. Find your own curiosity and let this inspire you to make exchanges with others. Let wonder, humility and a spirit of inquiry be the driving forces. Make alliances with locals. Use various inputs. Don't create a locked-in project but set time aside for flexibility and be ready to adjust and calibrate as reality unfolds. Leave the office and the computer behind and get out, instead, into the terrain. On the ground. Invest time and presence. Embrace chaos and complexity. Keep in touch. Keep on doing what you are doing. Relationships are gold. People can obtain power through working with art. Art is existentially important. We feel less lonely if we are part of a community where art is included.

Art grows and art works

During the summer of 2021, the artists Amr Hatem and Samara Sallam, Syrian and Palestinian refugees educated at the Academy of Fine Arts in Copenhagen, created an art garden together with the residents of a public housing project in the Nørrebro area of Copenhagen. A pergola, tables and benches, along with star-shaped beds and wickerwork fences were constructed. Children and adults planted olive trees, herbs, flowers and bushes. An informal garden group started to convene and manage the garden; originally, the garden was created as a temporary project, but to this day it continues to be a place for working, holding meetings, enjoying food and playing.

It is a Saturday in the month of October. The sunshine is surprisingly warming, and I have never tried to plant bulbs before. James, the unofficial leader of the garden project, has bought 600 bulbs and we are choosing for ourselves which of the bulbs we want to plant, where we want to do this, and how. Together with a woman who lives high up in the apartment block, with her window facing out toward the garden, I choose two different varieties of crocus bulbs. We are getting help from a young woman who resolutely grabs hold of a long-handled rake and starts scraping away the grass in circles. After various attempts, our collectively shared form emerges from the brown soil: a spiral pattern into which we place the bulbs at appropriate distances. Conversation is flowing around and between us: politics, gardens, home, food. Family, flowers, language. Karl Marx and crocus plants. It is as if we can leap from large to small with a special nimbleness, precisely because we are sitting hunched over, with our eyes trained on the ground, as our hands are busy working.

Power to the participants

Who is deciding? The Austrian art mediator and curator Nora Sternfeld is always asking where the power lies. She is critical about the way user involvement is practiced inside art institutions: “How are we to understand this participation, which aims to include as many people as possible, but without giving them any possibility of having an impact on the decisions made?” She also criticizes the use of the word “participation”: “Participation is not simply about joining in the game,” she explains. “It is also about having the possibility to question the rules of the game: the conditions under which education, the public realm and representation within institutions happen. And, when understood in this way, participation can indeed make a difference.” All power to the participants. All power to the non-planned, the non-expected. Welcome new forms of engagement.

This is a checklist that I use for projects—an attempt to avoid the pitfalls

1 Why does the project exist? Who is defining the goals, success criteria and perspectives?
2 Who is defining the frame for the project?
3 Whose needs are going to be satisfied by this project?
4 How is participation and co-creation being defined and practiced in the project?
5 To what extent does the project avoid individualizing structural problems?
6 To what extent does the project set its focus on something other than reinforcing the institution’s own legitimacy and reputation?
7 Does the project manage to avoid obscuring power conflicts and avoid diverting focus from fundamental conflicts of interest? Does it avoid delaying and preventing understanding and relevant effort?
8 Who is participating and is this participation real? Or are the participants simply providing pseudo-participation and fitting neatly into already established structures?
9 Are educated and qualified social workers and other relevant professions being represented?
10 To what extent does the project address the risk of putting participants on display and contributing to further marginalization?
11 What words are being used in the project about goals, participants and methods?

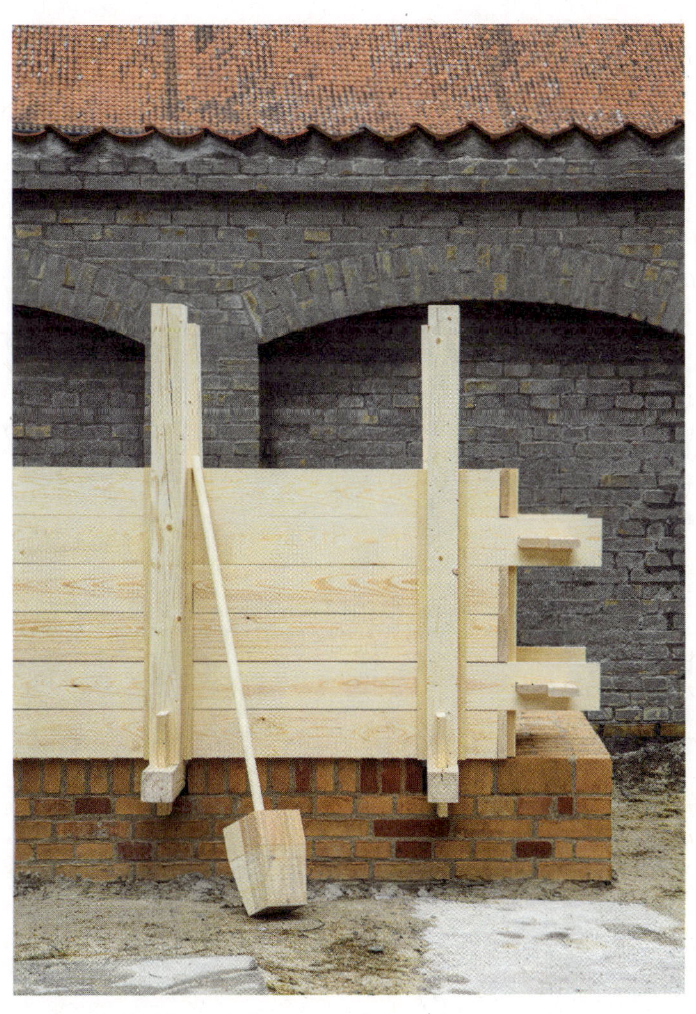

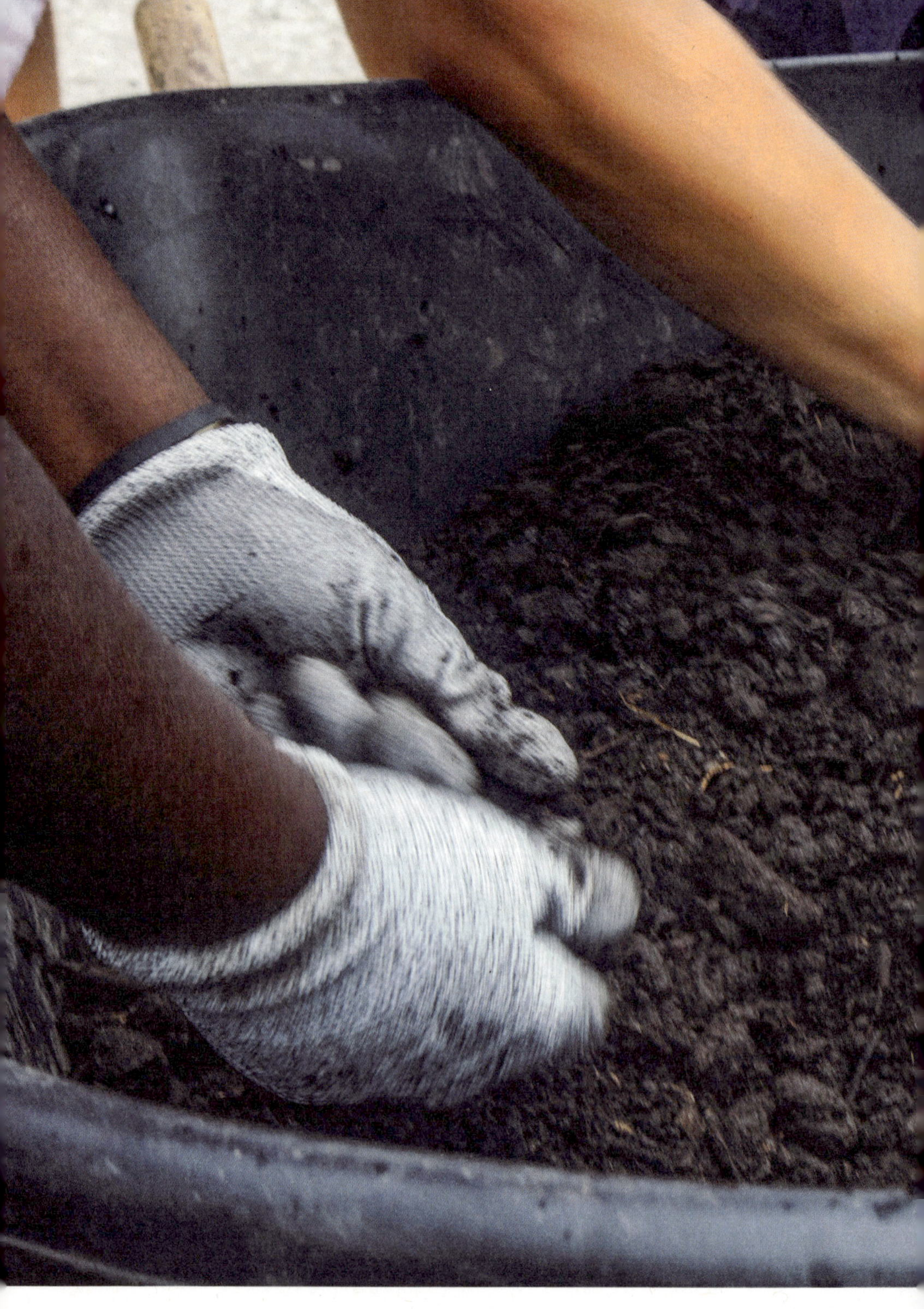

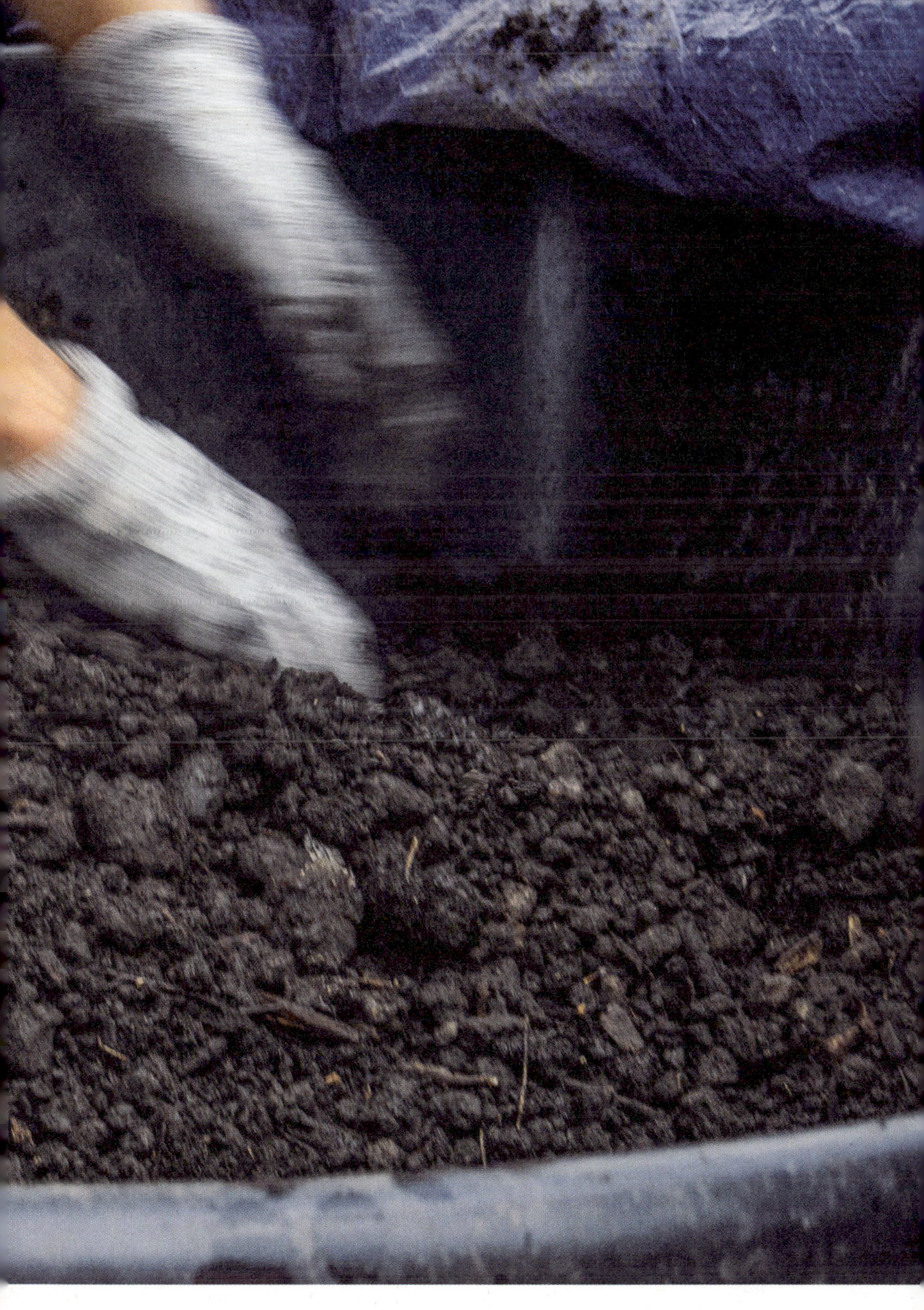

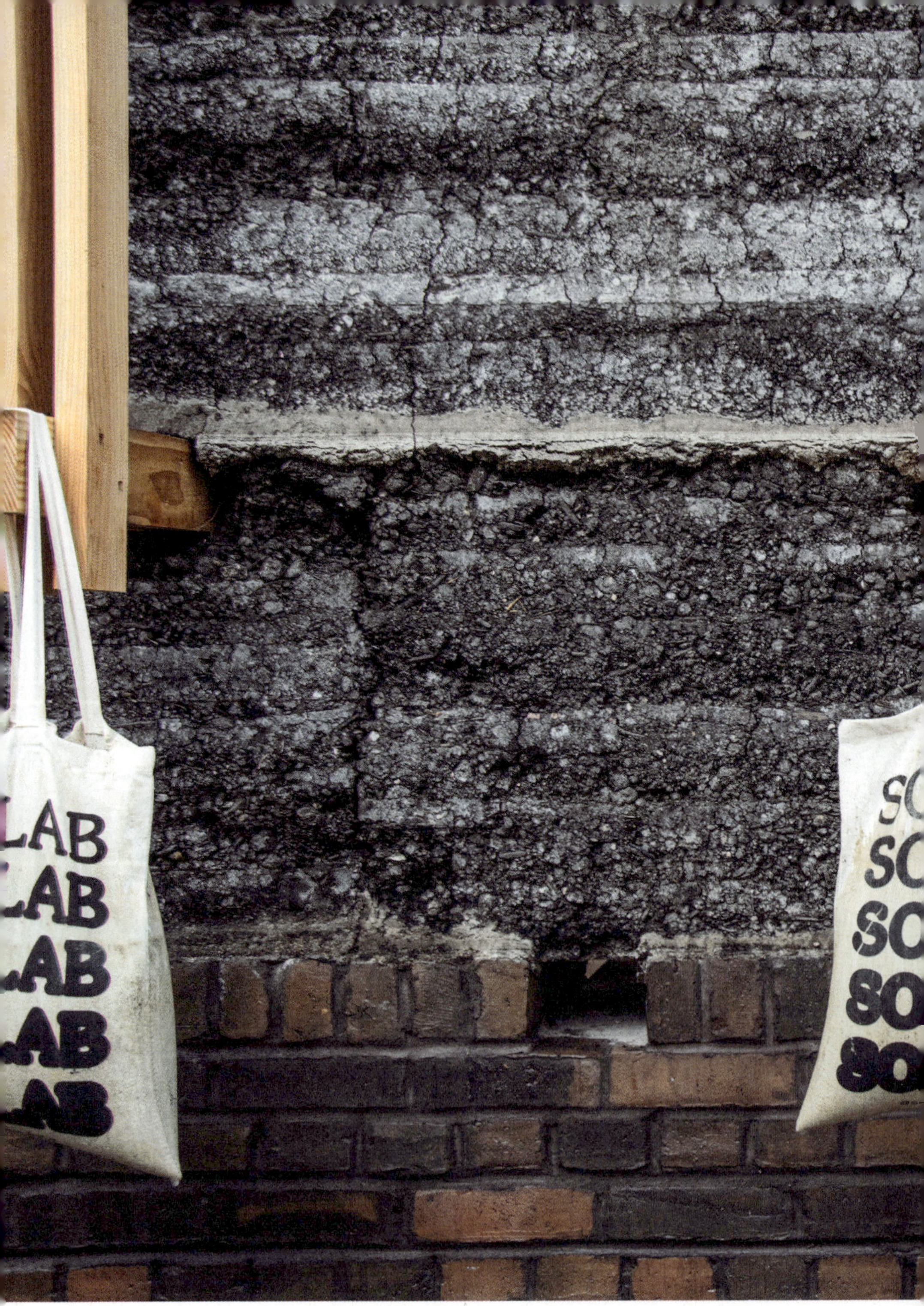
LAB

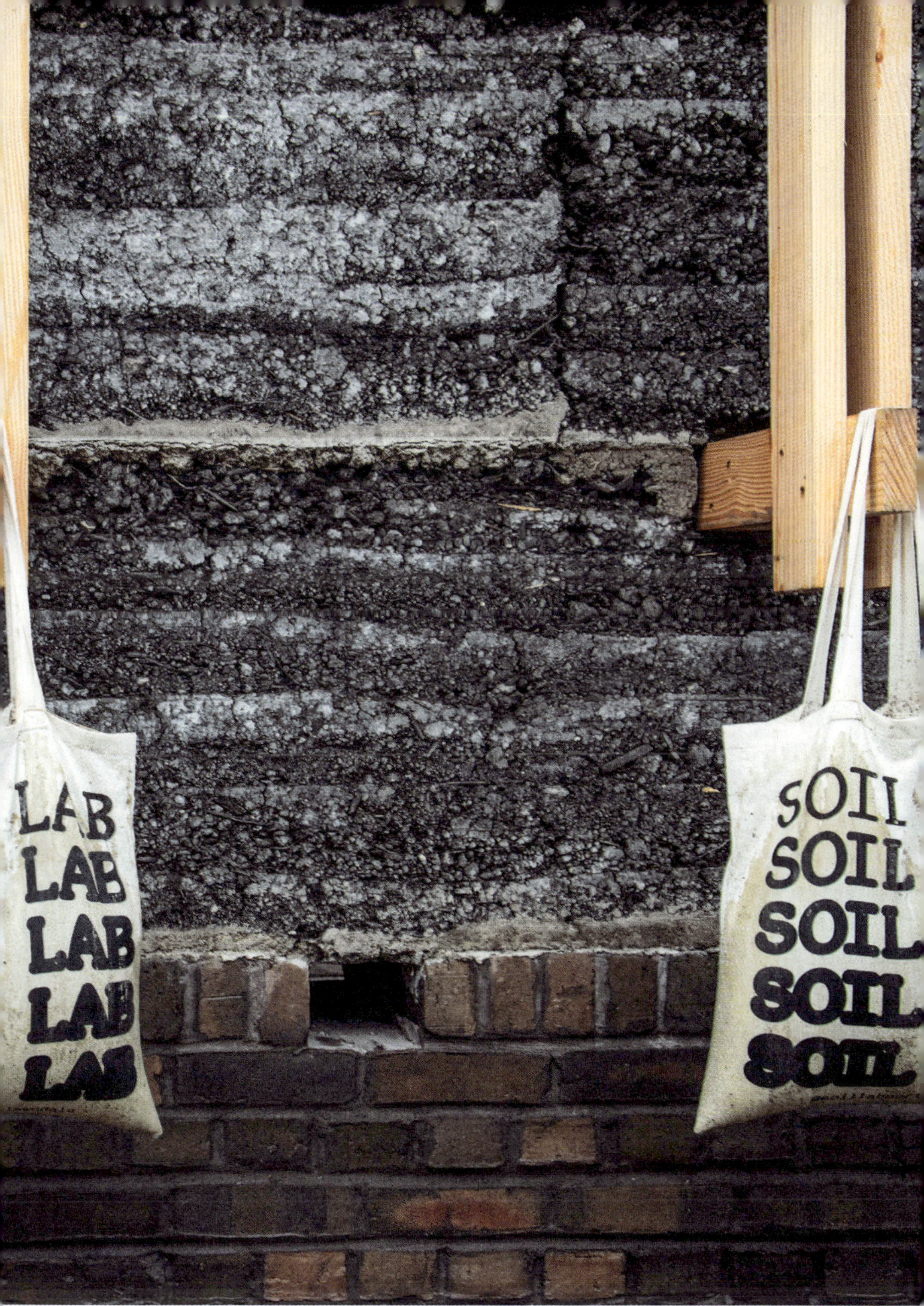
LAB
LAB
LAB
LAB
SOIL
SOIL
SOIL
SOIL
SOIL

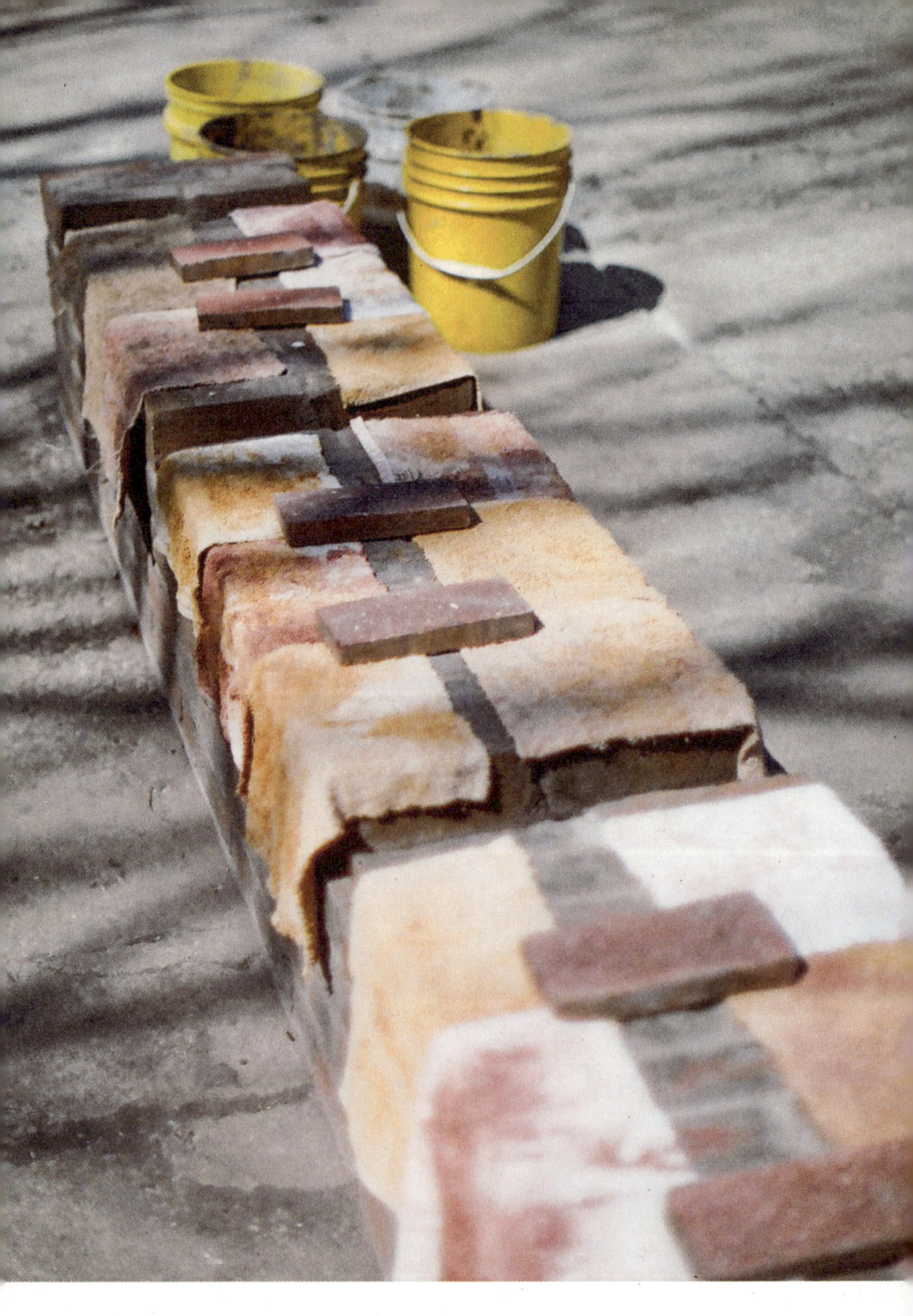

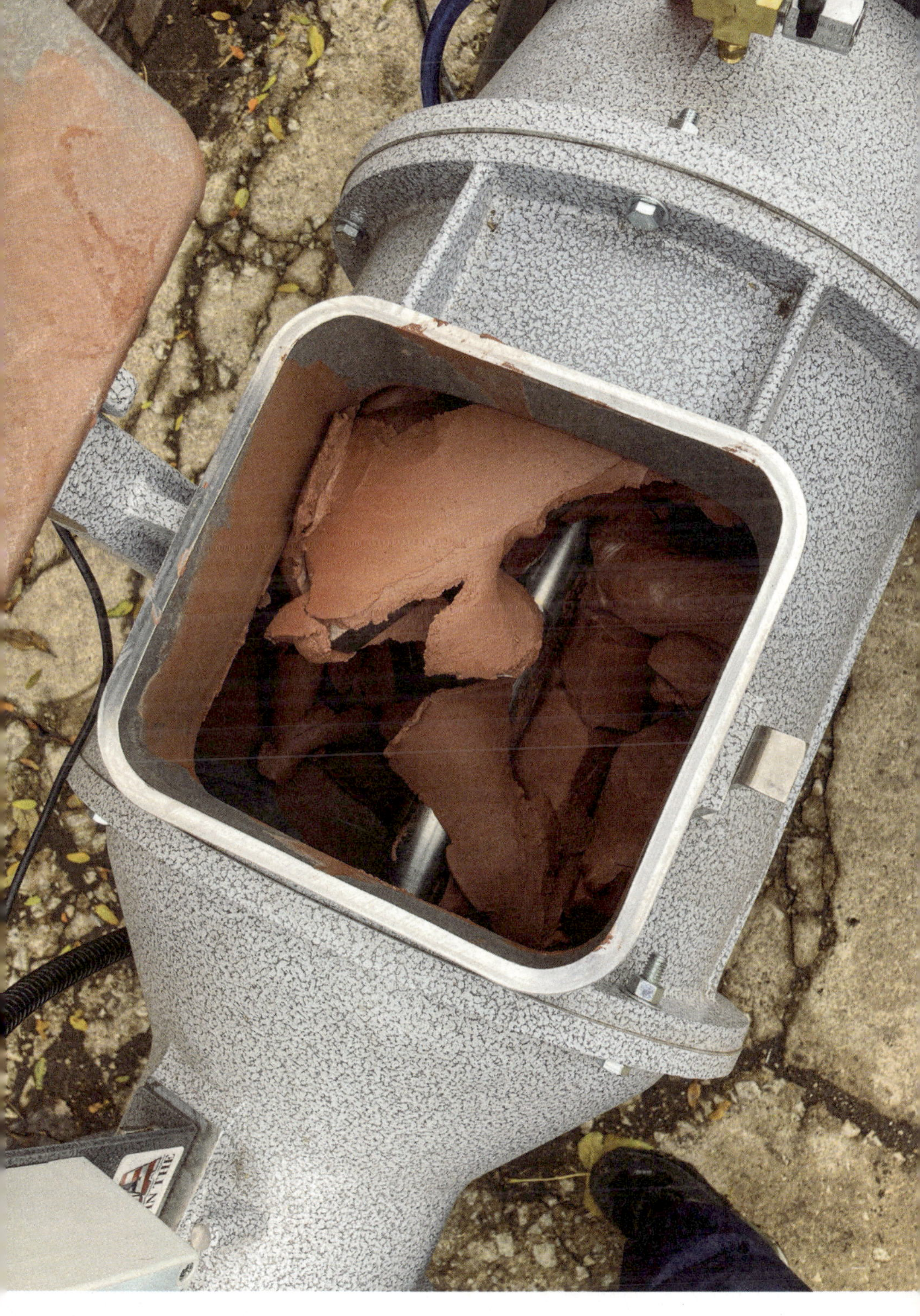

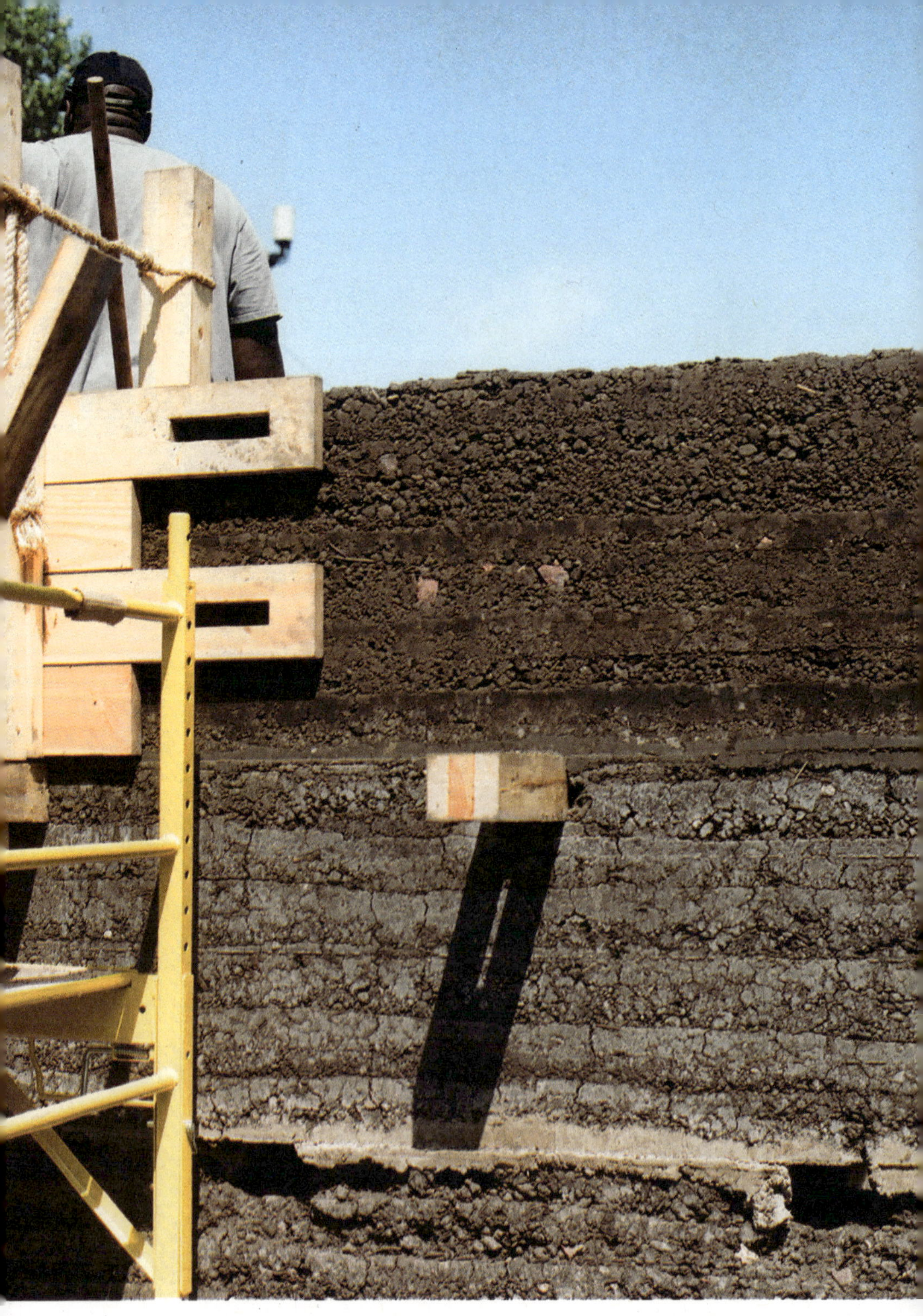

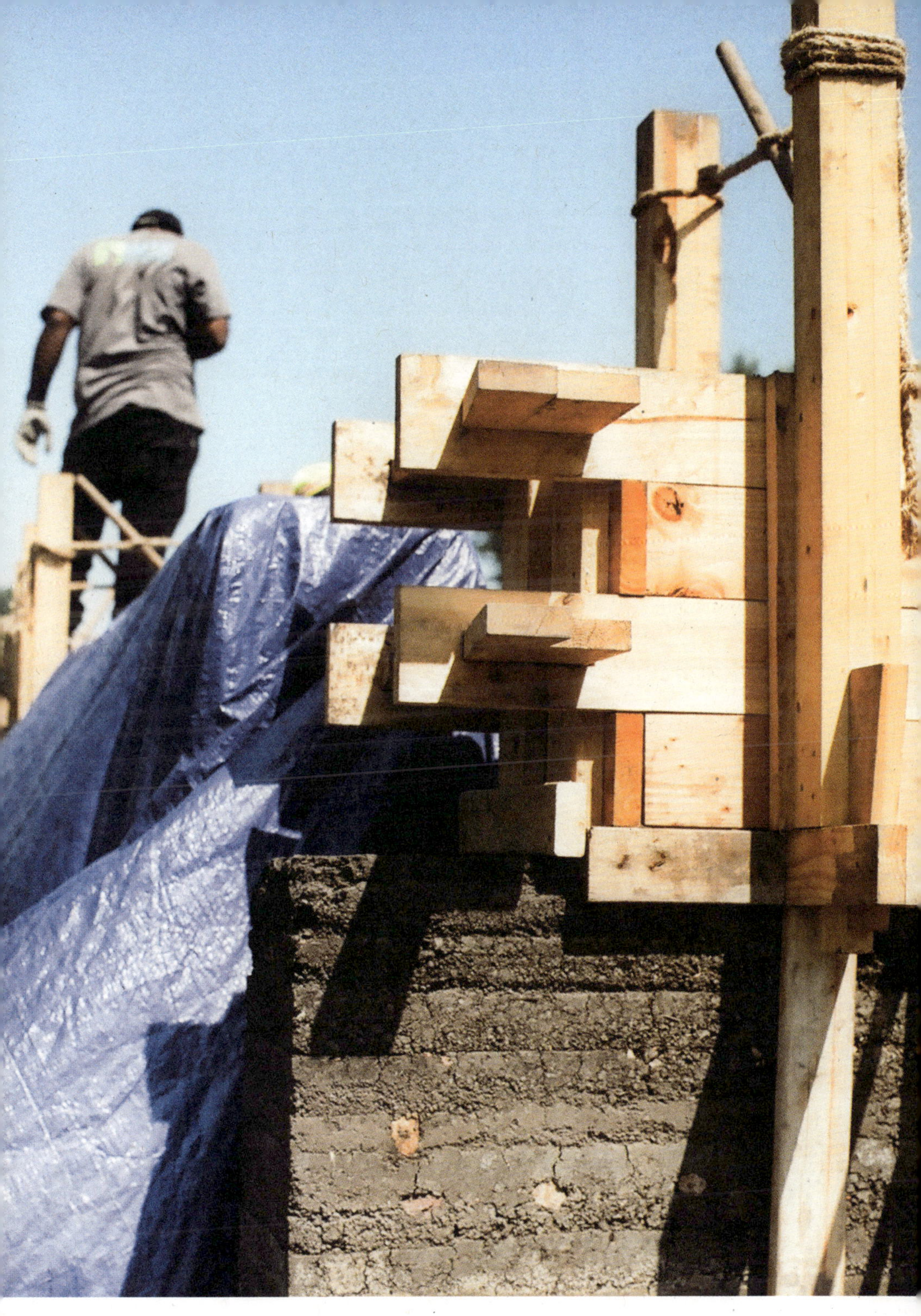

Amara Abdal Figueroa

ON THE SURFACE: CLAY HARVESTING AND PROCESSING WILD MATERIALS

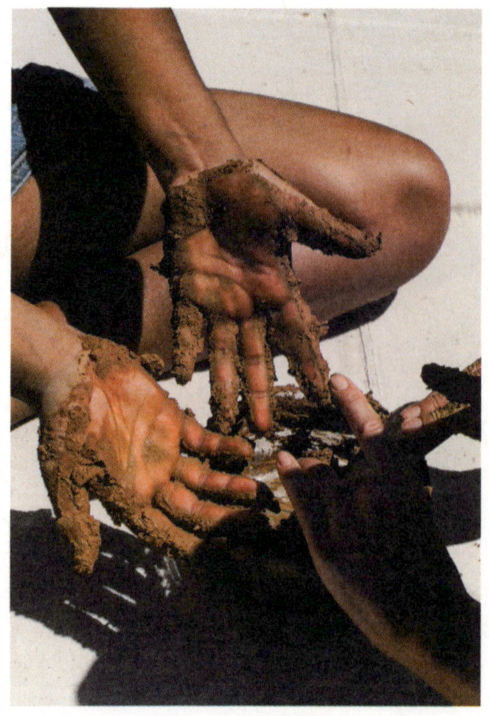

Amara Abdal Figueroa, of Tierrafiltra—a social and technical project based on the island of Borikén (Puerto Rico)—was invited to join the Soil Lab build to share her practice and tactile approach to clay. Through playful and intuitive experimentation with wet clay, the community was introduced to Amara's holistic approach to the material.

Soil Lab's ambition revolved around creating activities and workshops on the site. We did not want to create a biennial contribution in the sense of the classic exhibition, but a living and exchanging environment where skilled and unskilled people, along with the local community, could experiment as a unity. Clay is an accessible material and through this essay Amara contributes an experience-based step-by-step guide on how to harvest clay.

Barro es ente colaborador
Clay is a collaborating entity

Honra la tierra que tan abundante y generosa es
Honor the land for her abundance and generosity

Soil is incredibly diverse, differing in particle size, color, texture, structure and more. Working with clay is an invitation to discard attachment to specific results, and to open up to a process of getting to know natural materials intimately. It is a process of honing your senses, primarily—but not exclusively—observational and tactile skills.

I would like to share instances and processes of such an abundant and available material, through my intuitive trajectory, mainly encountering clay that has traveled. Touch and connect to the soil to unlock your personal inhibitions. Dig deeper at your own pace. Take cues from nature and adjust your practice to your surroundings.

Step 1: identifying (an interest in) clay

Consider where you are harvesting clay from and only take what you are committed to. If this is completely new to you, I'd strongly recommend small batches until you get a better understanding of what these processes entail. Be considerate. Some terrain is very prone to erosion and we should try to minimally impact these deposits.

I will always avoid extracting from a source on a path so as not to interrupt anyone's journey, nor from a roadcut or river edge that may cause a landslide. Recently I have collected clay deposits from a mudslide spilling onto a road as a result of extreme rain and poor road planning, and which needed removing anyway. Clay can take thousands of years to form from rock breaking down. Please, keep this in your heart.

Clay holds. If you see a chunk of drying or already dry earth defying gravity, it is likely to be a material that has the structural capacity to keep the form it is shaped into, may that be a vessel or a sculpture. Sand, on the other hand, will hold when damp, like when building a sandcastle, but will easily collapse when dry. Molecularly, this is explained by the form of the particles: clay particles are extremely small and laminar and stick together due to opposing electrical charges.

Clay swells with the presence of water and shrinks when it is absent; the cracks formed on a drying puddle are a result of surface tension. Sand particles are round, touching each other at tangential points. Water will filter through sand, in contrast to clay where it will saturate it. Silt, to me, is still somewhat a mystery. Soils usually consist of a combination of these three. For our purposes, we are looking for a predominance of clay.

If a material you see sticks to your curiosity and your fingers, start by making an earthworm and wrap it around your finger to test its elasticity. Make a small sphere with your palms and try to pinch it. In some instances, the clay will already be wet. In others, you will need to add a bit of water to make these field tests.

Step 2: safety and harvesting / harvesting safely

For your lungs and for your back, negotiate between an optimal humidity and excessive water weight when harvesting clay.

It is very important to mention safety while working with these materials. Airborne dry clay particles can easily suspend in the air we breathe, taking 24 hours to settle. It is highly recommended to wear an adequate mask to prevent scarring in the lungs due to this sedimentation. When possible, work in well ventilated areas and/or keep airborne clay particles low with a water mister or an air vent. Work with wet rags and a mop instead of brushing, sweeping or vacuuming. Do not underestimate the presence of particles that can be invisible to the eye.

Step 3: break it down and in(tro)spect!

In the field or in my studio, I like to open a canvas and start to get to know the wild clay with either a wire cutter, some tools or even my fingertips.

With the wire cutter, I like to cut raw slabs that can be read like an earthen book; often its contents are just speculations in my long-term studies.

Some contents can be problematic in ceramics during or after firing, like calcium-based limestone or gypsum. Testing for this early on will help us decide if the clay is one we want to harvest to begin with, and to what extent we might want to process the clay while wet.

To test the questionable calcium-based material—what appears to be white rocks—apply vinegar to a small portion and watch for bubbles. To better understand what I am saying, try making something with clay containing these contents anyway. Depending on the size and amount of the granular material present and the firing temperature, you may observe anything ranging from surface-level "pop-outs" to complete crumbling in less than two hours, subject to the humidity of your surroundings. Soluble salts only become visible after firing, as the fired clay will likely bloat or melt prematurely. Because of this, it is important to sift it out, not physically but metaphorically: are you grabbing a sample near salt or brackish water? Do not be discouraged if something doesn't work out. Remember to harvest small and test rigorously before you commit to harvesting larger amounts of material.

While I am breaking the harvested clay down, I like to become familiar with its feel. Get to know it in its crudest and freshest state. If I find rocks or twigs that are big enough and easy to grab with my fingers, I will remove them; if they are too small, I will catch them later on while sieving.

I've come to suggest breaking things down in this way because, personally, I find it more enjoyable and safer than doing it dry. It can seem time-consuming but if done with other curious people, it can form a constellation of shared readings. There is a point at which the clay is still a bit humid but super hard: it will take a lot of effort to cut with a wire and likely stick to your mallet. At this point, I'll let the chunks dry completely for breaking down later. Patience here saves physical effort in the long run.

Step 4: oversaturating clay in water or water in clay

If the harvested clay is already bone dry, crush and grind with a stick or stone or brick or mallet, and remember health and safety. Crushing the clay carefully into small chunks will increase the surface area for water to penetrate, which will break down the clay faster. This is called slaking.

The drier the clay, the stronger the pull for it to get wet. You can hear your clay sizzling, releasing air bubbles as clay begins to soak up

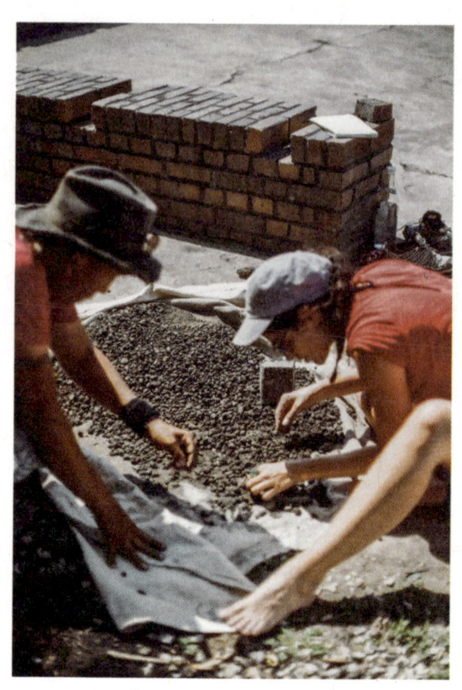

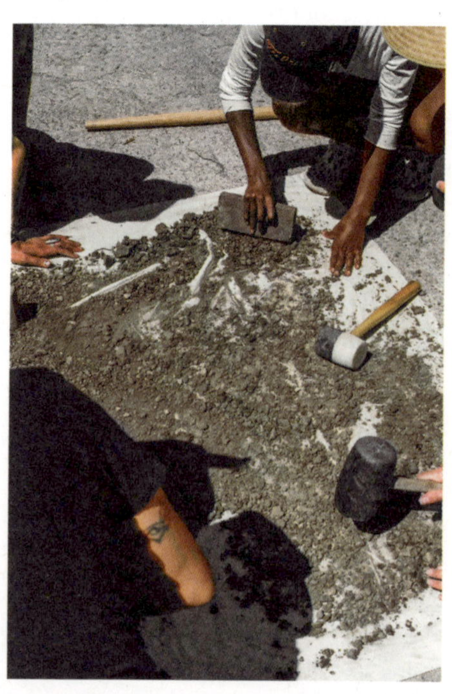

water, as water fills invisible air cavities. If the clay is still moist, it will take longer to break down.

If I'm in the studio doing multiple things and relaxed about time, I'll leave it in water overnight or for another time later when I can get to processing it. If rushed, using a drill with a mixer bit will accelerate the separation of clay particles from sand, fine gravel and rocks. Materials like roots and twigs will begin to float. It is probably easiest to remove some of this material now with your hand or the sieve on the surface of the water.

Patience/time saves physical effort in the long run (again).

Step 5: remove small rocks / an ideal consistency for wet sieving

Once the clay has been mixed to a green, juice-like consistency, I like to use a pasta colander to isolate larger rocks and chunks of clay requiring more water or agitation to break down. The water will run clear off the gravel once the clay is entirely washed out. There is so much to appreciate at this stage. Fine gravel will have passed through. If there is no calcium carbonate and you want to try working with the clay and the coarse sand, this may be enough processing.

If there are problematic minerals, I'll often use a kitchen sieve and sieve to a finer degree; some ceramists will go much finer. Using the different colander sizes avoids clogging the finer sieve and makes this task smoother. I remember earlier in my practice I simply used to discard this material. With time and experience I've been able to catch fine translucent quartz gravel and pick out spherical manganese nodules without knowing what they were. Befriending and collaborating with soil scientists and geologists has added so much depth to my practice. The process of inquiring into these is one way to acknowledge territory and its indescribable diversity.

Step 6: decanting water

Let the clay particles rest in order for them to settle. In a span of hours, clay and turbid water will be noticeably separating. Over 24 hours, that water will clear as the particles sediment. Gently decant this water into another pail. Try not to disturb the sediment or you will lose clay particles in the pour. Reuse water as much as you can.

Step 7: making clay workable

An ideal consistency for clay is when it sticks more to itself than to your hands but is still soft. Doing this task is easier and more enjoyable on hotter days. Trying to dry clay on rainy days is going against the current. Negotiate with the climate; have patience.

A common trick is to make clay arches to increase the surface area for drying. When time is in my favor, I will wrap clay in fabric over a mesh and get back to it after a few days with no problem if it is humid and not in direct sun. If you are rushed, a fan might help. Remember to flip the clay to dry it evenly. Clay could harden beyond the optimal consistency if it dries too much. In this case, you will have to rehydrate.

Wedge the clay the opposite way to how you would knead bread—we want to remove the air, not trap it. The goal is to end up with a homogenous mass without air pockets. Start by throwing the clay onto your wedging surface and making it into a cube. Although tricky when you are first starting, it is a swing and rhythm that improves with time.

Table height is key: too low and you will be bending over and too high you will have your shoulders hunched. Push your body weight into the clay and then pull the mass back to you so it stands up. Push the clay into itself again and keep on repeating, spiraling the clay toward you. Fast forward and you will have a mass that you can cut with a wire to inspect for air and consistency. Slap the cuts together and repeat a bit more wedging and wire-cutting to check it rigorously. Slap the clay together again, wedge, and you are ready.

If you're new to ceramics, welcome to this beautiful craft. If you're new to wild clays, welcome to getting to know your surroundings in such a sensible way. To both, it's a process of trial and error. Take GPS coordinates, look for soil surveys, play with different clays to have a way to compare them, write notes so that you can repeat a process you enjoyed or just play. There is no one way to do any of this. Be curious, savvy and creative.

Consider the elements: earth as medium, water as means, air to dry and fuel fire. An atmosphere of sustained heat will sinter clay, meaning it is no longer reversible to a malleable state. For this, you will need a decent pit fire or an accessible kiln. Different clays sinter at different temperatures. Otherwise, celebrate raw and endlessly reconfigurable clay.

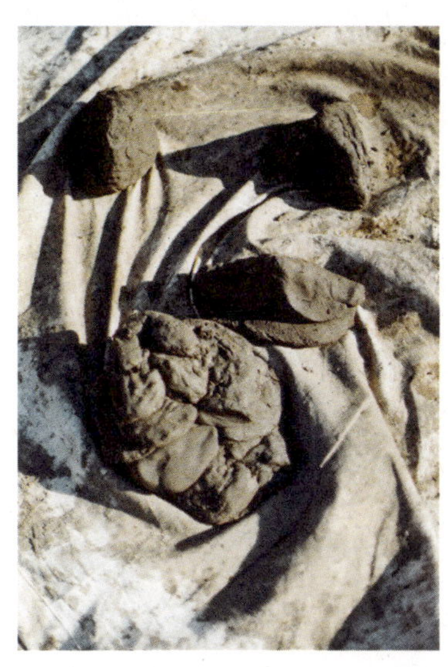

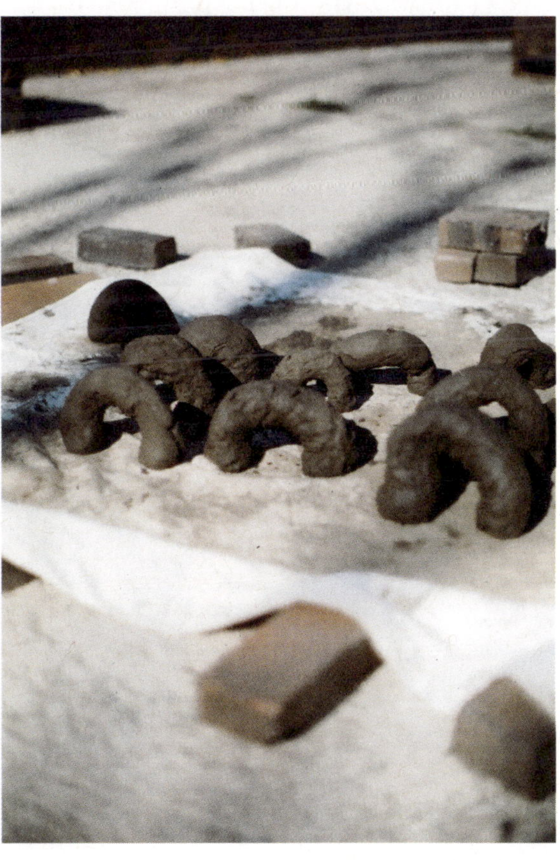

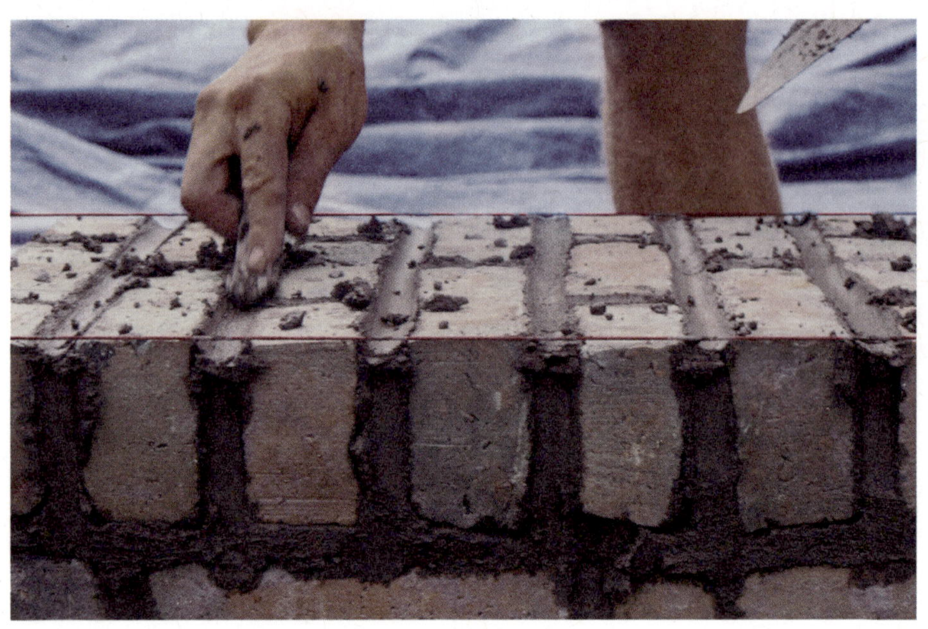

Will Quam

COLLECTING **BRICKS**

Will Quam was first introduced to us as an architectural photographer, and he made a lot of the images that feature on the pages of this publication. It was through his visits to site that we got to know Will and learn of his love for bricks. Through his *Brick of Chicago* walking tours, Will shares his knowledge and enthusiasm for bricks and the buildings that make Chicago's neighborhoods. Here he writes about his own brick collection, from the Chicago common brick to the brick special; he shares the stories that bring meaning to these humble building materials.

Collecting bricks seems like one of the most unlikely and strange hobbies one could have. A brick is a large, very heavy object, which naturally limits its collectability. Besides, how many different types of brick can there really be?

The answer is there are quite a lot of different bricks and even more reasons to collect them. A brick is more than just a piece of building: it is a piece of place and a piece of the Earth transformed by human force. Bricks have been made for thousands of years and in countless localities, each one bearing testament to the geological conditions, technologies and fashions of its maker. Some are stamped with a manufacturer's name; some are given special colors or textures; some were placed into the walls of buildings that became famous; some might come from places that are meaningful to a collector. A collector might collect only paving bricks made in Nebraska, or only decorative bricks from the 19th century, or collect indiscriminately. For many collectors it begins by looking for old bricks to build a garden path and then spirals from there. I have only about 60 in my collection inside my second-floor Chicago apartment, but some collectors have upwards of 4,000, and one German collector has over 8,000.

My collection began small with an admittedly boring brick left over from the remodeling of a dry cleaner's facade. I had just begun paying closer attention to the brick buildings in Chicago and wanted to have a little piece of the city for my own. A week later my collecting began in earnest when I scooped up a Chicago common brick from the alley behind my home. Chicago common bricks, like their name implies, were readily available and nothing special during the time they were produced (roughly between 1830 and 1970), but I love them anyway. The faces of Chicago common bricks are incredibly varied in color, ranging from yellow to pink to black with soot. Little pebbles dot the surface and create cracks. These qualities caused architects to look down on them and use them only for the sides and backs of buildings throughout Chicago, but they used a lot of them because they were so cheap. Chicago commons only cost about $12 per 1,000 in the early 20th century, compared to $50 or more per 1,000 for the nicer bricks used on the front of buildings.

The particular Chicago common brick in my collection was probably made around 1910 out of clay from a clay pit somewhere in Chicago. That pit has long since gone and been filled in, paved over and topped with something else (my local park, for example, was once a clay pit—so was the site of Chicago's largest high school). Beyond the historical connection that interests me, there is the geological oddity of it. The clay from my brick was deposited 14,000 years ago by glaciers in the last ice age. As they moved across North America, these glaciers carved out pieces of the Earth and mixed them together before they stopped where Chicago now sits and melted, allowing all that clay and stone to settle on the land, the water receding into Lake Michigan. The stones visible in my brick are part of that churn: pieces of limestone plucked from the Niagara Escarpment, a long ridge of stone that cuts across the northern United States. The stones in my brick are made of the same stone, the exact same stone, that makes up the cliffs of Niagara Falls.

The variety of material found in a Chicago common brick becomes all the more odd when compared to bricks from nearby. Milwaukee is less than a hundred miles north of Chicago but its geologic conditions produced clays and bricks that are wildly different to those of Chicago. Known as Cream City bricks, Milwaukee bricks are smooth, almost chalky to the touch and a consistent soft yellow color. They bear none of the chaotic variation and pebbles of Chicago's bricks. My particular Cream City brick came from the former Pabst Brewing Complex, a series of a dozen or so buildings in Milwaukee in which Pabst Blue Ribbon beer was produced. As the buildings were gutted and converted to condos and restaurants, the internal bricks were removed and placed in the median between the sidewalk and the street. That's where I grabbed mine, the third brick in my collection.

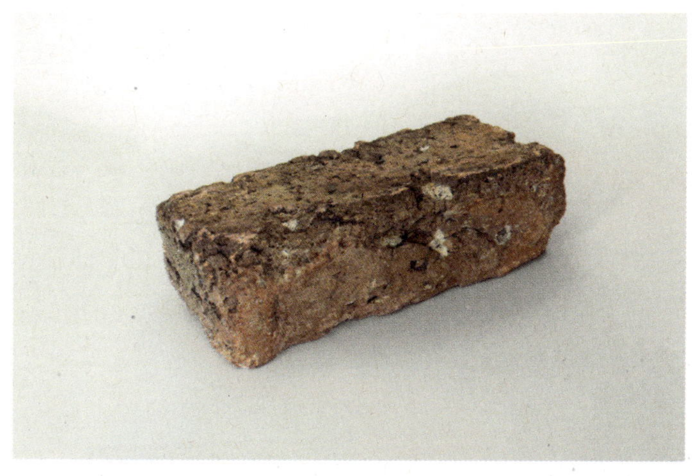

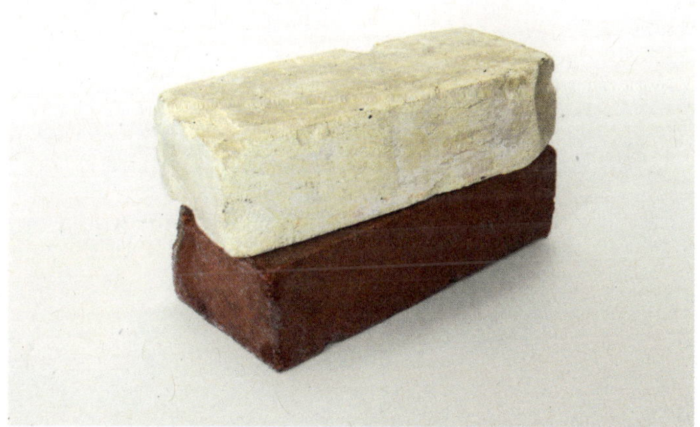

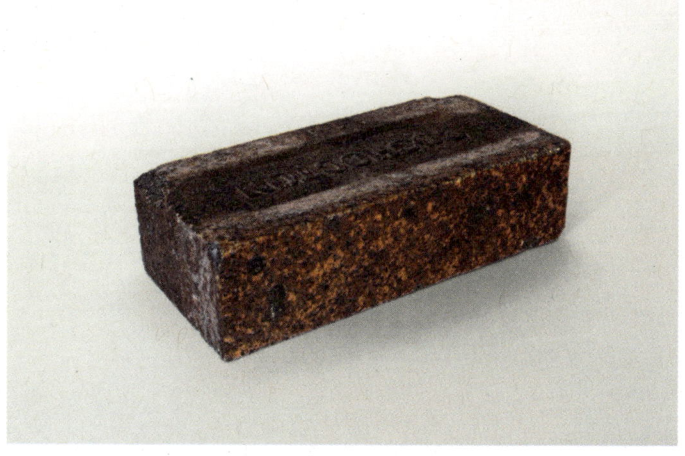

Chicago common brick   Cream City & St Louis   ironspot

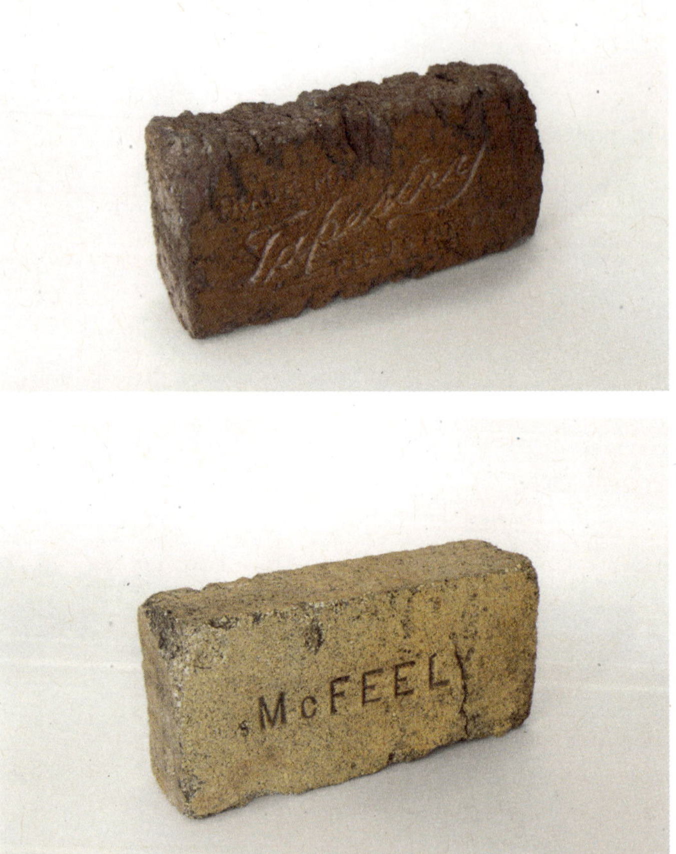

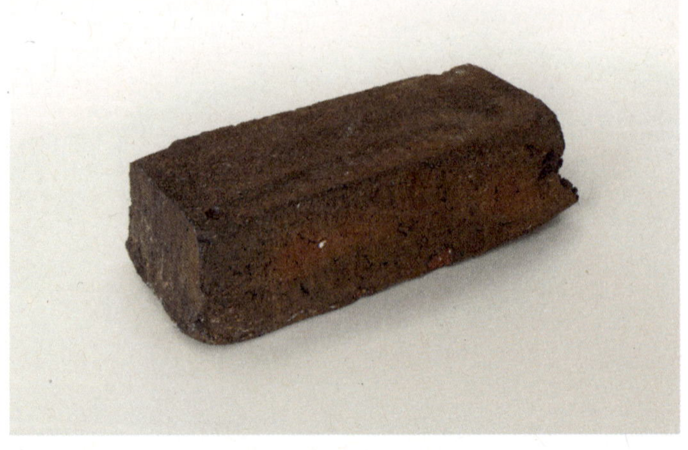

 Tapestry brick McFeely fire brick Soil Lab brick

The consistency and color of Cream City bricks made them exceptionally popular in mid-19th-century Chicago as a facing brick, bringing them in by the thousand before there was even a road between the two cities. Architects used cheap Chicago common bricks on the sides and in the guts of their buildings but covered the street facade with the more aesthetically pleasing Cream City bricks. Chicago's oldest surviving church, Old St Patrick's (built in 1853), is clad in Cream City bricks on two sides.

Three hundred miles to the south of Chicago, the clays and brickmakers of St Louis produced bricks very different to those from either Chicago or Milwaukee. The clays were incredibly fine and free from particulates, and bore consistent levels of iron oxide (the stuff that makes bricks red). Late-19th-century brickmakers used new tools like pugmills and hydraulic presses to make smooth, uniform bricks with razor sharp edges.

Architects in turn wholeheartedly embraced these red bricks as a technological marvel and they dominated the scene throughout the end of the 19th century. An architect could specify St Louis bricks and trust that they would receive a material of all one color and with such sharp edges that they could use thin mortar joints to create a homogenous facade. Brickmakers also used special molds of all sorts of decorative shapes with the knowledge that the fine clay and hydraulic presses would produce bricks that could hold their edge. I have a few of these red bricks in my collection, gifted to me by my friend Jay, a retired art teacher and lifelong St Louisian.

Those red bricks, once considered the apex of fashion, slowly fell out of style and were replaced by new colors and textures. I, in turn, looked to find good examples of these other types of bricks for my collection. I found a wonderful example of the next generation of popular brick while passing an apartment in the process of being demolished. I dug through a dumpster and plucked out a rough, shiny ironspot brick. Ironspot bricks were (and still are) produced from iron-rich clays found in parts of Nebraska and Ohio. When fired with the right mix of heat and oxygen, the iron impurities in the clay come to the surface as pockmarks and pebbles, giving the brick an almost volcanic appearance. For architects like Frank Lloyd Wright, ironspot bricks had the appearance of a much more natural material than the smooth red bricks of the earlier generation. The iron also gives the bricks a subtle sheen, and I love how my brick almost glows throughout the day. It is also meaningful to me because it was made just a few miles from where I went to college.

As the 1910s pressed into the 1920s, architects sought more variety in color and texture for their bricks. New methods of production like extrusion allowed brickmakers to cut into the face of the bricks with textures like bark, waffle, stipple, ripple and velour. One particular manufacturer, Fiske of Boston, made a brick called the Tapestry brick. The rough face was meant to emulate the quality of fabric and they published gorgeous color catalogs comparing their brick to Persian rugs and medieval textiles. The texture and name were widely copied so Fiske trademarked the name, stamping the tops of their bricks with a script logo and a prominent reminder of their legal ownership of the name. I love that this incredibly ornate piece of work can be found on a regular brick and in a place that no one except a bricklayer would see. Once on site, this ornate top would be covered in mortar and placed among a thousand other bricks.

I received my Tapestry brick by mail from a fellow collector in Pennsylvania. A $15 flat rate US Postal Service box can comfortably fit three bricks and this Tapestry brick was tagging along with the real gem I was after. Inside the box and wrapped in newspaper was a McFeely fire brick. Fire bricks are bricks that can withstand tremendous amounts of heat and are used to line kilns and furnaces. McFeelys were made in Latrobe, PA and used in the coke and steel furnaces of western Pennsylvania. The reason I was after this brick, however, was not because of its use but because of its maker. McFeely on its own might not ring a bell, but the company was founded and run by the family of legendary public television host Mister Rogers (full name Fred McFeely Rogers). Rogers was the creator, showrunner and host of *Mister Rogers' Neighborhood*, an influential children's program which ran on public television from 1968 to 2001. I was a teacher before I was a brick collector and Rogers has always been a hero of mine. Today, my McFeely fire brick sits atop my desk in a place of honor, a physical reminder of Mister Rogers' kindness and enthusiasm.

My collection also contains bricks from buildings long gone. I have one from Harpo Studios (where Oprah Winfrey recorded her talk show for decades); a splotchy brick from the modernist Cenacle Retreat & Conference Center, demolished to make way for condos; a brick painted International Orange by the late designer Virgil Abloh for a Louis Vuitton pop-up store; and a green and white terra cotta pillar from a 1920s movie palace. Each one is a small reminder of a history and a place that is no longer there, and I'm grateful to be a caretaker for these little remnants. For every brick I have from a demolished building, however, there are dozens more out there that I failed to save from the crusher or the scrap heap.

Finally, there's my brick from Soil Lab. The bricks used in this project are modern bricks but they are made in a style much closer to a

Chicago common brick than the mass-produced brick I found outside my dry cleaner. They were made by a company in Vermont using the water-struck process, where molds are lined with a liquid solution (which serves like butter in a baking tin) and clay is packed in by hand. When the bricks are removed from the molds, the wet faces of the bricks slump slightly, each taking on a unique texture and shape. They are stacked by hand and many bricks have spots from where they were stacked against each other in the kiln. This unique process means that no two bricks from Soil Lab are the same. Each one tells a slightly different story of the hands that shaped it and the heat that hardened it.

Every brick in a wall is unique, bearing witness to the conditions it was made in and embodying the physical legacy of the building it was a part of. Though buildings may fall, bricks can serve as reminders of what once was, as physical embodiments of fashion trends and glacial history. Each brick is a little sculpture with a history and a purpose.

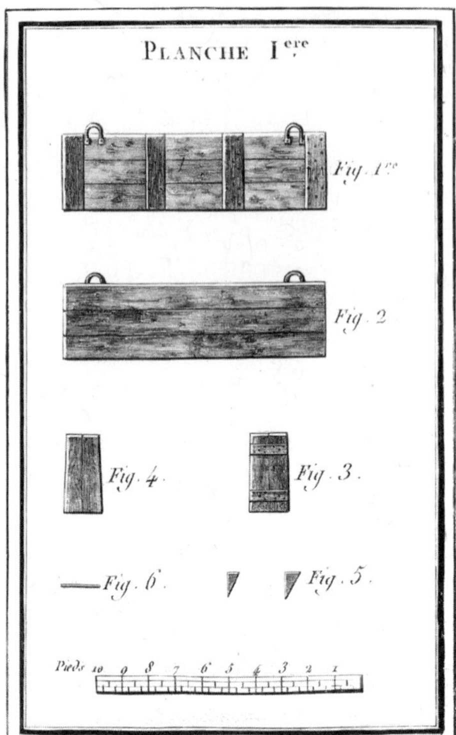

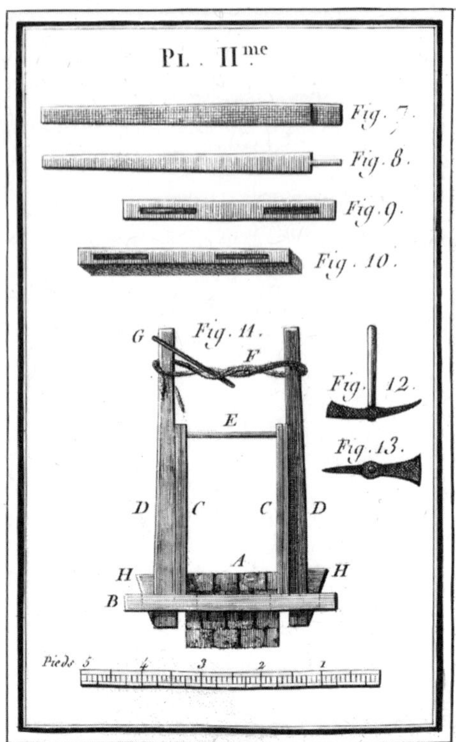

Soil Lab

MAKING,
A **START**

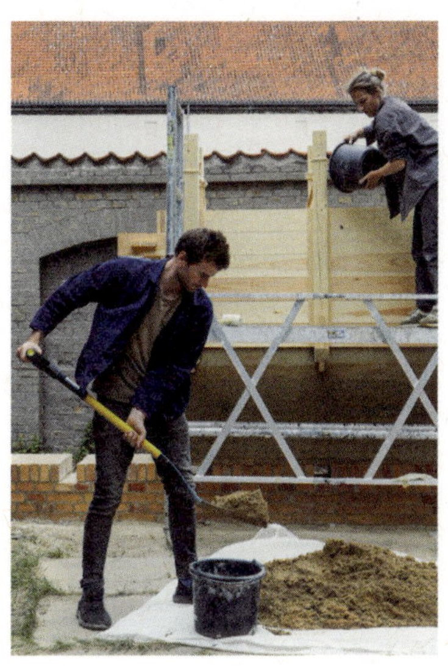

At the beginning of May 2021, with four months to the biennial opening, the four of us began a month-long residency at the Statens Værksteder for Kunst (National Workshops for Arts) in Copenhagen. There, in a sunny yard, we started by making a 1:1 mockup using an 18th-century rammed earth building manual.

The do-it-yourself publication, one of 72 booklets relating to rammed earth construction made by François Cointeraux, a Lyon-based architect, was a direct revolt against the rapidly developing industrialized processes of the 18th century. Its goal was to promote rammed earth construction as a self-building method and to enable and empower people to build their own homes with simple and affordable means using an available and local resource: “This type of construction has already been brought to such perfection and ease of use that every farmer is able to build his own dwelling himself… without spending much more that his effort and handiwork.” We were inspired by the ambition and goal of these publications and encouraged by the ease of production it promised.

Using the drawings, we built a formwork, and with the formwork we built a wall. It was a shot in the dark. We built in order to develop a project based on the material and the process, and to establish what we could feasibly accomplish with our own physical bodies and those of the people who could be persuaded to join us.

We built to understand the weight of the lines drawn by Cointeraux, and to tease out the embedded knowledge between them. We built to provoke discussion and ideas, and to solve together the problems that were not immediately apparent in the manual. We built to assess the energy required of a day's work, to calculate the amount of sweat that went into a rammed earth block. We built to understand what we would be asking of the workshop participants when we would soon arrive in Chicago. We built to understand what we would be asking of ourselves. We built to start.

Needless to say, we didn't become experts during this intensive month-long period. But we did begin to understand some of the complexities and constraints that we would have to grapple with, and we made peace with them. Toward the end of our residency, one evening after dinner, exhausted from the day spent filling the box, we decided that we had to become comfortable with the unknown and agile to overcome whatever obstacles lay ahead. We acknowledged that while the work was physically demanding—and was only exacerbated by the heat of the summer sun—a conscious effort would need to be made to keep morale high on-site: cool refreshments, flowing conversation and rhythmic tunes. In order to realize the social ambition of the project, and for a community of rammed earth builders and brickmakers to flourish, we would need to make it enjoyable. We would have to let go of the schedule and accept that some days wouldn't be as productive as others. Despite our month in the yard, we were starting from scratch—again. We were completely vulnerable but now we could see that this vulnerability was our strength. On August 9, on an empty lot in North Lawndale, we started by introducing ourselves as novices and invited participants to join us in learning together through building. It was to be a collective learning experience, a built experiment.

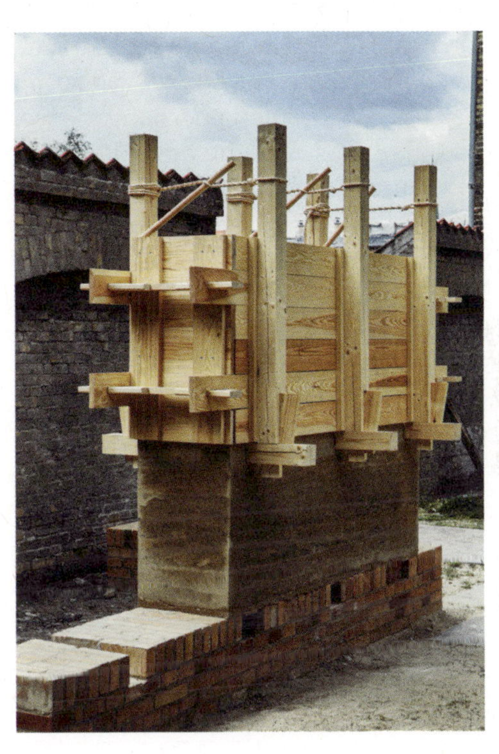

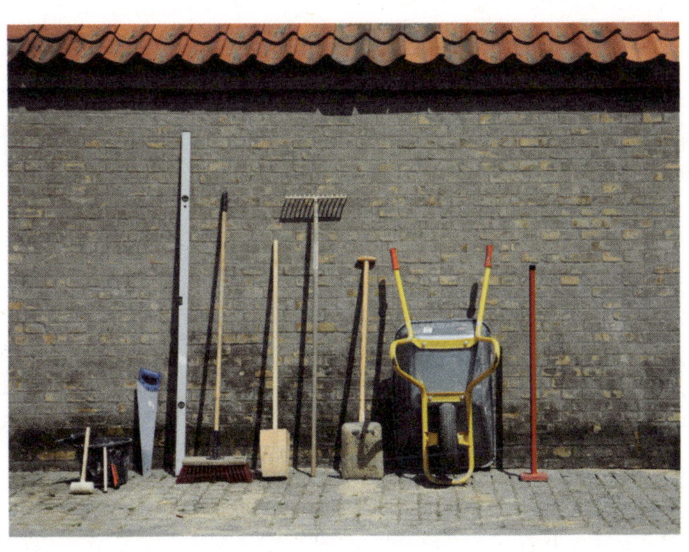

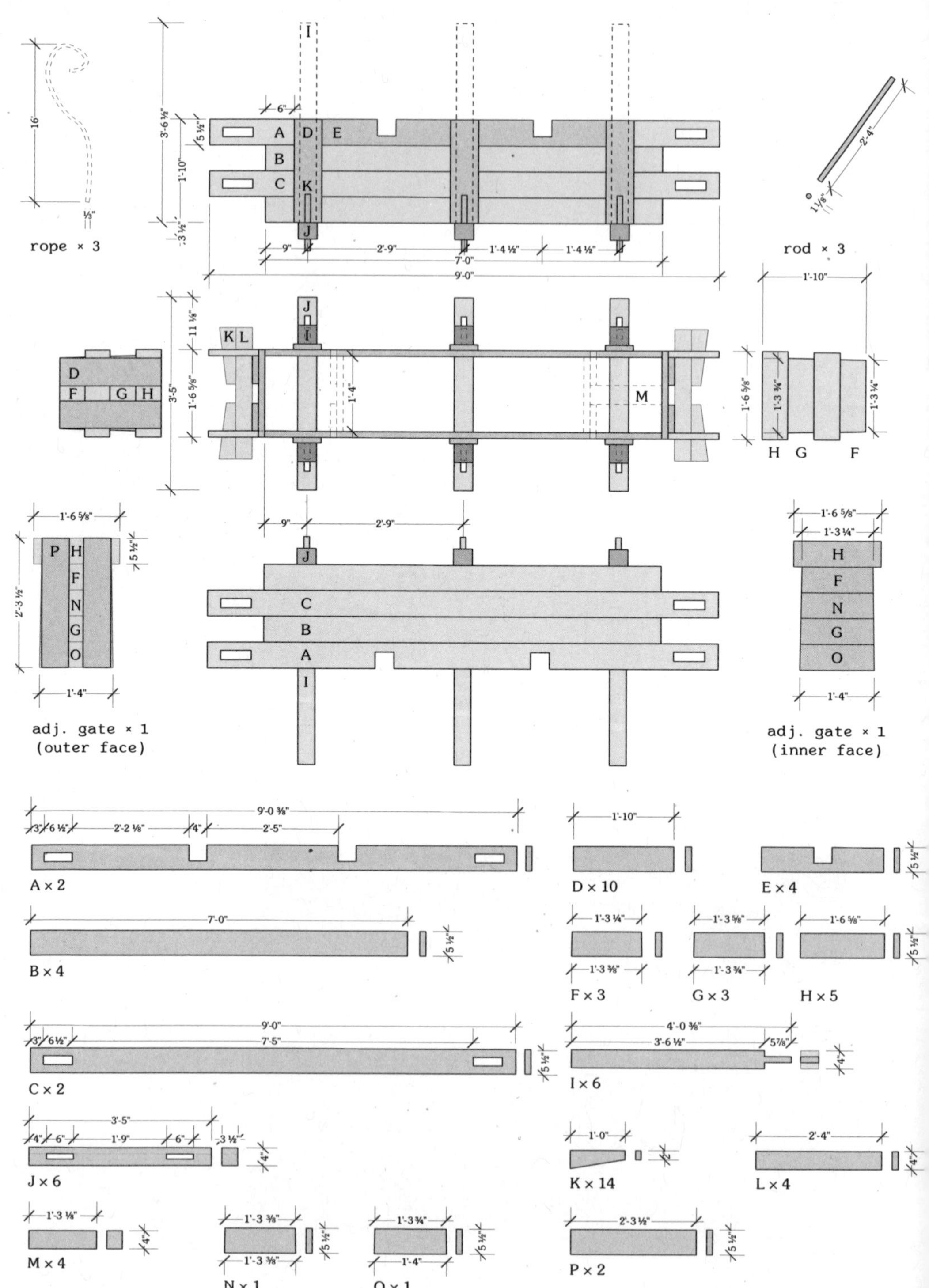

rope × 3
16"
⅓"
rod × 3
2'-4"
1 ⅛"
3'-6 ½"
1'-10"
3 ½"
5 ½"
6"
I
A
B
C
D
E
K
J
9"
2'-9"
1'-4 ½"
1'-4 ½"
7'-0"
9'-0"
1'-10"
11 ⅛"
3'-5"
1'-6 ⅝"
1'-4"
K L
M
F
G H
1'-6 ⅝"
1'-3 ¾"
1'-3 ¼"
H G F
1'-6 ⅝"
5 ½"
2'-3 ½"
P H F N G O
1'-4"
adj. gate × 1
(outer face)
1'-6 ⅝"
1'-3 ¼"
H F N G O
1'-4"
adj. gate × 1
(inner face)
9'-0 ⅜"
3"
6 ½"
2'-2 ⅛"
4"
2'-5"
A × 2
1'-10"
D × 10
5 ½"
E × 4
7'-0"
5 ½"
B × 4
1'-3 ¼"
1'-3 ⅜"
F × 3
1'-3 ⅝"
1'-3 ¾"
G × 3
1'-6 ⅝"
5 ½"
H × 5
9'-0"
3"
6½"
7'-5"
5 ½"
C × 2
4'-0 ⅜"
3'-6 ½"
5⅞"
4"
I × 6
3'-5"
4"
6"
1'-9"
6"
3 ½"
4"
J × 6
1'-0"
2"
K × 14
2'-4"
4"
L × 4
1'-3 ⅛"
4"
M × 4
1'-3 ⅜"
1'-3 ⅜"
5 ½"
N × 1
1'-3 ¾"
1'-4"
5 ½"
O × 1
2'-3 ½"
5 ½"
P × 2

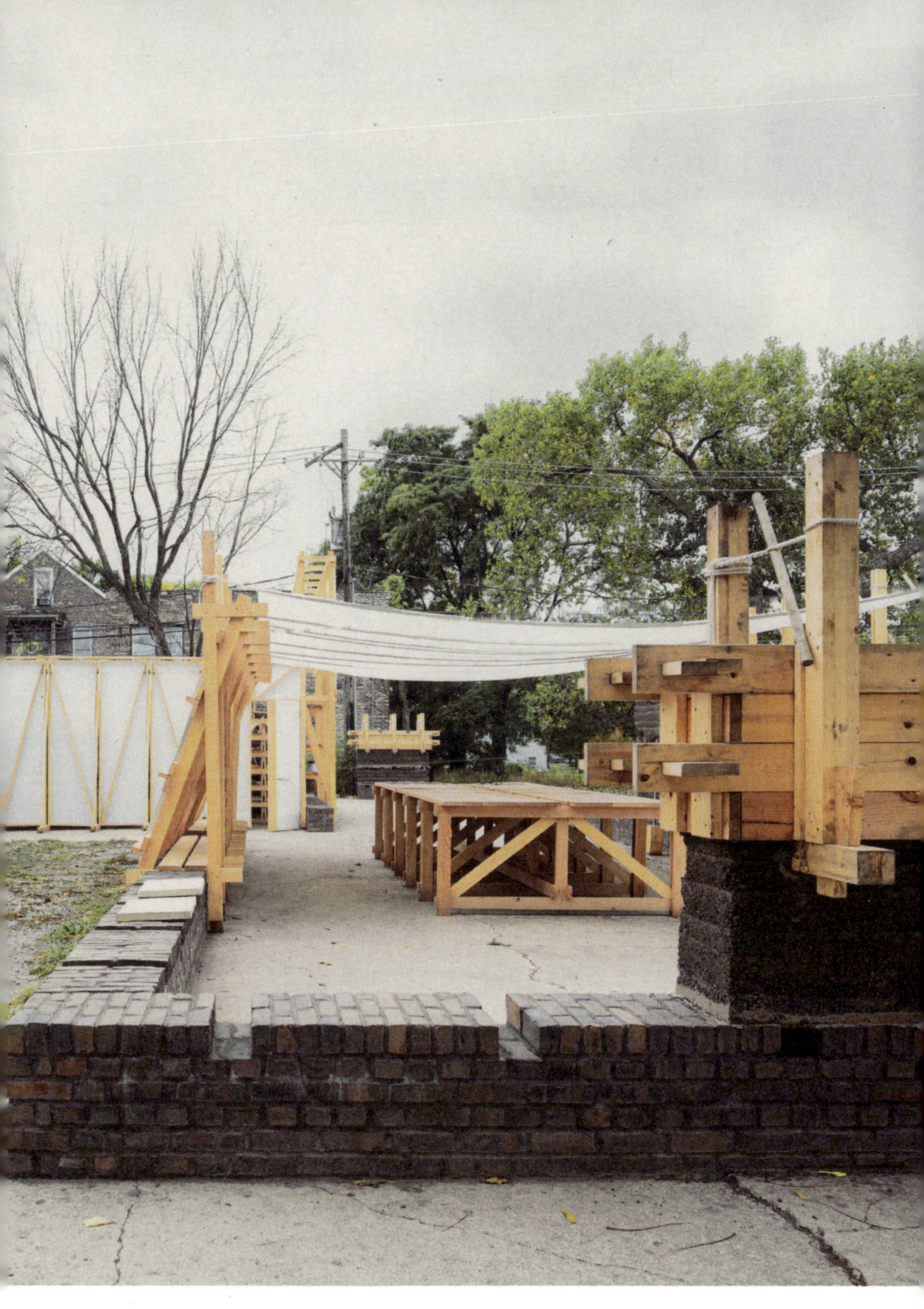

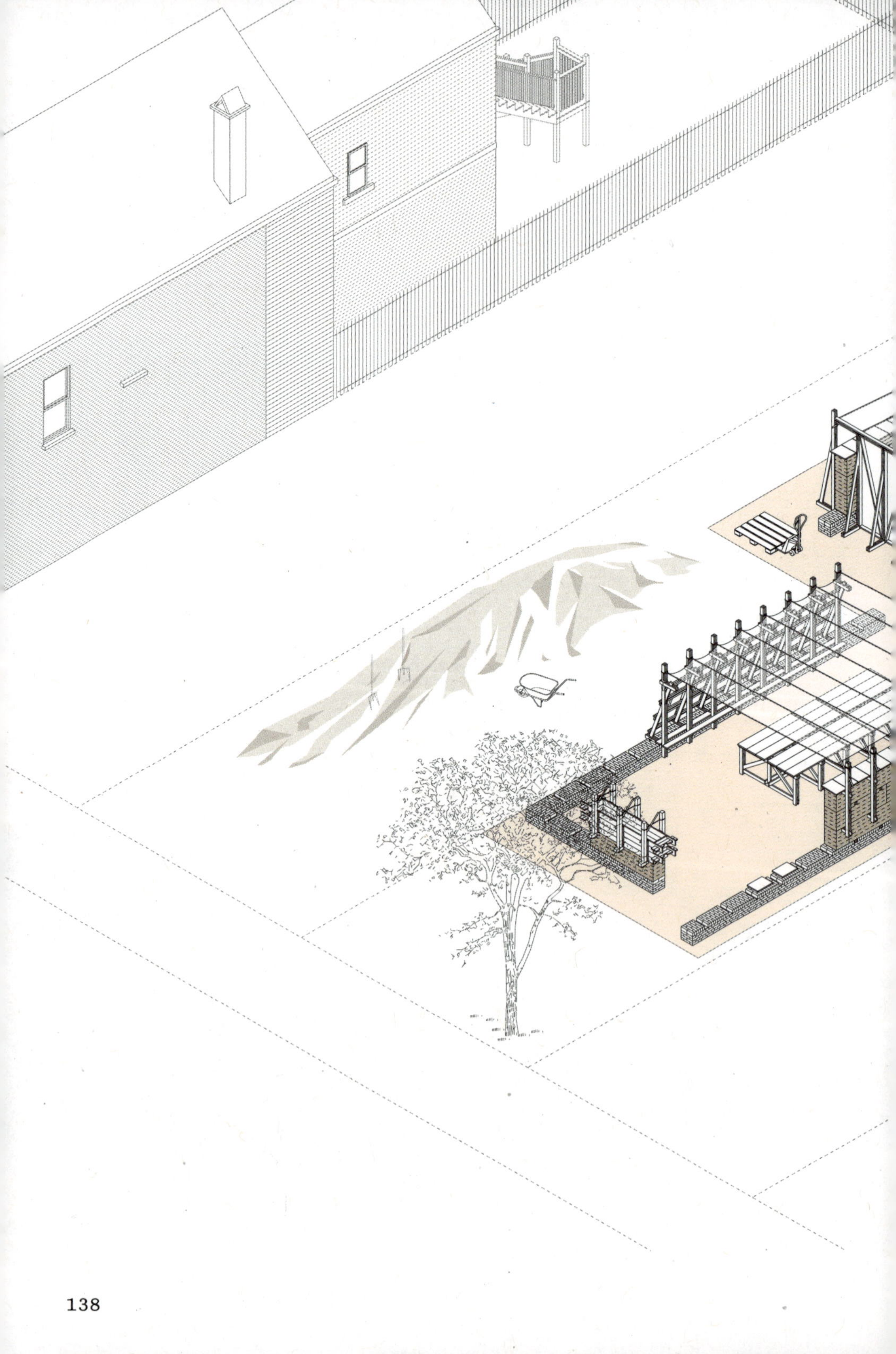

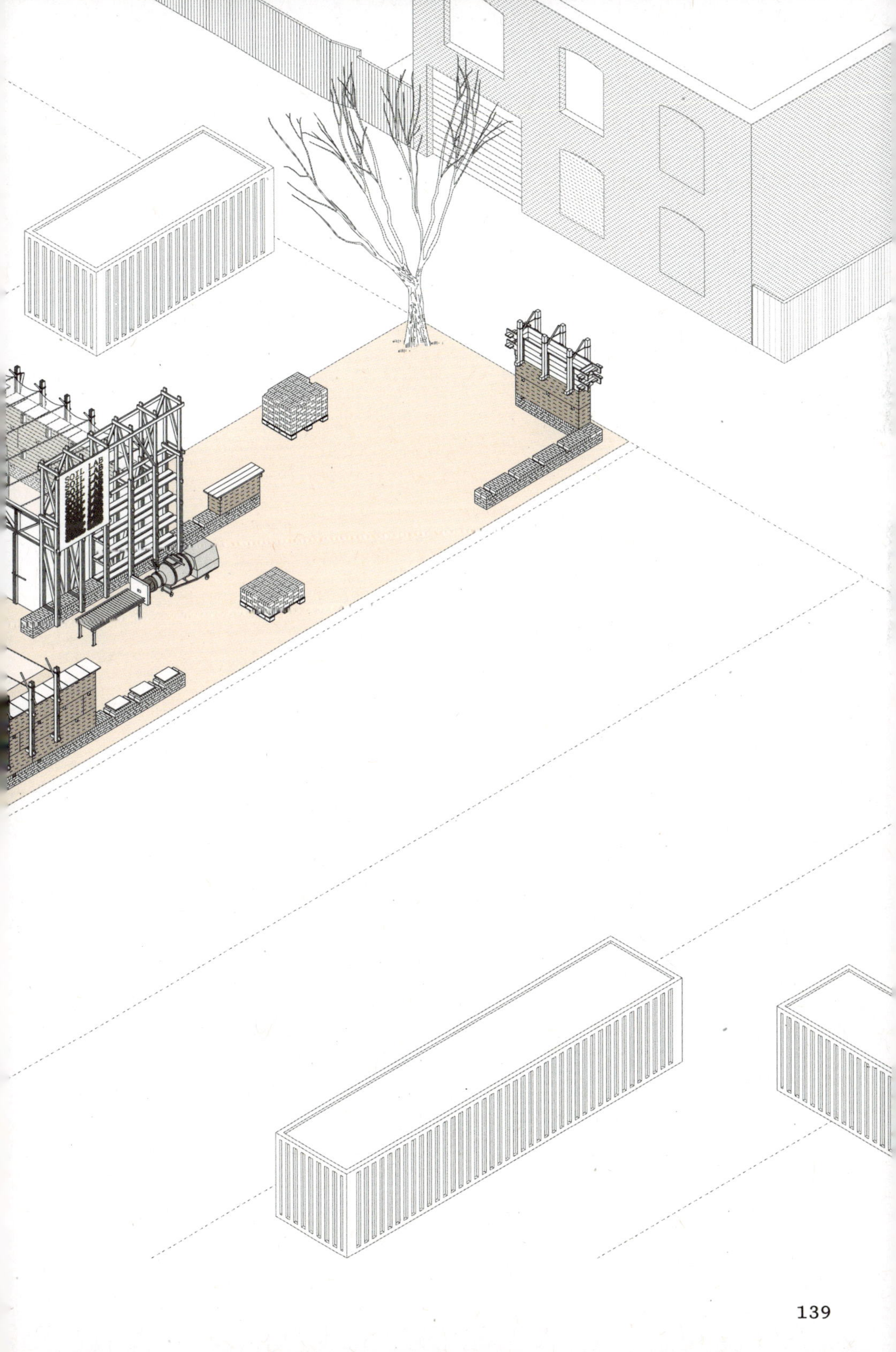
SOIL LAB

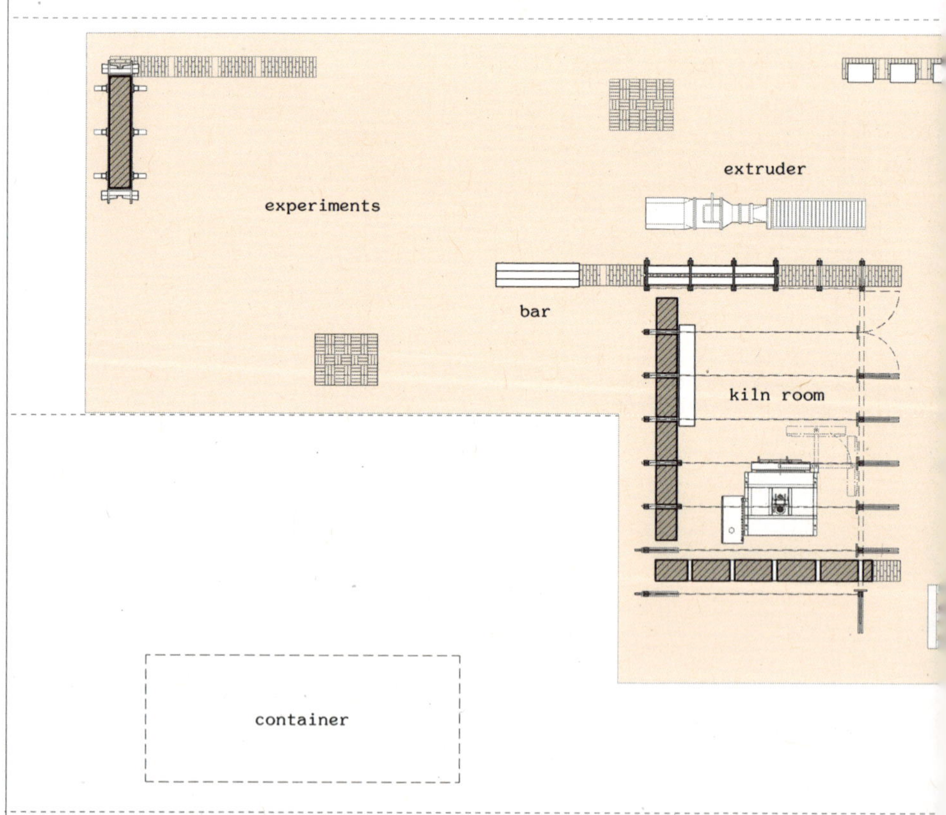
alley
experiments
extruder
bar
kiln room
container

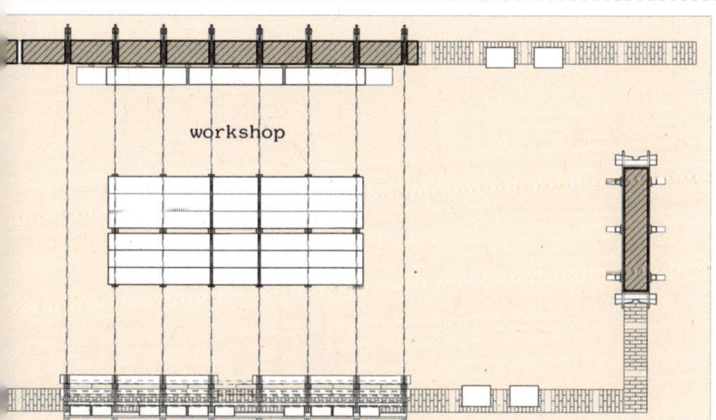

arrival

side walk

soil heap

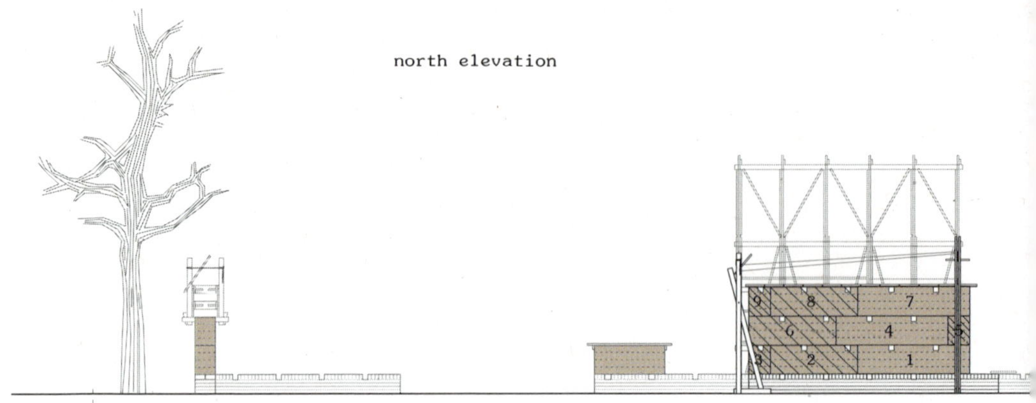
north elevation
alley
kiln room wall #1
9 days

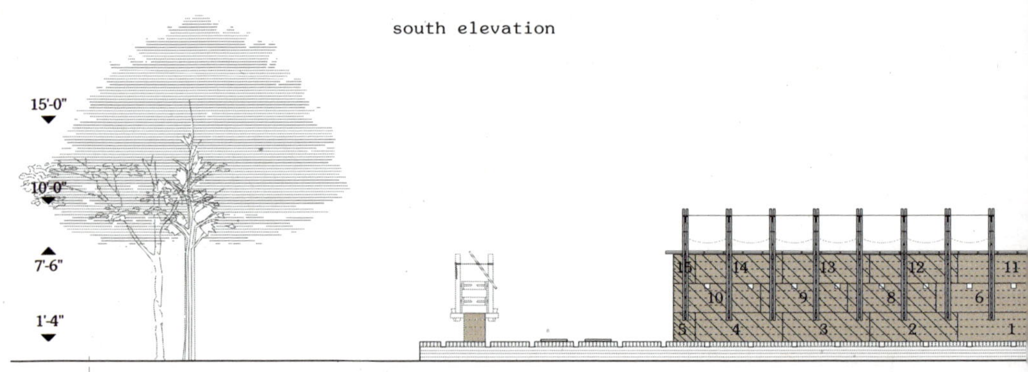
south elevation
15'-0"
10'-0"
7'-6"
1'-4"
sidewalk
workshop wall
15 days

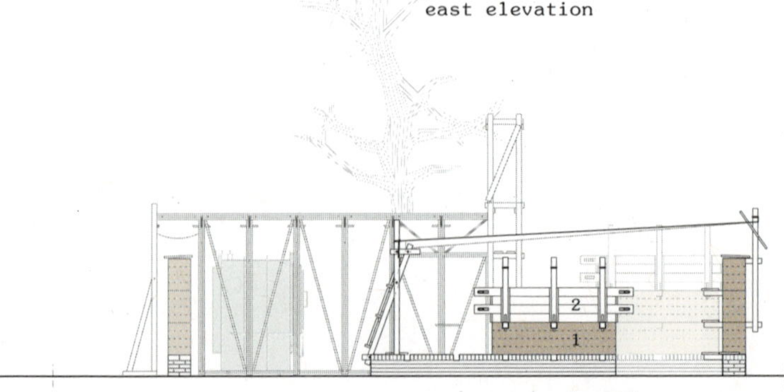
east elevation
east wall
2 days

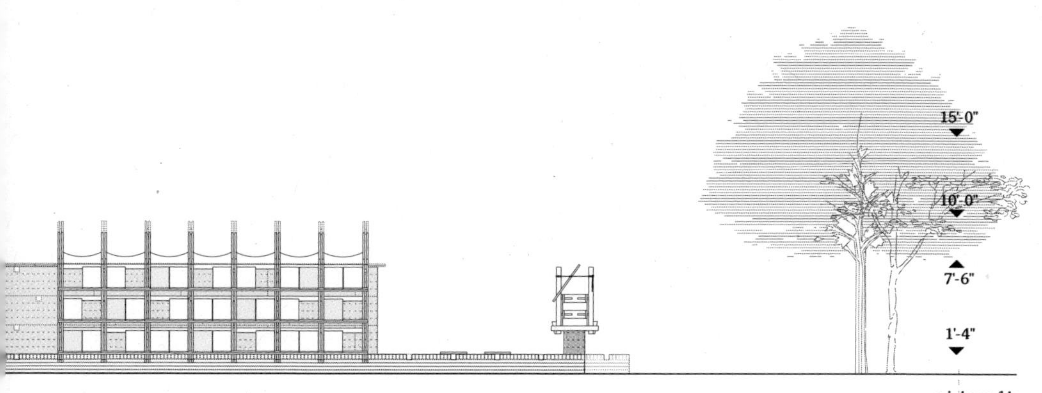

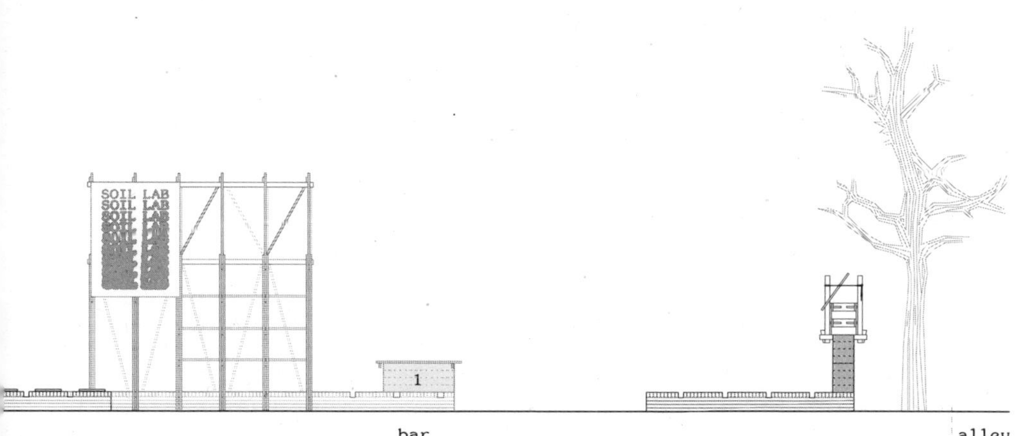

west elevation

15'-0"

10'-0"

7'-6"

1'-4"

3
2
1

10 9 8
7 6 4 5
3 2 1

west wall
3 days

kiln room wall #2
10 days

kiln room

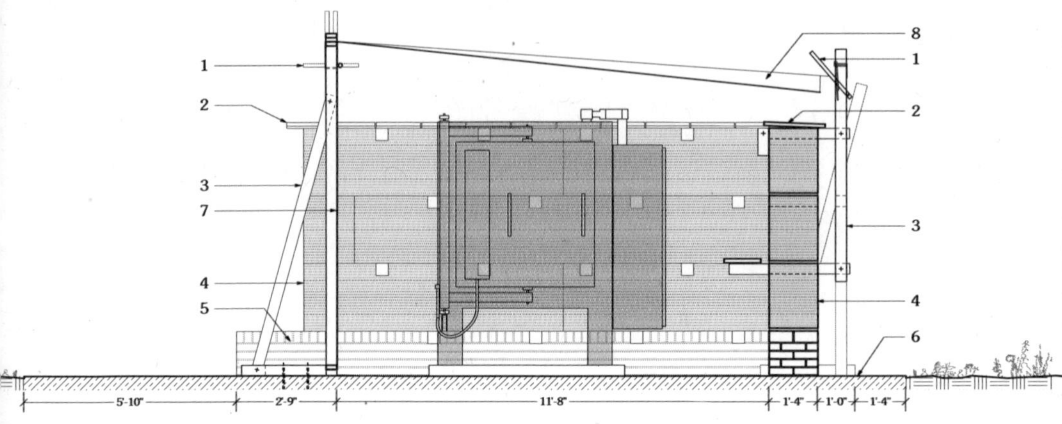

ceramic workshop

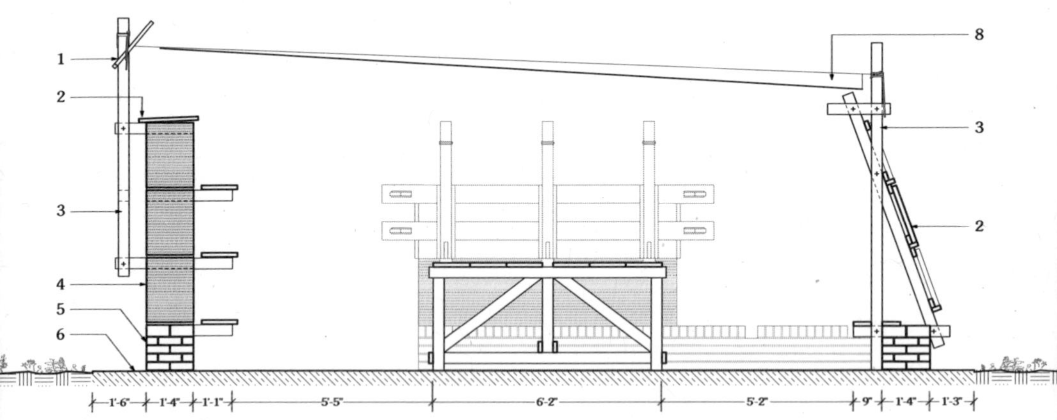

1 28mm round bar (to tighten sisal rope)

2 350 × 500 × 40mm Tommerup ceramic tiles (15kg)

3 Douglas Fir timber structure

4 rammed earth wall

5 brick plinth with tradition lime mortar

6 existing concrete slab

7 flamesafe tarpaulin screen

8 flamesafe tarpaulin canopy

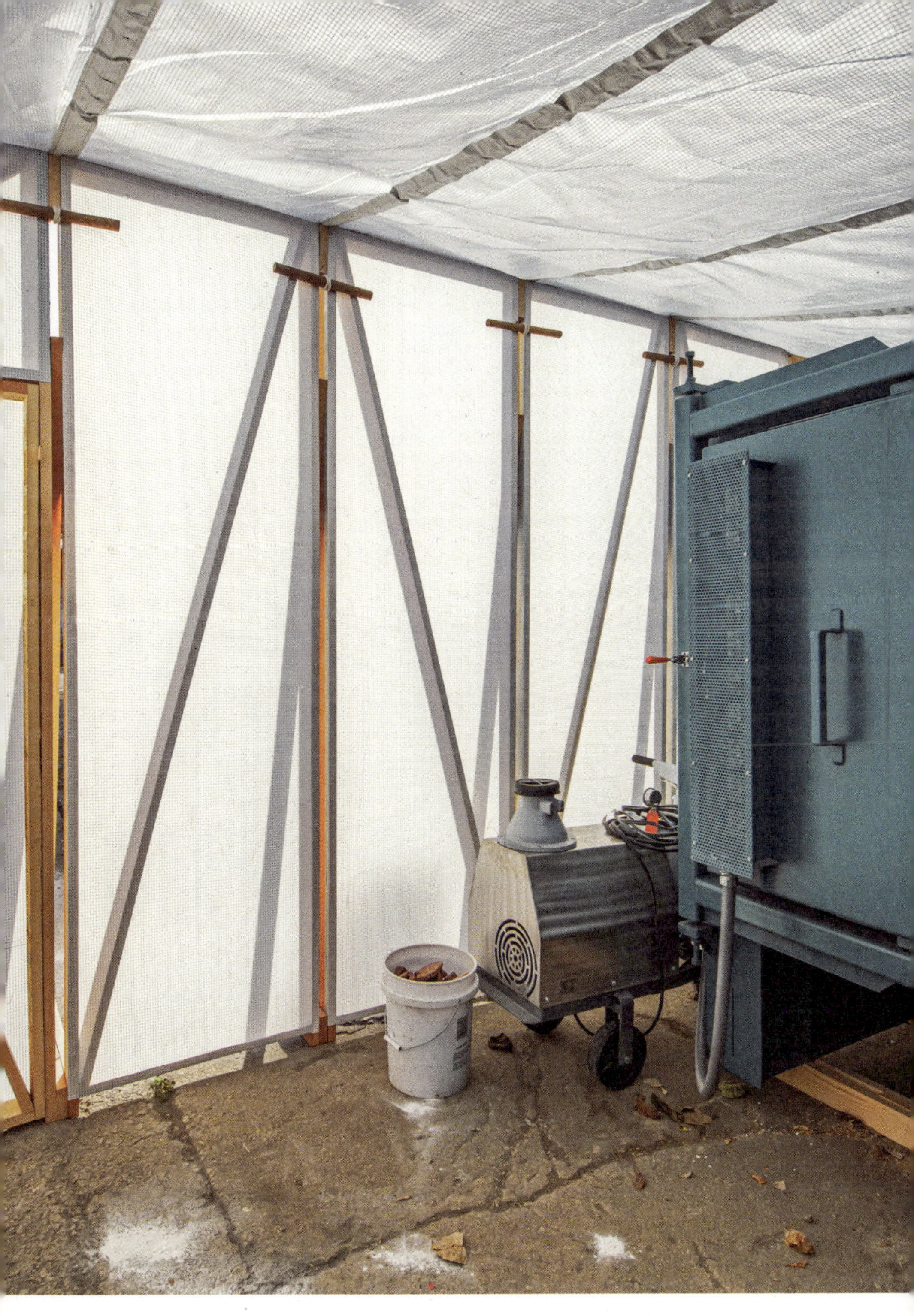

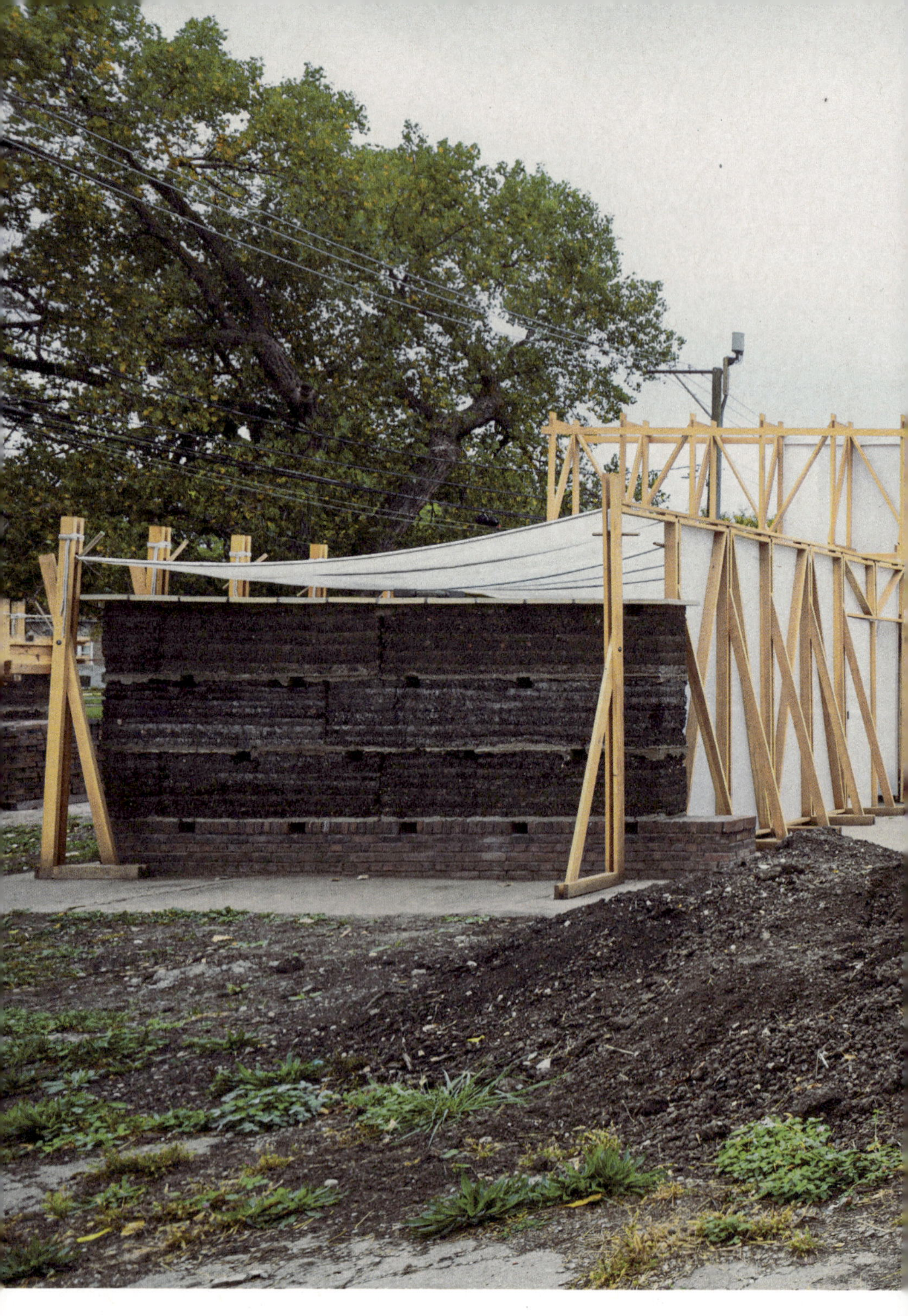

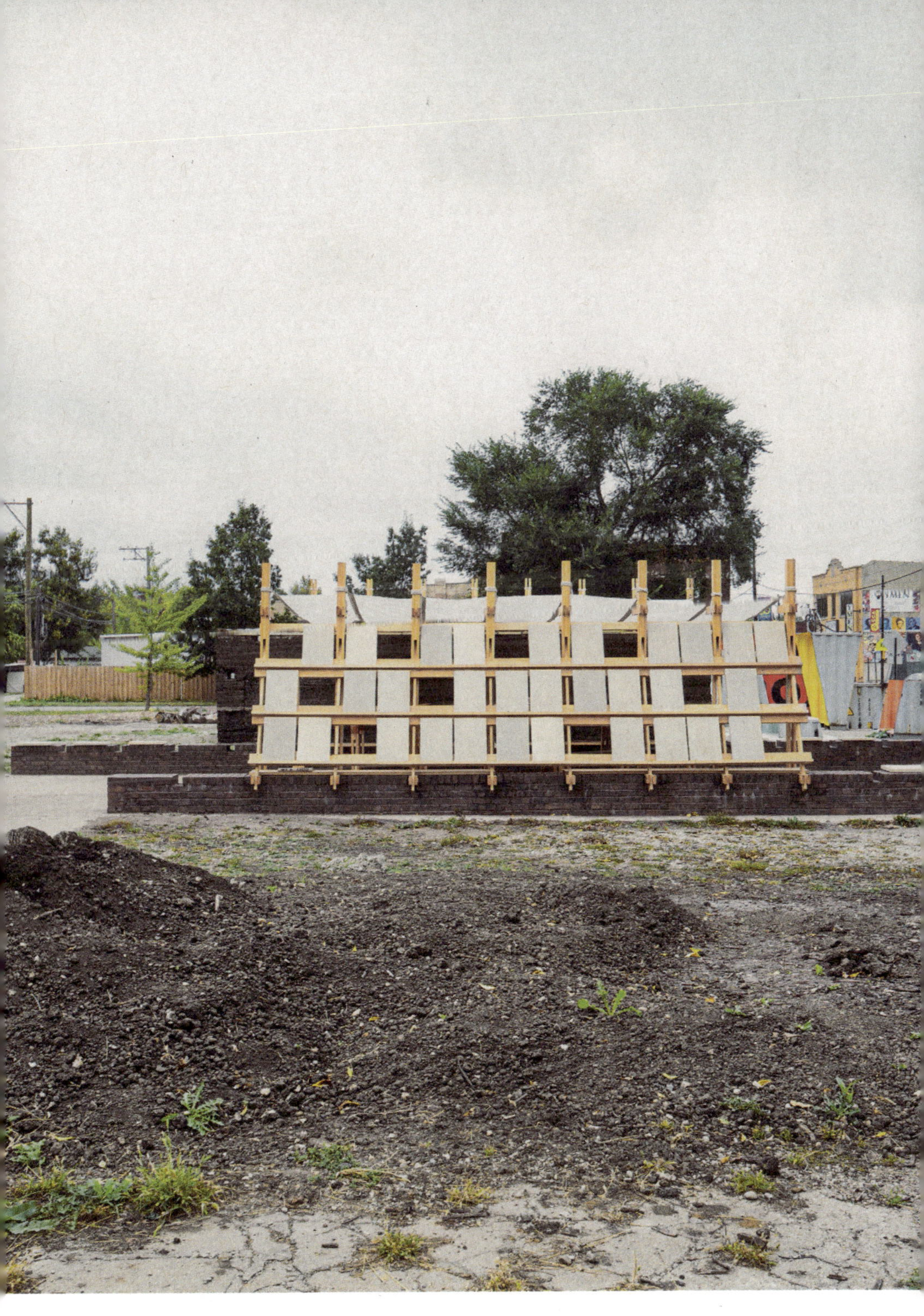

workshop table

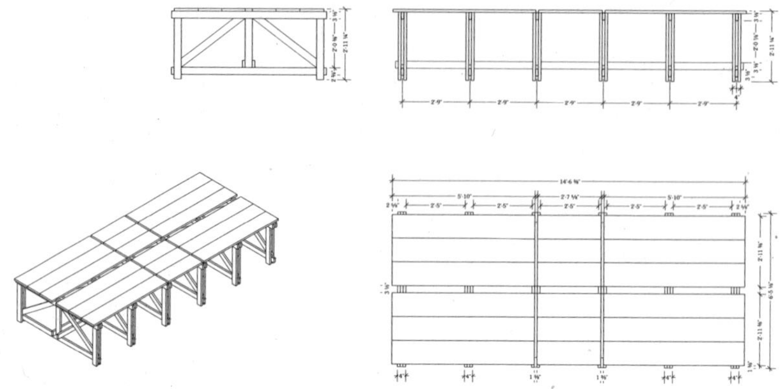

workshop wall (north)

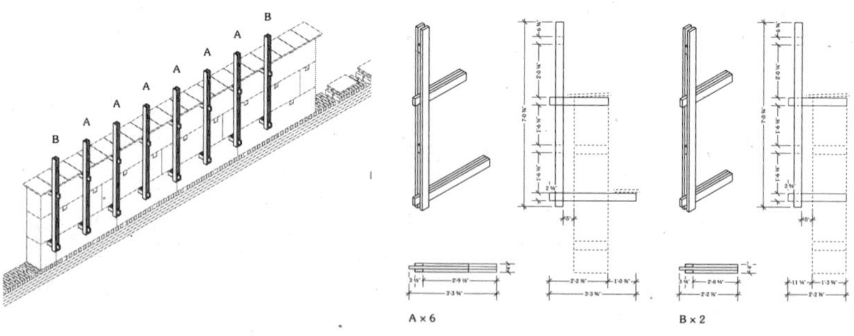

workshop wall (south)

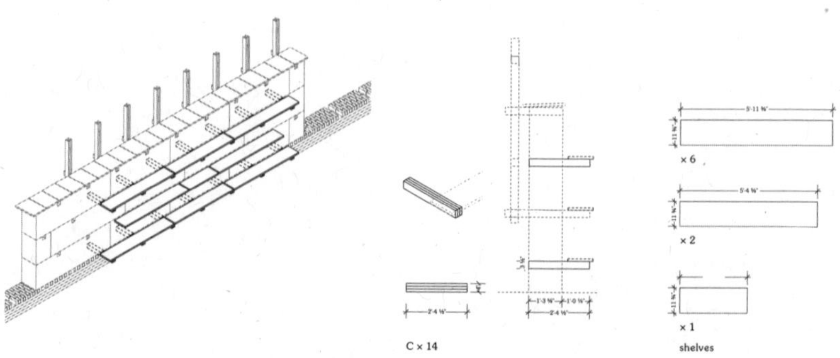

billboard

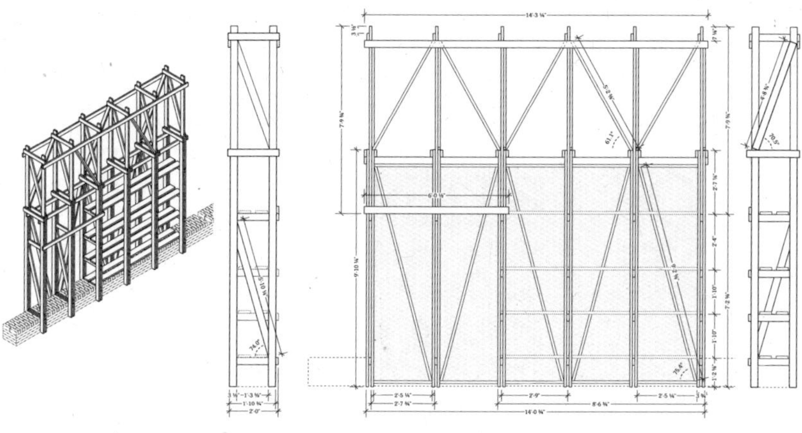

billboard (exploded)

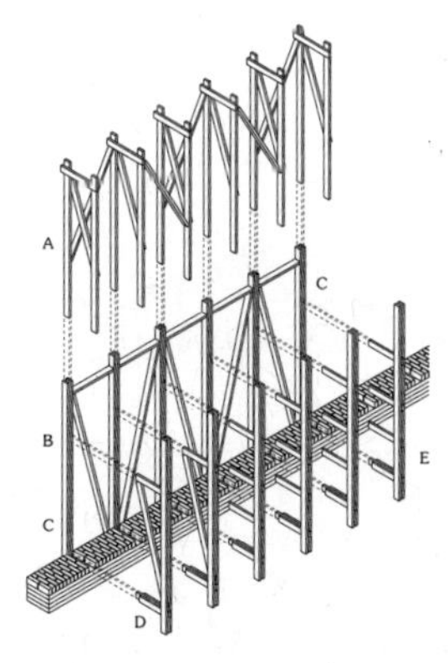

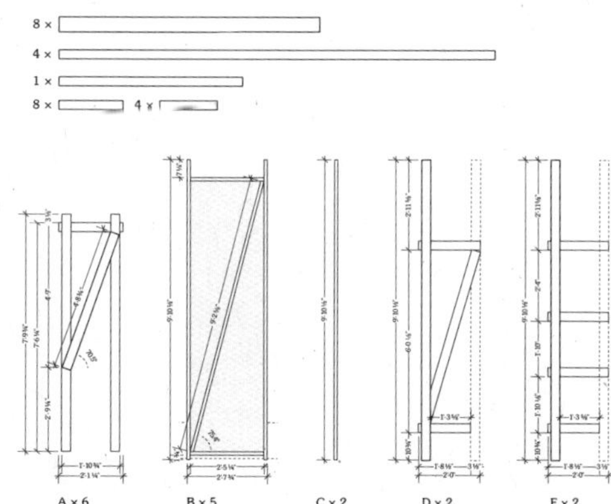

kiln room wall (west)

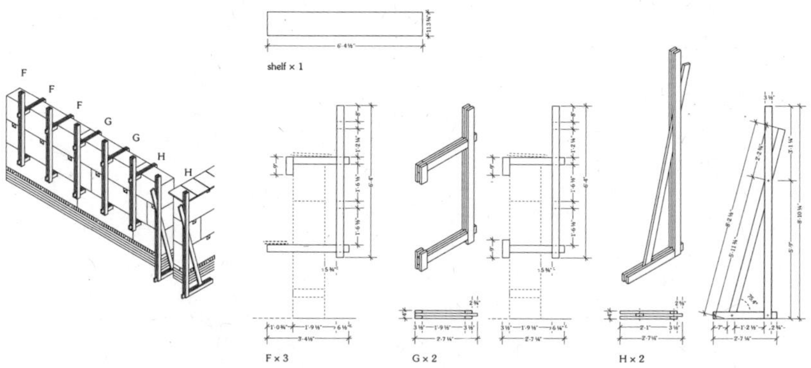

Ellen Braae

THE EXPANDED FIELD OF BIENNIALS: SOIL LAB ENABLING CHANGE

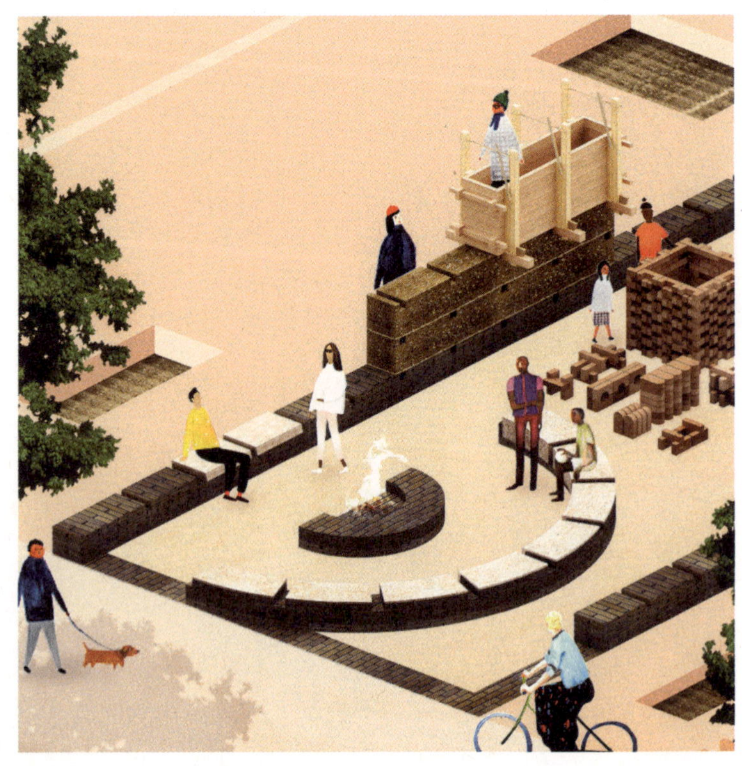

In September 2021, artisans, designers and architects got a unique opportunity to create the official Danish contribution to the Chicago Architecture Biennial, through an open call by the Danish Arts Foundation. As chair of the Scholarship Committee for Architecture, Ellen Braae was presented with the early ambition of Soil Lab. Here, she provides insight into the selection process and the work of the jury. She elaborates on the strengths and challenges of the Soil Lab entry and reflects on the sustainable society of the future.

Denmark's participation in the Chicago Architecture Biennial (CAB) was a unique opportunity to ask questions about what a biennial can be and what architecture is and can do. While biennials are held largely on specific, enclosed sites, designated for the event, the Danish entry to CAB in 2021 was allocated a site in North Lawndale, an urban district on Chicago's West Side and just one of the city's 10,000 vacant lots.

A total of 23 teams submitted entries responding to the theme of CAB 2021, *The Available City*, despite the short announcement period of six weeks. The jury, with members from both Denmark and Chicago, looked for applications that showed critical and ethical awareness of the task and setting, demonstrated courage to challenge disciplinary boundaries, and were adjustable to respond to community input.

Right from the start, the jury was fascinated by the Soil Lab proposal due to its special atmosphere, the idea behind it and the fact that it touched upon the material culture shared by both Denmark and Chicago: bricks and brickwork. Not only did the proposal meet all the criteria, it also questioned what "availability" might mean in terms of resources, skills, knowledge and spatial interaction.

But Soil Lab was a high-risk project due to its creative, open and co-creative dimension—it was not conceived as an "in-full-control-ready-made-object" to be dropped into the empty plot in North Lawndale.

The jury was uncertain whether the Soil Lab team would be able to get local people to fully engage with the soil—pounding the earth, building bricks, molding ceramics. The jury continued to weigh up other projects whose results were easier to imagine. If the jury had known in advance that the winning entry would have to contend not only with challenges on-site but also with a long period of pandemic lockdown, they probably would have chosen a different project. But it is hard now to imagine any other project team working so persistently under such difficult circumstances or being so open to engagement on so many levels.

The idea to focus on local relationships between people and place originated in Denmark's CAB 2019 entry, *Cabbage Patch* by Gamborg and Magnussen, which consisted of planting and growing 10,000 cabbage plants, with an outdoor kitchen where the cabbages were then cooked. In being part of an everyday living environment entangled with local community groups, the project made a widespread and lasting impact, reaching beyond a traditional biennial entry.

Similarly, Soil Lab's collaboration in 2021 broke new ground for what architecture biennials can enable; it provided a physical, spatial structure that straightforwardly involved local people, taught that learning is a collaborative process, and showed that arts and crafts can empower people and places. Soil Lab enabled shared learning and mobilized the material and social resources found in the everyday realm. The project points to the importance of trust and talk if we wish to overcome cultural differences, keep an open mind and make the city available: an ethos that heralds the sustainable society of the future.

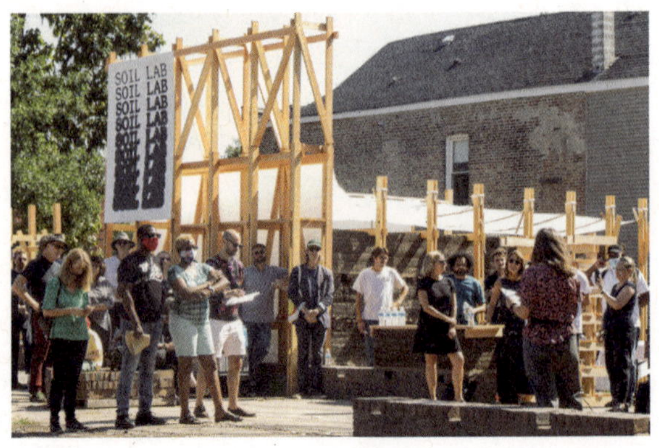

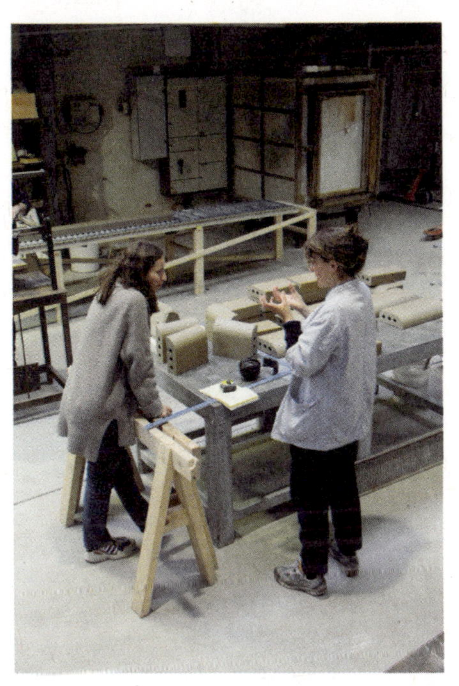

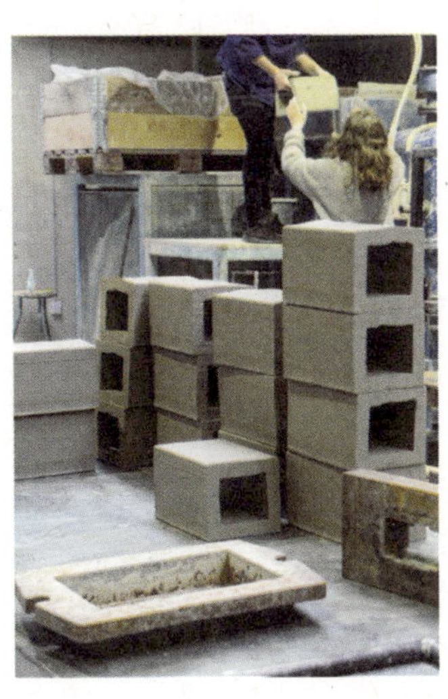

Soil Lab

TOMMERUP

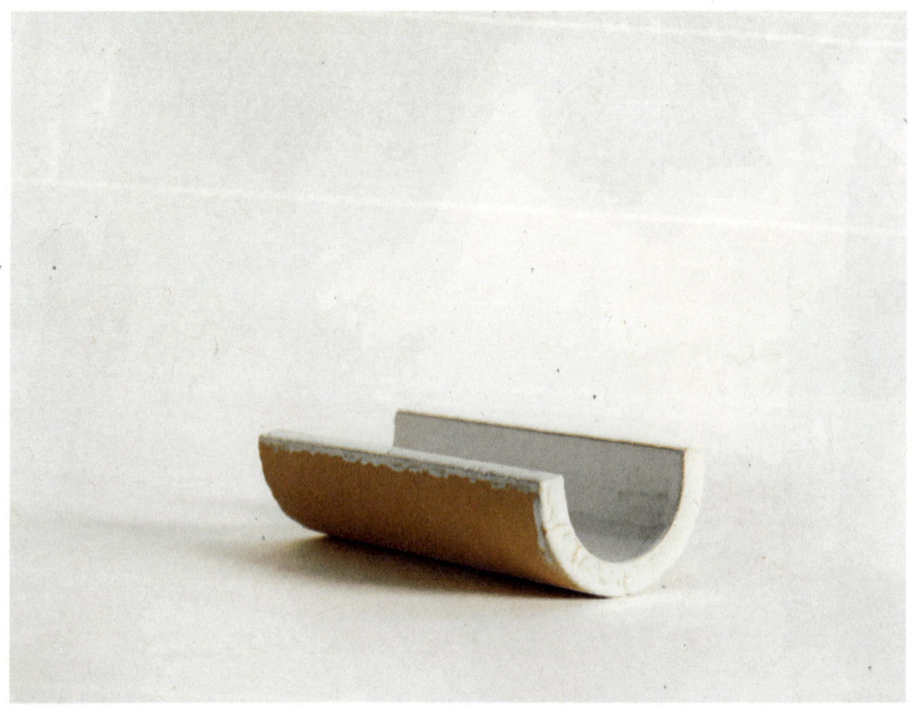

Early in the process we decided to involve Tommerup Ceramic Workshop because of their extensive knowledge of brick production. Their large-scale ceramic workshop on the Danish island of Funen has worked with ceramics and the production of tiles and bricks for more than 30 years. In their workshop, it became possible for Soil Lab to expand the knowledge of extruding bricks and test what an interim ceramic workshop could look like when moved to North Lawndale. With guidance from Per, Søren and Henrik, we mapped Soil Lab's needs for equipment and material. During these visits we discovered Tommerup's extensive library of collected and self-produced bricks. We were kindly allowed to document and study parts of the collection and share them here.

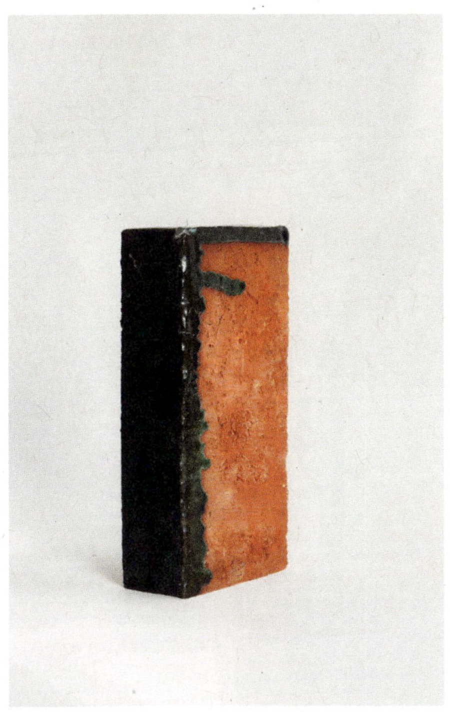

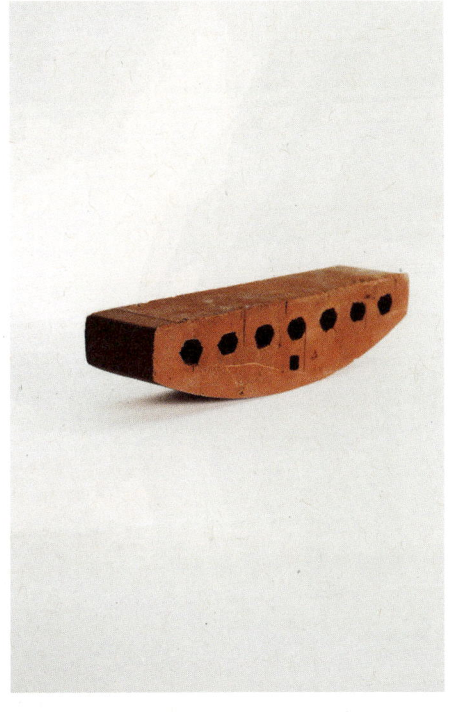

standard glazed brick

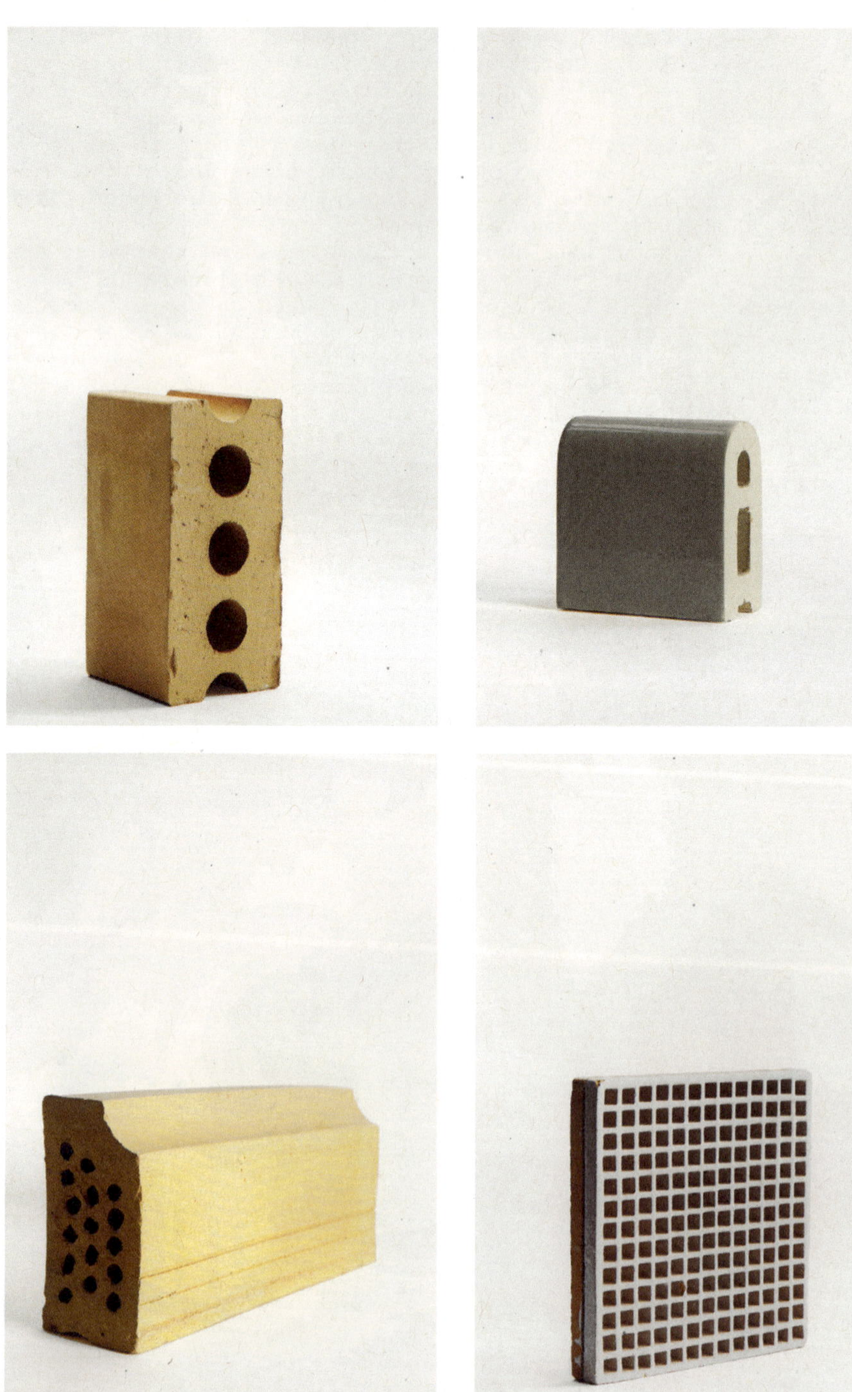

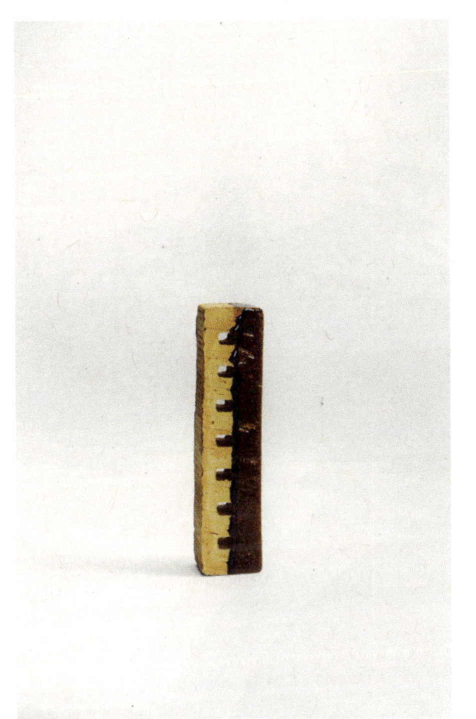

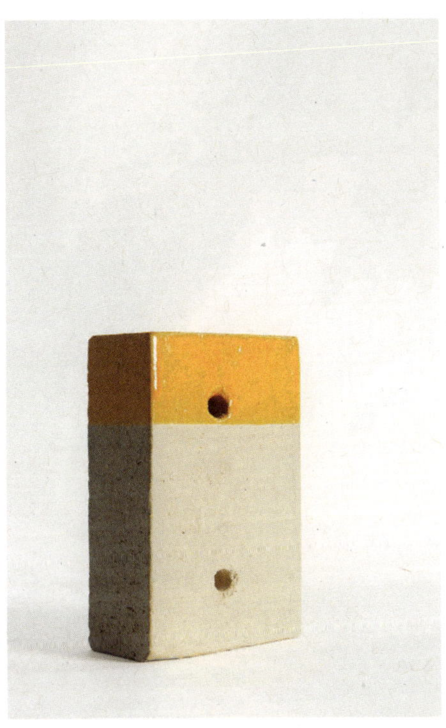

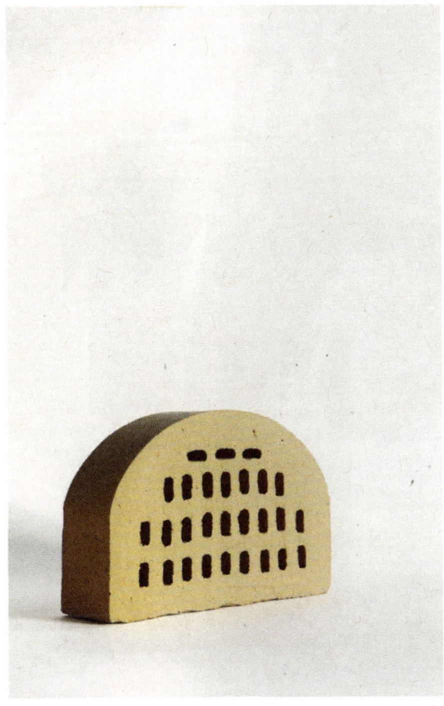

for edging

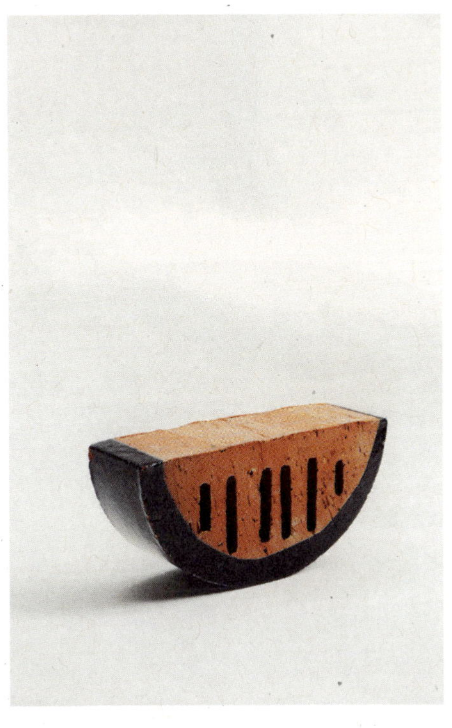

for ornamentation

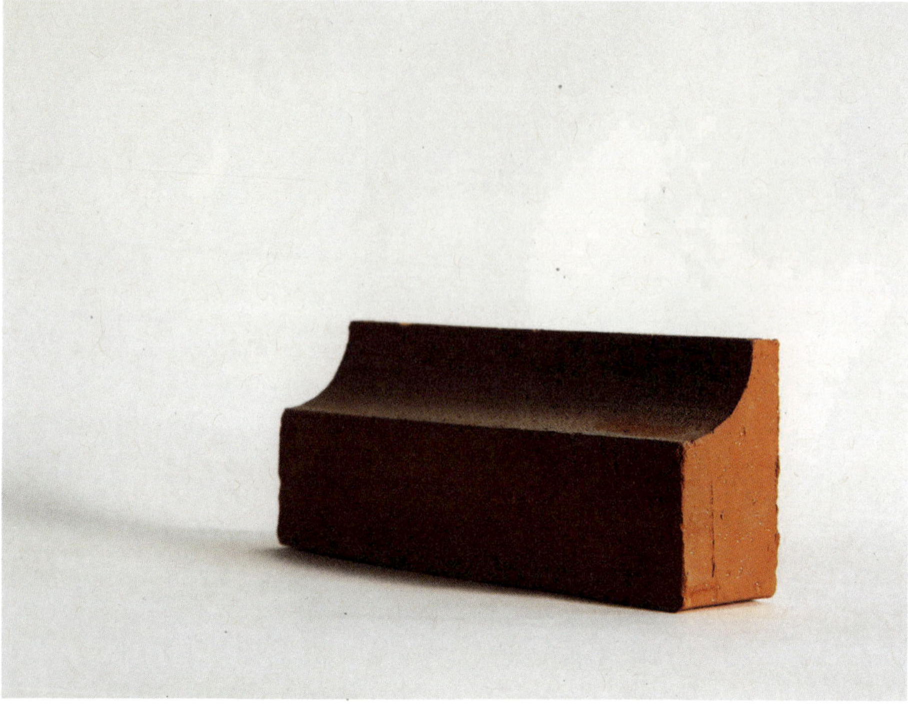

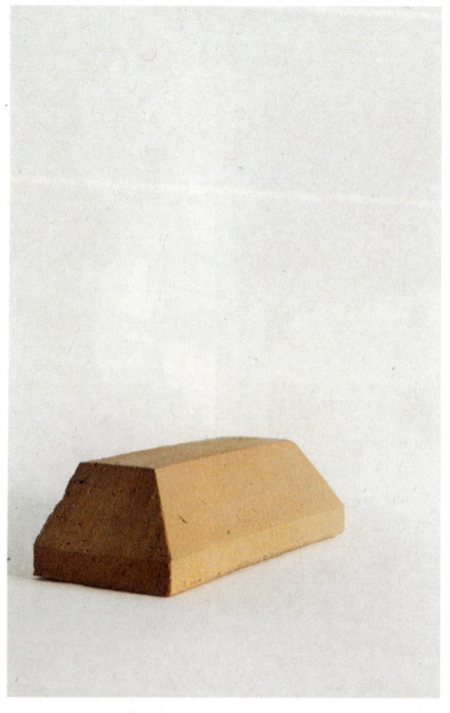

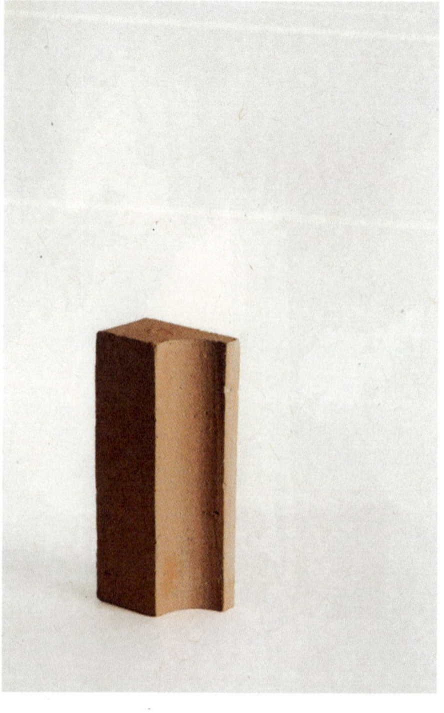

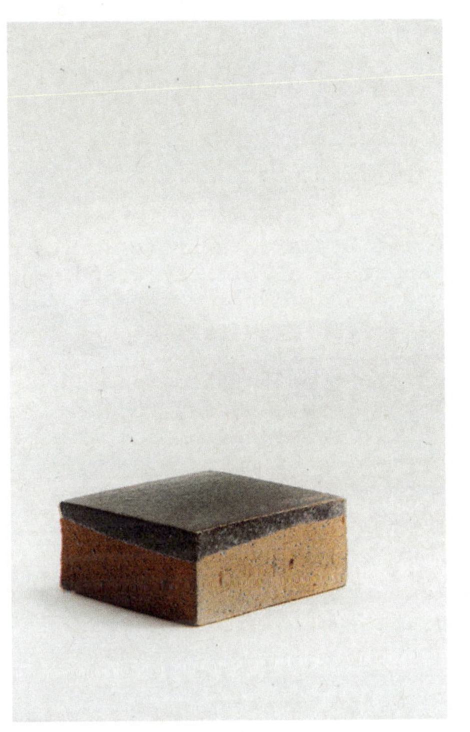
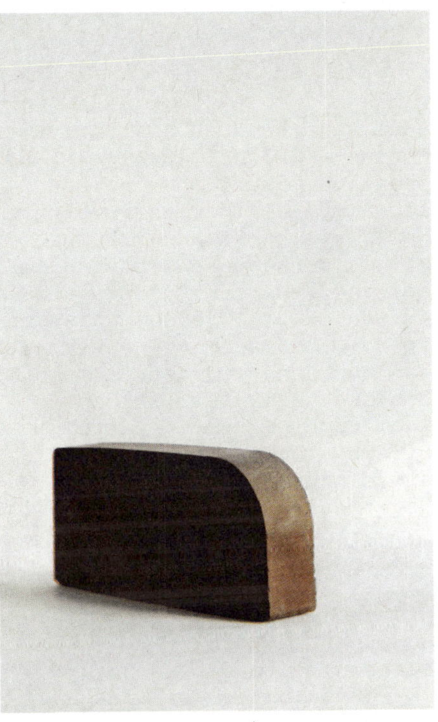
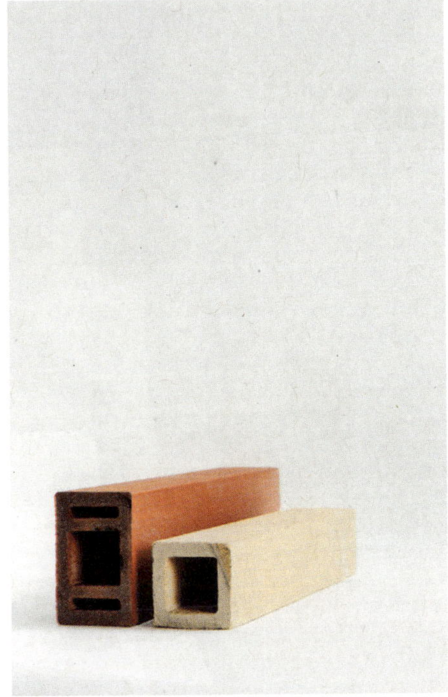
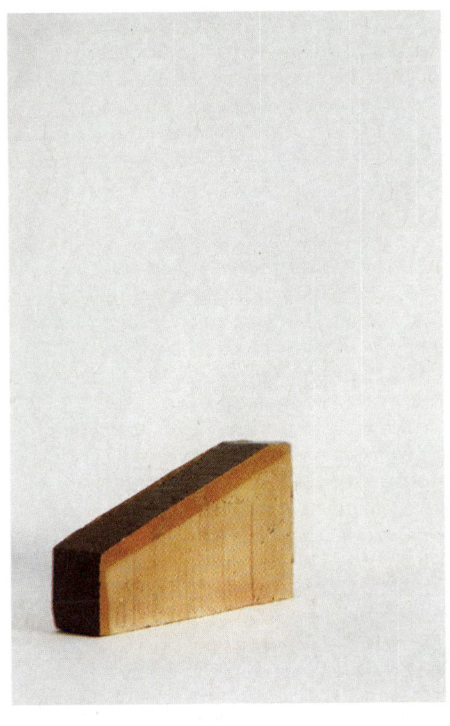

BIOGRAPHIES

Sami Akkach is an Australian-Syrian architect, designer and creative maker, specialized in rammed earth construction and sustainable architecture. He has worked as a freelance designer between Europe and Australia, and is now an architect for pioneering Austrian earthen construction firm Lehm Ton Erde Baukunst. Akkach's knowledge of rammed earth offers a unique approach to sustainability, bringing together technological innovation, local materials, regional building culture and vernacular building techniques. His cross-cultural experiences and understanding enable him to bring into design unique insights that intertwine eastern and western creative traditions. Akkach has been consulted by architecture practices across the world and in his appointment as adjunct professor at Columbia University has trained graduate students in the rammed earth technique.

Eleanor Beaumont is deputy editor at London-based international architecture magazine *The Architectural Review*. First printed in 1896, the AR's current editorial agenda is informed by tireless curiosity, questioning and dialogue, scouring the margins and evolving a careful and rigorous mode of editorial practice. She studied architecture at the University of Cambridge and the School of Art, Architecture and Design at London Metropolitan University. She is a passionate south Londoner and believes that architecture is made as much with words as bricks and mortar.

Ellen Braae is a professor of landscape architecture and the head of the research group Landscape Architecture and Urbanism. With a background in architecture and landscape architecture, Braae focuses on the preservation and transformation of post-industrial urban landscapes. Her research explores cultural heritage, ecology, aesthetics and the relationship between landscapes and urban development. Braae's expertise encompasses landscape theory, design theory and historical perspectives on landscaping tools. She investigates the meaning, appearance and function of open spaces in urban contexts.

Maria Bruun is a furniture designer, joining a long-standing design tradition. With sincere respect for classic Danish furniture, Bruun builds on this foundation with an innovative approach, creating her designs in close dialogue with skilled craftspeople. She often devotes her work to the refinement of the individual elements and persistently seeks out new possibilities in her field. Bruun was awarded the Wegner Prize in 2022, and the prestigious Danish Finn Juhl Prize in 2021. She co-founded MBADV with Anne Dorthe Vester, where between 2013 and 2022 they collaborated on projects at the intersection of architecture, design and fine art.

Bruun holds an MA in furniture Design from the Royal Danish Academy of Fine Arts, School of Design.

Ta-Nehisi Coates is a renowned American author, journalist and educator known for his profound insights on race and social issues. Growing up in a politically conscious household, he gained prominence through his thought-provoking essays on systemic racism and the experiences of Black Americans. Coates's work as a journalist, including his contributions to *The Atlantic*, sparked intense discussions on race relations. As an influential author, his memoir *Between the World and Me* received critical acclaim, examining the Black experience in America. Coates's contributions to literature and his thought-provoking commentary continue to challenge prevailing narratives and advocate for a more just society.

Catherine Fennell is an anthropologist, specializing in the cultural transformation of the American welfare state and its impact on citizenship, belonging and race within redeveloping cities. Her ethnographic research focuses on how changes in urban environments shape people's understanding of social difference and their forms of social care, concern and intimacy. Fennell investigates the sensory and affective qualities of urban life, cultivating personal attachments to place and fostering connections with its associated communities. Her research encompasses topics such as public housing reforms, "post-welfare" social belonging and the ethics of sustainable urban redevelopment movements.

Amara Abdal Figueroa is an agroceramist, artist and environmental advocate living between Borikén (Puerto Rico) and Kuwait. Her practice focuses on the interconnectedness of nature and culture, examining the effects of ecological collapse on conflict. Abdal Figueroa's work explores material sourcing, transformation and reuse, primarily using locally identified clay bodies. She currently studies the ground in Puerto Rico to filter the island's water through her project Tierrafiltra. Abdal Figueroa continues the legacy of Ron Rivera's (Potters For Peace) work on his native island, emphasizing regenerative and intergenerational approaches.

James Albert Martin is a registered architect with the Royal Institute of the Architects of Ireland and Grade 3 Accredited in Architectural Conservation. He has taught at the Aarhus School of Architecture and at University College Dublin where he is currently a Design Fellow. Martin is interested in the act of making, and his work is informed by this collaborative act. He holds an MA from the Aarhus School of Architecture, and has also undertaken courses in joinery at the school for craft and design Capellagården. Since graduating he has worked with international studios Sou Fujimoto Architects, Herzog & de Meuron and Grafton Architects.

Eibhlín Ní Chathasaigh is a registered architect with the Royal Institute of the Architects of Ireland. She teaches at both University College Dublin and Technological University Dublin. Since graduating from the Aarhus School of Architecture, Denmark, she has worked at Atelier Peter Zumthor in Switzerland and Grafton Architects in Dublin, Ireland. Ní Chathasaigh is interested in the social act of architecture and design as a collaborative conversation.

Will Quam is an architectural photographer, writer and researcher with a deep appreciation for the beauty of bricks. He is captivated by the unique characteristics of each brick, from its intricate details to the effects of weathering and aging. Quam's documentation of bricks aims to inspire others to pay closer attention to the world around them. He believes that everything, including physical structures like buildings, carries an impact and deserves appreciation. Quam offers captivating tours focused on bricks and architecture, sharing his expertise and passion with participants. Through his work, he unveils the hidden narratives embedded in buildings and encourages a deeper understanding of our built environment.

Anjulie Rao is a Chicago-based journalist and critic specializing in the built environment. With a background in art history, she explores the intersections between visual art, architecture, infrastructure and political narratives. Rao's work delves into the complexities of post-industrial cities, connections to place and land, and the transformative power of architecture and landscapes. She holds teaching positions at the School of the Art Institute of Chicago and the Illinois Institute of Technology. Rao's writing focuses on livable built environments, equitable design, architecture criticism and urbanism. She sheds light on the challenges and possibilities of post-industrial cities, with a particular emphasis on the winter landscape.

Emmett Scanlon is an architect with a diverse creative and design practice, spanning building and spatial design, public art, exhibition making and curation, research, education and writing. His work aims to make architecture accessible and culturally relevant, emphasizing its social impact. With experience in independent practice and previous roles at Grafton Architects and as Assistant to the Curators for the Venice Architecture Exhibition, Scanlon combines practice, research and teaching.
He advocates for architects' creative development and broader inclusion in architectural discussions and processes.

Annette Skov is an art facilitator and advisor, using art as a method for change and community building. Collaborating with various organizations, she promotes equality in access to society's values and resources. Skov has served as the Head

Contemporary and worked as an art facilitator at the National Gallery of Denmark. She believes art holds significant democratic potential, encouraging interpretations, emotions and understandings. Through art facilitation, she aims to create new encounters, strengths, agency and joy. Skov has a background in language, literature and art history. Besides her role as an art facilitator, she is a creative visual artist and a member of the Visual Artists' Association (BKF). Skov often works on site-specific projects involving actions, installations and words. She is also a member of the exhibition group Efterkommere ("Descendants").

Craig Stevenson is Chicago-based and passionate about the mind-body-spirit connection and using arts and culture, business, education, leadership development and design as tools for social change. He is dedicated to building thriving, sustainable communities using creative placemaking. Stevenson works at the intersections of arts and culture, community healing, storytelling, social impact and spatial design. Along with creative strategy with CRADLE ideas, he continues his advocacy as the Co-Chair of Open Architecture Chicago. As a systems change and futurology practitioner, Stevenson was ranked in *Newcity* magazine's Design 50 2022 in Chicago.

Anne Dorthe Vester is a masters graduate from the Royal Danish Academy of Fine Arts, School of Architecture, and studied for her BA at Aarhus School of Architecture. She has a background in craft and has taken courses in fine woodwork at KTS (Copenhagen Technical College). Whether large or small in scale, her work seeks to unfold the inherent qualities and technical potential of materials. Her work is developed through an experimental and exploratory approach, grounded in the Danish design tradition. Anne Dorthe Vester founded her own studio with a focus on architecture and design in 2012. She co-founded MBADV with Maria Brunn, where between 2013 and 2022 they collaborated on projects at the intersection of architecture, design and fine art.

Traci Wile is a badass feminist activist architect who works to empower people, students and communities through collaboration, design and inclusive engagement. She is currently Assistant Professor of Architectural Design at James Madison University. She received her BFA from the Massachusetts College of Art and Design in Boston in 1997 and her Master of Architecture from the School of the Art Institute of Chicago in 2011. In her former life, she was an organizer, artist, restaurant snob, Apple Mac Genius and movie extra. Her claim to fame: she worked on *The West Wing* and *Pirates of the Caribbean*.

THANK YOU

Ebere Agwuncha, Per Ahlmann, Ellen Alderman, Amoriona Allen, Deshaan Alston, Ana Amaya, Tormod Amundsen, Henriette Noermark Andersen, Rikke Krogh Andresen, Alexandra Antoine, Blanca Aviles, Stefan Badovsky, Michael Baldwin, Berit Basse, Eleanor Beaumont, Ulrik Bebe, Danielle Becker, Jacob Blecher, Henrik Boe, Frederik Bo Bojesen, Corniki Bornds, Ellen Braae, David Brown, Derek Brown, Marcus Buchanan, Andreas Carlsen, Leo Bruun Carlsen, William Bruun Carlsen, Linda Chavez, Chandra Christmas-Rouse, Alice Clancy, Trevor Clarke, Odile Compagnon, Susana Coré, Magnus Cortsen, Solange Carla Crudo, Eddie Davis, Gregory Davis, Rob de Boer, Maiken Tandgaard Derno, Ricardo Devesa, Philip Dodd, Sergey Dorokhov, Jeremy Dunne, Ann Engh, Valentina Espinoza, Jose Estrada, Catherine Fennell, Amara Abdal Figueroa, Antwan Fipps, ‘Nini’ Calvinita Fipps, Tim Frederich, Mika Friis Amundsen, Ronan Gallagher, Brandon Glass, Rebecca Graff, Mamie Grey, Chad Hagedorn, Ida Harden, Frederik Hardvendel, Roxann Harry-Potter, Lauren Hartman, Sonja Henderson, Sara Heymann, Andrew Hockenberry, Sheila Holmes, Sheila Holmes, Gregory Hubert, Livia Hurley, Hiroki Ito, JoVanna Jackson, Mikael Jackson, Jaclyn Jacunski, Frank Jensen, Salvador Jimenez, Willie Johnson, Ernest Jones, Anton Bech Jørgensen, Rachel Kaplan, Jonathan Kelley, Angela Key, Jimmie Kimble, Donail Kirby, Nance Klehm, Tess Landon, AnnaMaria Leon, Rebekka Lewin, Mirek Malarick, Benita Marcussen, Philip Martin, Salvador Martinez, Stephen Martinez, Kathleen McCarthy, Fiona McDonald, Miki McDonald, Flemming Meier, Daisy Mertzel, Parish Mitchell, Colm Moore, Max Kejser Mortensen, Eric Nedreberg, Cecilie Nellemann, ‘King’ Ronnell Newbern, Caitríona Ní Chathasaigh, Lasse Koefoed Nielsen, Vibeke Hejgaard Nielsen, Morten Nybo, Eoin Ó Cathasaigh, Liam Ó Cathasaigh, Olisaemeka Okakru, Annelie Grimwade Olofsson, Juan Manuel Paz. O, Anicia Peden, Craig Perry, Pauline Personeni, Mikkel Wittenburg Petersen, Will Quam, Doug Rappe, Maxwell Rodencal, Manny Rodriguez, Samuel Rodriguez, Cristina Román, Gunhild Rudjord, Alfonso ‘Piloto’ Nieves Ruiz, Myra Sampson, Mister Sanchez, Sonia Saxon, Brittany Scales, Brent Schmitt, Jay Simon, Annette Skov, Steve Smith, Stuart Smyth, Craig Stevenson, Melissa Stroud, Patti Swanson, Walter Terrazos, Sara Thetmark, Stefan Thorsteinsson, Søren Thygesen, Birthe Tinning, Michael Trout, Jim Turnbull, Andrea Wittenburg Vester, Mads Wittenburg Vester, H.C. Warfield, Jim West, Traci Wile, Marcus Woods, Marguerite Wynter, Andrea Yarbrough, Alyssa Zhan, Nancy Zook.

EPILOGUE

After the end of the biennial, the recycled soil was gifted to the Pilsen Housing Cooperative gardens for landscaping purposes. The kiln found a permanent home in Little Black Pearl Art & Design Academy, a public high school located at the crossroads of the historic Kenwood, Oakland and Bronzeville communities. The handmade clay tiles and extruder also joined the ceramic department at the high school. Clay and tools suitable for art classes were donated to the CCA Academy in North Lawndale, and all building site equipment, scaffolding and shovels were donated to the tools library at Stone Temple Baptist Church, also in North Lawndale.

Soil Lab
A Built Experiment

Editors
Eleanor Beaumont,
Maria Bruun,
James Albert Martin,
Eibhlín Ní Chathasaigh,
Anne Dorthe Vester

Graphic Design
Studio Atlant

Text Contributions
Sami Akkach
Ellen Braae
Ta-Nehisi Coates
Catherine Fennell
Amara Abdal Figueroa
Calvinita Fipps AKA Nini
Will Quam
Anjulie Rao
Emmett Scanlon
Annette Skov
Soil Lab
Craig Stevenson
Traci Wile

Proofreading
Eleanor Beaumont

Translation
Dan Marmorstein

Printing and binding
Gràfiques Jou

The publication is kindly supported by
Realdania

The Soil Lab project is kindly supported by
Realdania
Statens Kunstfond
Chicago Architecture Biennial
Consulate General of Denmark in New York
Dreyers Fond
Culture Ireland
Irish Arts Council
Dinesen
Sal's Hand Car Wash

Published by
Actar Publishers, New York, Barcelona, www.actar.com

Distribution
Actar D, Inc. New York, Barcelona

New York
440 Park Avenue South, 17th Floor
New York, NY 10016, USA
T +1 2129662207
salesnewyork@actar-d.com

Barcelona
Roca i Batlle 2
08023 Barcelona, Spain
T +34 933 282 183
eurosales@actar-d.com

Photographs and illustrations
Maria Bruun 153
François Cointeraux 132
Frankie Dintino 99
Lehm Ton Erde 34
Amara Abdal Figueroa 14, 15, 62, 112, 114-115, 116, 120, 123
Bruno Helbig 38
Sonja Henderson 65
Lorenz Kastner 52, 54-55, 57-60
Wallace Labs 31
Hanno Mackowitz 37
Benita Marcussen 8, 76-84, 86, 88-89, 90, 92, 107, 133, 135, 154-159
James Albert Martin 110, 136, 138-144, 148-150
Eibhlín Ní Chathasaigh 24, 28, 68, 70, 102
Carlos Javier Ortiz 94
Will Quam 1-2, 20-23, 40-45, 50-51, 67, 127-128, 137, 146, 167-168
Jay Simon 16, 32, 102, 108, 124, 152
Sandra Steinbrecher 18-19, 46-49, 145, 146
Anne Dorthe Vester 113

Indexing
English ISBN: 978-1-63840-106-3
Library of Congress Control Number: 2023940879

Printed in Europe
First edition, July 2023